BEST PRACTICES: EVALUATING THE CORPORATE CULTURE

By
James Roth, PhD, CIA, CCSA

The Institute of Internal Auditors
Research Foundation

Disclosure

Copyright © 2010 by The Institute of Internal Auditors Research Foundation (IIARF), 247 Maitland Avenue, Altamonte Springs, Florida 32701-4201. All rights reserved. Printed in the United States of America. No part of this publication may be reproduced, stored in a retrieval system, or transmitted in any form by any means — electronic, mechanical, photocopying, recording, or otherwise — without prior written permission of the publisher.

The IIARF publishes this document for informational and educational purposes. This document is intended to provide information, but is not a substitute for legal or accounting advice. The IIARF does not provide such advice and makes no warranty as to any legal or accounting results through its publication of this document. When legal or accounting issues arise, professional assistance should be sought and retained.

The Institute of Internal Auditors' (IIA's) International Professional Practices Framework (IPPF) comprises the full range of existing and developing practice guidance for the profession. The IPPF provides guidance to internal auditors globally and paves the way to world-class internal auditing.

The mission of The IIARF is to expand knowledge and understanding of internal auditing by providing relevant research and educational products to advance the profession globally.

The IIA and The IIARF work in partnership with researchers from around the globe who conduct valuable studies on critical issues affecting today's business world. Much of the content presented in their final reports is a result of IIARF-funded research and prepared as a service to The Foundation and the internal audit profession. Expressed opinions, interpretations, or points of view represent a consensus of the researchers and do not necessarily reflect or represent the official position or policies of The IIA or The IIARF.

ISBN 978-0-89413-682-5
02/10 First Printing
08/11 Second Printing

Dedication

To Sally, who makes all things possible.
To Katrina and Megan, who make all things worthwhile.

CONTENTS

About the Author ix
Acknowledgments xi

Executive Summary 1
    Objective and Central Findings of This Study 1
    Use of the Term "Best Practices" 2
    Summary of the Chapters 3
    Final Word 4

Chapter 1: Introduction to Soft Controls 5
    "Definition" of Soft Controls 5
    The Importance of Soft Controls 6
    Why Internal Auditors Should Evaluate Soft Controls 6
    Evaluating Soft Controls: Basic Principles 8
    Overview of the COSO Report 11
    Examples of Soft Controls 12
    Chapter Summary 16

Chapter 2: Surveys Used During Audit Projects 17
    University of Minnesota 17
    Precision Drilling Corporation 19
    Boeing 19
    Lowes 21
    New York State Comptroller's Office 22
    Guidelines for Using Soft Control Surveys During Audit Projects 24

Chapter 3: Participative, Risk-based Audit Projects 27
    Allina Hospitals and Clinics 27
    Securian 30
    ING 35
    TD Ameritrade 41
    Guidelines for Evaluating Soft Controls on Participative, Risk-based Audit Projects 43

Chapter 4: Structured Entity-level Interviews 49
    Precision Drilling Corporation 50
    Kaiser Permanente 51
    Anonymous 52
    Aquila Inc. 53
    Guidelines for Entity-level Interviews 54

Chapter 5: Entitywide Surveys 55
    Ameritech 56
    United Stationers 58
    BP PLC 59
    The City of Austin 61

Best Practices: Evaluating the Corporate Culture

  Lennox International 63
  Robeco 64
  Guidelines for Entitywide Soft Control Surveys 70

Chapter 6: Combination of Techniques 73
  A Fortune 500 Company 73
  WorkSafeBC 76
  Sarasota County 79

Chapter 7: Soft Control Audit Report Comments 85
  Report Excerpts A to K 87
  Guidelines for Formal Reporting of Soft Control Weaknesses 116
  Conclusion 116

EXHIBITS

1A.	SA at BellSouth: The Afterlife	119
2A.	University of Minnesota Employee Survey	124
2B.	Precision Drilling HR or "Happiness" Survey	126
2C.	Boeing Customized Survey	128
2D.	Lowes IT Project Management Survey Statements	130
2E.	New York State Comptroller's Office Internal Control Survey Guidelines	(CD only)
2F.	New York State Comptroller's Office Audit Report	(CD only)
3A.	Allina Annual Risk Assessment Interview Guide	135
3B.	Allina Audit Planning Document	138
3C.	Allina Audit Program Excerpts	140
3D.	Securian Auditing Department Core Values	143
3E.	ING Group Audit Strategy Memorandum	144
3F.	ING Business Line Audit Strategy Memorandum	(CD only)
3G.	ING Organizational Unit Audit Strategy Memorandum	(CD only)
4A.	Precision Drilling Entity Level Interview Guide	150
4B.	Precision Drilling Ethics Training	157
4C.	Kaiser Permanente Audit Committee Presentation on Entity-level Controls	171
4D.	Kaiser Permanente Criteria for Governance Committee Review	175
4E.	Interview Guide for Compliance Audit	177
4F.	Aquila COSO-based Capabilities Maturity Assessment	181
5A.	Ameritech Entity-Wide Soft Control Survey	188
5B.	United Stationers Survey Invitation Letter	194
5C.	United Stationers Survey Statements and Structure for One Group	196
5D.	United Stationers Survey: Differences Among the Groups	(CD only)
5E.	"Risk Watch" Article on City of Austin Ethics Audit	202
5F.	Lennox International Entity-Wide Survey	208
5G.	Robeco Entity-Wide Survey	213
6A.	WorkSafeBC Pre-Interview Handout	218
6B.	WorkSafeBC Pre-Interview Presentation	227
6C.	WorkSafeBC Soft Controls Questionnaire	232
6D.	WorkSafeBC Divisional Audit Report	(CD only)

6E.	WorkSafeBC Executive Interview Material	241
6F.	WorkSafeBC Manager/Employee Survey	247
6G.	Sarasota County COSO-Strategic Risk-HPO Framework Cross-Reference	251
6H.	Sarasota County Executive Director Meeting Agenda	252
6I.	Sarasota County Procurement Card Audit Material	(CD only)
6J.	Sarasota County Overall Assessment of Management Control Form	254
6K.	Sarasota County Audit Report — Explanation of COSO Criteria	256

ABOUT THE AUTHOR

James Roth, PhD, CIA, CCSA, is president of AuditTrends, a training firm devoted to identifying and communicating the best of current internal audit practice. He has three decades of progressive internal audit experience as practitioner, author, and presenter. Roth is the 2008 recipient of The Institute of Internal Auditors' (IIA's) Bradford Cadmus Memorial Award for his contributions to the internal audit profession.

AuditTrends' primary service is a program of seminars, including:

- *Internal Audit's Role in Corporate Governance: How to Evaluate Soft Controls*
- *Best Practices in Internal Auditing*
- *Operational Auditing: A Risk and Self-assessment Based Approach*
- *Implementing the COSO ERM Framework: A Practical Approach*
- *Relationship Building Skills for Auditors*
- *Leadership and Supervision Skills for Auditors*
- *Skills for the New Internal Auditor*
- *Report Writing*

Roth has published 13 major products for The IIA, as well as numerous articles on internal audit, control, risk management, and governance. He is a frequent speaker at international conferences.

Contact:

James Roth, PhD, CIA, CCSA
AuditTrends
9787 Manning Ave. S.
Hastings, MN 55033
USA
Phone: +1-651-459-7573
Fax: +1-651-459-1643
E-mail: jamesroth@audittrends.com
Web Site: www.audittrends.com

ACKNOWLEDGMENTS

I would like to thank Bonnie Ulmer, Erin Weber, and Lee Ann Campbell of The Institute of Internal Auditors Research Foundation staff, as well as the Project Advisory Team, for their contributions to this book. I would also like to thank Norman Marks and Gerald Wu for the anecdotes that enrich the guidelines at the end of Chapter 3.

Most of all, I would like to thank the 19 organizations that are included in this study, and the people within those organizations who gave generously of their time and energy helping me understand their practices. These include three whose organizations wish to remain anonymous. The people I can name who contributed the most are:

Allina Hospitals and Clinics
Vicki L. Phipps

Boeing
Theodore W. Wills

BP
Kevin Casey

ING
Berry Wilson and Berdie Heinrich

Kaiser Permanente
Cindy Overmyer

Lennox International
Gary McGuire

Lowes
Carolyn Saint

New York State Comptrollers
Dave Hancox

Precision Drilling
Robert Kuling

Robeco Groep
Rick Mulders

Sarasota County
Mark Simmons

Securian
Mark Sievers

TD Ameritrade
Michael Head

United Stationers
Sandy Kruse

University of Minnesota
Gail Klatt

Worksafe BC
Jerry Mah and Suzanne Dunn

PROJECT ADVISORY TEAM

John Harris, CIA
Steven Mezzio
Susan Driver, CPA, CIA, CISA, CFE
Katherine Sidway Homer, CIA
Claire Beth Nilsen, CRCM, CFE, CFSA, CRP, AMLP

EXECUTIVE SUMMARY

This book argues that evaluating the corporate culture is an internal audit best practice and gives practical examples of how this can be done. To make the case that evaluating the corporate culture is a best practice, we need only look at the long history of major business frauds and failures. Root cause analysis leads inevitably to the culture of the organization. At the time of this writing we have a macro-level example — the global financial meltdown caused by the "culture of greed" on Wall Street.

Internal auditing's stakeholders want assurance that their organization will not be the next highly publicized failure. To give them that assurance, the potential causes of such failures must be identified: weaknesses in the corporate culture.

But how can internal auditors evaluate something as vast and intangible as the culture? The short answer is that we cannot evaluate the culture as a whole, but we can evaluate specific elements of the culture. Throughout this book the term "soft controls" is used to refer to the informal, intangible levers of control such as tone at the top, the organization's ethical climate, and management's philosophy and operating style that together make up the corporate culture.

Evaluating soft controls, which are inherently subjective, and reporting weaknesses to those accountable is perhaps the greatest challenge internal auditors have ever faced. Traditional auditors believe we cannot and should not try to do this, but best practice audit departments like those featured in this book have found ways to do so.

The Institute of Internal Auditors' (IIA's) *International Standards for the Professional Practice of Internal Auditing* (*Standards*), in fact, points to the need to evaluate soft controls. If we are to "evaluate and improve the *effectiveness* of risk management, control, and governance processes (italics added)," we need to determine whether these processes are having the desired *effect*. For example, governance processes include the dissemination of ethics policies. To be effective, such policies must be understood, accepted, and acted upon by employees. That is, they must be integrated into the culture of the organization.

A specific example of ineffective ethics policies is worth mentioning here. Enron is the company whose failure in 2001 kicked off a wave of public scandals and led to the U.S. Sarbanes-Oxley Act of 2002 and similar regulations in other countries. This company's formal governance structure and practices were a model of excellence, but the informal communications and behavior of management created a culture that was almost diametrically opposed to the stated values. A good internal audit department (Enron had outsourced theirs to Arthur Andersen) focused on evaluating soft controls could have identified the gap between the stated and real corporate values.

Objective and Central Findings of This Study

This research report began as an update to the author's 1997 study, *Control Model Implementation: Best Practices.* That book was part of the vibrant control self-assessment (CSA) movement of the

1990s, which was fostered in large part by the first Committee of Sponsoring Organizations of the Treadway Commission (COSO) report, *Internal Control–Integrated Framework*.

The COSO framework, which has become the globally accepted criteria for evaluating internal control, emphasized the central importance of soft controls, especially the control environment. In the early 1990s the only well-known technique for evaluating soft controls was the CSA workshop. In fact, many people still equate the term CSA with the workshop technique. *Control Model Implementation* showed that other techniques were beginning to emerge. These techniques included surveys, structured interviews, and risk-based audit approaches that identify both hard and soft controls.

Current research suggests that soft control evaluation has evolved further from CSA workshops toward simpler survey and interview techniques, and is being integrated into the fabric of audit departments' routine audit work. I believe this evolution reflects the improved image and credibility of internal auditing. Auditors no longer need a dramatically innovative technique — in which they carefully avoid expressing their own opinions — to surface soft control issues. The best audit departments are accepted as business partners whose opinion is listened to rather than fought against. This does not mean that they can venture baseless opinions, but it does mean that when they have solid evidence, even if some subjectivity is involved, they are taken seriously.

I should add that CSA workshops have not disappeared from the internal auditor's tool bag completely. Five of the 19 audit departments presented in this book use workshops. Two do so selectively, when a particular situation calls for it. Two do so in combination with interviews and surveys. One used workshops with executives for an entitywide review. In general, though, workshops have evolved from an internal audit tool into a central technique in enterprise risk management (ERM) programs.

Use of the Term "Best Practices"

The term "best practice" is commonly used and easily misunderstood. Taken literally, it implies there is only one "best" way of doing something. Identifying the single best way would require defined criteria and some sort of contest. This is not, of course, how the term is used. In common usage, "best practices" are techniques that consistently produce better results than others and are benchmarks to strive for.

I believe that evaluating soft controls is a best practice. Consider the following hierarchy of audit techniques and findings:

- At the lowest level are techniques that only identify errors.
- At the next level are techniques that identify the control weakness that can lead to the errors.
- At the highest level are techniques that identify the root cause of the control weakness.

Another obvious hierarchy is the significance of the findings, ranging from minor errors to business failure. As stated before, root cause analysis often leads to weaknesses in soft controls, and this is especially true when major risks such as business failure are examined.

No practice is best for everyone and in every situation. Everything internal auditing does, and especially soft control evaluation, must be done in the "best" way for the particular organization it serves.

The evaluation technique must fit the size, environment, industry, and culture of the organization, and it must also be useable by the audit staff.

This book presents soft control evaluation techniques from a variety of organizations. All have proven effective in their environment. Hopefully, readers will gain insight into how to tailor a technique to their own organization by seeing how similar results are achieved in different organizations. Chapter 3, for example, shows how soft control evaluation is integrated into routine audits in two small audit shops and a very large audit shop. Allina and Securian (10 and 14 auditors respectively) succeed informally, by hiring auditors with business savvy and providing hands-on leadership. ING, with 700 auditors spread across the world, had to develop a sophisticated formal process to get similar results.

Summary of the Chapters

Chapter 1, "Introduction to Soft Controls," elaborates on what I said above about the nature of soft controls and why internal auditors need to evaluate them. It also provides some basic principles that should be followed regardless of the specific technique used. It provides a brief overview of the first COSO report, because several of the techniques presented in this book use its terminology and structure. It ends with several pages of specific soft controls. These may be helpful in providing content for the reader's development or enhancement of soft control evaluation techniques.

So far I have talked about soft controls as making up the corporate culture, which is an entitywide issue. But managers create subcultures with their own areas. When a subculture is dysfunctional in some way (i.e., has a soft control weakness), a host of problems can arise. Surveys can be a simple way to measure elements of the subculture and identify dysfunctions. Chapter 2, "Surveys Used during Audit Projects," shows how four audit departments and one internal consultant use surveys to evaluate soft controls while reviewing a specific area or process. Their circumstances and method of application vary widely. The surveys also vary and are included as exhibits. The chapter concludes with guidelines for developing and applying similar surveys.

Chapter 3, "Participative, Risk-based Audit Projects," shows how four audit departments integrate soft control evaluation into their everyday audit work. As mentioned above, two are small and one is very large, and their approach varies accordingly. The fourth is an audit department whose participative, risk-based approach became the basis for the organization's ERM program. The chapter ends with guidelines for evaluating soft controls during audit projects, including techniques for effective soft control interviews.

Chapter 4, "Structured Entity-level Interviews," shows how four audit departments evaluate entity-wide soft controls through structured interviews at various organizational levels. It concludes with guidelines for entity-level interviews that augment the interview guidelines in Chapter 3.

Chapter 5, "Entitywide Surveys," presents six approaches to evaluating entity-level soft controls with surveys. Ameritech's is a "classic" example that has been used as a model by many other organizations. United Stationers' is a direct descendant, but its value has been lessened by a human resources (HR) survey that covers much of the same ground. BP shows how an audit department can use the results of an HR-administered survey. The City of Austin shows how internal auditing can enhance an existing HR-administered survey. Lennox International shows how a survey developed by internal auditing can be transferred to another function. And Robeco shows a highly disciplined approach to developing a survey to fit a specific organization. The chapter ends with guidelines for developing and using an entitywide soft control survey.

Chapter 6, "Combination of Techniques," profiles three audit departments that used a combination of surveys, interviews, and workshops. One does so for audit projects and one for entitywide reviews. The third has an integrated, COSO-based approach from entity-level risk assessment through audit execution. There are no guidelines in this chapter because the relevant guidelines were presented in previous chapters.

Chapter 7, "Soft Control Audit Report Comments," discusses the challenges involved in disclosing soft control weaknesses in written audit reports. It presents three complete audit reports and 14 excerpts that address soft control weaknesses. It also references three audit reports included in previous chapters. Together, these report comments represent six audit departments with six different approaches. None are likely to be perfect models for another audit department, but readers should be able to combine what they like from each and add their own creativity to develop an approach that might work in their own organizations.

Final Word

Obtaining reliable information about soft controls is a challenge, perhaps the greatest challenge internal auditors have ever faced. We will never be able to meet that challenge to the extent we can with hard controls, because subjectivity is involved. But our stakeholders' expectations and our professional *Standards* require that we try. As long as we use a "systematic, disciplined approach," work in partnership with those accountable, and are careful in drawing conclusions from available evidence, we can accomplish a great deal.

Hopefully, readers who have hesitated to evaluate soft controls because of the tremendous challenge involved will find what they need to get started. I hope that readers experienced in this realm will find something to help them do even better.

CHAPTER 1

INTRODUCTION TO SOFT CONTROLS

Readers who are already evaluating soft controls may not need to read this introductory chapter. On the other hand, the text might give them some ideas for how to explain their soft control work to others, and the examples of soft controls at the end might help them enhance their techniques. The sections of this chapter are:

- "Definition" of Soft Controls.
- The Importance of Soft Controls.
- Why Internal Auditors Should Evaluate Soft Controls.
- Evaluating Soft Controls: Basic Principles.
- Overview of the COSO Report.
- Examples of Soft Controls.
- Chapter Summary.

"Definition" of Soft Controls

The first question some readers might ask is "What is a soft control?" There is no strict definition of the term, nor is there a clear-cut dividing line between hard and soft controls. To some extent it is a matter of "I know it when I see it." But with that caveat, I will try to explain what I think is generally meant by this commonly used and very useful term.

Hard controls tend to be formal, objective, and quantitatively measureable. Soft controls tend to be informal, subjective, and intangible. *The Auditor's Dictionary* (David O'Regan, John Wiley & Sons, 2004) defines a soft control as, "An internal control based on intangible factors like honesty and ethical standards."

Examples are probably the best way to show the difference between hard and soft controls:

Hard Controls	Soft Controls
Policy/procedure	Competence
Organizational structure	Trust
Bureaucracy	Shared values
Restrictive formal processes	Strong leadership
	High expectations
	Openness
	High ethical standards

A colleague likes to say that hard controls are like a map that tells you what should be there; soft controls are the real terrain — what's really there inside people.

For example, an organization can have an excellent code of ethics, stated values, and related policies, but when an employee's supervisor or peers say "Well, that's the theory, but this is how it works in the real world...," the employee internalizes the "real world" values and behaves accordingly.

What this employee's colleagues are communicating is the corporate culture, which leads us to the next point.

The Importance of Soft Controls

All the soft controls in an organization together constitute its corporate culture. The corporate culture is the most powerful control in any organization. It influences every employee's behavior every moment of every workday in ways they may not even be aware of.

Why is the corporate culture important to internal auditors? We have been observing major organizational frauds and failures for three decades, from the Savings & Loan failures in the United States during the 1980s through Barings Bank in the United Kingdom and several Japanese banks in the 1990s, through the wave of financial reporting frauds starting in 2001 to the worldwide financial crisis starting in 2007 with subprime mortgages in the United States. In every case, the root cause is a weakness in the corporate culture.

Some might question that last statement and point to examples like Barings, in which one unethical trader, Nick Leeson, was in charge of both the front and back office of Baring's Singapore branch — a clear lack of segregation of duties. What is less well known, however, is that a formal control — an internal audit — detected this weakness six months before Leeson's scheme collapsed. The audit report recommended segregating the front and back offices and also sending a supervisor from the United Kingdom to oversee the branch. But the internal auditor was part of the corporate culture and politically astute. The audit report also said, "But the biggest risk to the Singapore branch would be losing the branch manager" (Leeson). The report went to the audit committee and no action was taken. In the Barings culture, as in so many others, no one wanted to offend the best salesman by looking too closely at what he was doing.

As Barings illustrates, even when there is a serious hard control weakness, the underlying root cause is usually a soft control weakness. In the worldwide financial crisis at the time of this writing (2009), it is commonplace and correct to blame the "culture of greed" on Wall Street.

Why Internal Auditors Should Evaluate Soft Controls

As our profession advances, we are becoming more strategically focused, dealing with bigger issues, and giving assurance at a higher level. At the highest level, audit committees and other oversight groups want assurance that the organization will not be the next big fraud case or failure. To give them that assurance, the root cause of such events must be evaluated: the corporate culture.

I am not suggesting an opinion on the corporate culture as a whole. It is too vast and complex for a blanket opinion. But it is made up of individual soft controls, and these can be evaluated.

Chapter 1: Introduction to Soft Controls

Another way to phrase the argument for soft controls is in terms of the *Standards*. The definition of internal auditing in the introduction says that we bring "a systematic, disciplined approach to evaluate and improve the effectiveness of risk management, control, and governance processes." The importance of culture to risk management and governance should be obvious, and it is just as important to control. Standard 2210.A3 states: "Adequate criteria are needed to evaluate controls."

The globally accepted criterion for evaluating controls is COSO's *Internal Control–Integrated Framework*. (I will refer to this document as "the COSO report." COSO has produced other reports, but they are all based on this one, and it is all that is needed for purposes of this book.) I give an overview of the COSO report later in this chapter, but for now I will consider the seven factors that make up the first component, the Control Environment:

- Integrity and ethical values.
- Commitment to competence.
- Board of directors and audit committee.
- Management's philosophy and operating style.
- Organizational structure.
- Assignment of authority and responsibility.
- Human resources policies and practices.

Three of the first four (excluding the board) are clearly soft controls, and evaluating the effectiveness of the others involves soft controls. For example, to evaluate the effectiveness of human resources policies and practices, you need to evaluate their effect on employees.

Although the COSO report is a United States document, the *Standards* incorporates COSO's Control Environment. A Glossary entry reads:

> **Control Environment** — The attitude and actions of the board and management regarding the significance of control within the organization. The control environment provides the discipline and structure for the achievement of the primary objectives of the system of internal control. The control environment includes:
>
> - Integrity and ethical values.
> - Management's philosophy and operating style.
> - Organizational structure.
> - Assignment of authority and responsibility.
> - Human resources policies and practices.
> - Competence of personnel.

A final argument for evaluating soft controls also comes from the *Standards*. Standard 2310 states, "Internal auditors must identify sufficient, reliable, relevant, and useful information…" Consider this statement in terms of hard and soft controls. The following chart shows which kind of control evaluation provides the best evidence for each of these four criteria.

	Hard Controls	**Soft Controls**
Sufficient	?	?
Reliable	✓	
Relevant		✓
Useful		✓

Sufficient, or how much information is needed, will vary from one situation to another. *Reliable* information can be obtained far more easily when evaluating hard controls. It can be objective, quantitative, and tangible. Because soft controls are inherently subjective, the same level of reliability can rarely, if ever, be achieved. But if the most powerful control is the corporate culture — and weaknesses in soft controls are the root cause of major hard control failures — then which is more *relevant* to a conclusion on the effectiveness of risk management, control, and governance? Surely soft controls. And which is more *useful* to the organization in achieving its objectives? Again, soft controls.

The point is that obtaining reliable information about soft controls is a challenge, perhaps the greatest challenge internal auditors have ever faced. We will never be able to meet that challenge to the extent we can with hard controls, but the extent to which we meet it is the extent to which we are meeting our professional responsibility and giving the assurance that our key stakeholders really need.

The goal of this book is to give readers tools, techniques, and guidelines for meeting this challenge. I will begin with some basic principles and anecdotes.

Evaluating Soft Controls: Basic Principles

A respected colleague says that integrity, competence, understanding, and commitment are *attributes*, not controls. Controls are the things management does to create these attributes in their employees, and these are what we should evaluate. Although I do not agree, this is a valuable distinction worth exploring.

Standard 2110.A1 states: "The internal audit activity must evaluate the *design, implementation*, and *effectiveness* of the organization's ethics-related objectives, programs, and activities." (italics added)

Enron, the subject of the 21st century's first major financial reporting scandal, had extremely well *designed* and *implemented* ethics-related objectives, programs, and activities. In fact, those who have studied Enron in detail say it was a model of corporate governance from a formal, hard control perspective. The objectives, programs, and activities were not *effective* because the corporate culture was in many ways diametrically opposed to the stated values.

To explore this point of design and implementation versus effectiveness further, let's consider training programs in general. A training program can be seen as a hard control because it is a formal program. But the real question is: What did attendees internalize? Did they really understand and will they apply the principles they learned?

Internal auditors can test the *design* of a training program by comparing it to best practice models. For example, well-designed ethics training includes exercises in which attendees are given a concrete situation and have to make an ethical decision. The instructor then gives feedback on which decision is most consistent with the organization's ethical values. This sort of experiential training should help employees to really understand the values and be better able to apply them.

Internal auditors can test the *implementation* of a training program by checking the qualifications of the instructors, noting the percentage of employees who have taken the training, examining attendee evaluations, etc.

These are all good tests, but the training program is a waste of resources if it does not achieve the desired effect on attendees. The *effectiveness* of training can be tested in several ways, depending on the objectives of the training. If the objective was only to impart knowledge, the auditor can quiz attendees at a later date to see if they have retained the knowledge. If the objective was to build a skill, the auditor can observe employees on the job or look at their performance evaluations to see if their skill has increased. In both cases, the auditor needs to test the attribute (knowledge in one case, skills in the other) that is the objective of training to determine if it has been effective.

Returning to my colleague's view that things like knowledge and skill are attributes, not controls, we can see that it really does not matter in practical terms. If we use his definition, only the training program (what management does to create these attributes in their employees) is a control. However, we still have to test the attributes to fulfill the *Standards*' requirement that we evaluate the effectiveness of the control. In terms of what internal auditors need to do, we get to the same place.

In this book, I include both the actions management takes to create the desired attributes in employees (e.g., what management communicates to employees) and the attributes themselves (e.g., what employees "heard" and internalized) in the definition of soft controls, because I believe that is the way the term is most commonly used.

Now let's explore ethics training a little further. To test its effectiveness, we can pose situations requiring an ethical decision to attendees at a later date to determine whether they have internalized and retained the desired ethical values. But this is still not enough. They might give us the right answer because they know that is what they are supposed to say, but they might actually do something else if faced with that situation. Knowing the right thing to do and doing it are two different things.

We are now back to the employee described at the beginning of this chapter whose supervisor or peers say, "Well, that's the theory, but this is how it works in the real world…" Employees learn the stated or desired culture through training and other formal communications. They learn the real culture by informal communication and observing how others in the organization behave.

Evaluating soft controls means evaluating specific elements of the real culture as experienced by employees. To do this we must have tools and techniques that encourage employees to be honest with us about sensitive matters.

The first disciplined tool internal auditors developed for this purpose is the CSA workshop. I only present two workshop techniques in this book, from Aquila Inc. (Chapter 4) and WorkSafeBC (Chapter 6). There are three reasons. First, the CSA workshop is a well-known technique with a wealth of existing literature. Second, most internal auditors find the technique extremely difficult and perhaps impossible to implement within their corporate culture. Third, my research indicates that the workshop technique has evolved from an "audit thing" into a "management thing," as many early workshop advocates envisioned it would. Specifically, ERM programs are using workshops more frequently than internal audit departments. Exhibit 1A on page 119 is a reprint of an article by Glenda Jordan of BellSouth, one of the CSA workshop pioneers, on how this evolution occurred in her company.

My current research suggests that the essential elements of CSA workshops are being integrated into routine audit projects and entitywide reviews in ways that are simpler and more practical for most audit shops. The most common method for evaluating soft controls in a CSA workshop is to present a series of statements like "Management of my business unit demonstrates high ethical standards." Workshop attendees indicate their level of agreement/disagreement with each statement on a numerical scale using confidential voting technology. Then they discuss why they feel this way. The same technique is being used with surveys and producing excellent results for the audit departments featured in Chapter 2, "Surveys Used During Audit Projects," and Chapter 5, "Entitywide Surveys."

Even without a formal tool like a written survey, the audit departments featured in Chapters 3 and 4 are addressing the same issues and getting good results through interviews. For entitywide reviews (Chapter 4), these tend to be structured interviews with a standard set of questions. For audit projects (Chapter 5), each interview is different. They are successful because the audit department has a risk-based approach that focuses auditors on soft control issues and a participative relationship with audit clients that encourages candor. Chapter 6 presents audit departments that use a combination of these techniques.

All of these soft control evaluation techniques are really forms of self-assessment. That is, the information is volunteered by audit clients rather than from independent, objective testing. Four central principles of self-assessment are worth stating here because they apply to all the techniques in this book.

- **If employees fear retribution, they will not be honest about soft control weaknesses.** We will see how confidentiality in surveys and a participative relationship in interviews can lower or eliminate this fear.

- **The information gathered is employee perceptions.** This is powerful information because the organization's most powerful control — its culture — does not exist in the words and actions of executives. It exists in the perception of employees.

- **To use employee perceptions as audit evidence, auditors must validate them.** Perceptions are subjective, and employees can be wrong. To use perceptions as evidence for audit findings, auditors must confirm their accuracy.

- **Negative employee perceptions are themselves facts, even if they are wrong, and they can seriously damage a work unit.** Managers need to know what these perceptions are so they can deal with them appropriately. If auditors cannot validate employee perceptions, or even if they find contradictory evidence, they should report it to the manager directly responsible as a consulting service. Confidentiality, of course, must be preserved.

The guidelines at the end of Chapters 2 through 5 elaborate on these principles as they apply to the techniques presented in those chapters.

Overview of the COSO report

As I said above, *Internal Control–Integrated Framework* has become the globally accepted criteria for evaluating control. Its concepts and, in some cases, its words are included in the *Standards*. It has been a major influence in getting our profession to accept the challenge of evaluating soft controls.

Several of the evaluation techniques presented in this book are structured according to the COSO framework. Without going into the details of this well-known report, it may be helpful to present its five components and 16 factors for readers not intimately familiar with it. They may want to use this as a reference point to help them understand the structure of those techniques.

Control Environment
Integrity and ethical values
Commitment to competence
Board of directors and audit committee
Management's philosophy and operating style
Organizational structure
Assignment of authority and responsibility
Human resources policies and practices

Risk Assessment
Objectives — entitywide
Objectives — activity level
Risks
Managing change

Control Activities

Information and Communication
Information
Communication

Monitoring
Ongoing monitoring activities
Separate evaluations
Reporting deficiencies

The COSO Framework consists of these components and factors. At a more detailed level, COSO also presents over 300 "points of focus" which are more specific controls — hard and soft — that evaluators *might* focus on when evaluating internal control. While these are not an essential part of the Framework, they can be helpful in developing and applying evaluation tools and techniques.

Examples of Soft Controls

In this introductory chapter I addressed the topic of soft controls in terms of basic principles. I said the sum of soft controls make up the organization's culture. The culture is too vast and complex to evaluate as a whole, but internal auditors can and should evaluate specific soft controls. I have not yet identified many specific soft controls.

To generate examples of specific soft controls, I went through COSO's "points of focus" as well as other reports and evaluation tools found in this and previous research projects and put together the following list. It is by no means exhaustive, but it will give readers a more concrete idea of what we are all dealing with.

More than perspective, this list might provide content for readers who want to develop or enhance formal evaluation tools like surveys. Even readers who want to evaluate soft controls during audit projects without a formal tool might find it useful. Often, the detection of a soft control weakness begins when an auditor senses something is wrong in the work environment, but has difficulty identifying exactly what the issue is. Skimming through some of the soft controls listed here might help. The list is organized according to the COSO framework to facilitate using it as a reference tool.

CONTROL ENVIRONMENT

Integrity and Ethical Values

- Quality of policy statements (codes of conduct, etc.) — comprehensive, meaningful.
- Management proactively (formally and informally) communicates the organization's values.
- Management's behavior exemplifies the values — "walk the talk."
- Employees understand the values and behave accordingly.
- Performance targets are realistic. Employees are not unduly pressured to meet targets "whatever it takes."
- Management deals appropriately with expensive problems (e.g., hazardous waste, potentially defective products).
- Management has created a "perception of detection" by appropriate policies, informal communication, and responding appropriately and publicly to violations of behavioral standards.
- Exceptions to policy are allowed only under clearly defined conditions. When they occur, they are documented, explained, and reviewed.

Commitment to Competence

- Quality of job descriptions (accurate, complete, up-to-date) — job descriptions may be formal or informal, depending on the environment.
- Employees understand their job descriptions.
- Employees have the skills and experience they need.
- Employees are committed to excellence in performing their jobs.
- The organization and its employees are committed to continuous improvement.

- Bonus packages and other performance measures reward the right behavior (e.g., include quality as well as volume measures).

Board of Directors or Audit Committee

- Members understand the industry and the organization well enough to oversee management effectively.
- Regular reports to the board provide sufficient information in a sufficiently user-friendly format for members to monitor key operations.
- Members receive sufficient information before meetings that they can come fully prepared to discuss relevant issues.
- Members do their homework (i.e., read the material sent to them and come to meetings prepared).
- Members are not only structurally independent of management but have an independent state of mind — willing to ask the tough questions.
- Members do ask challenging, probing questions of management and are not satisfied until they receive complete answers.
- The board receives sufficient and timely information about sensitive issues.
- The board and audit committee are involved sufficiently in evaluating the effectiveness of the "tone at the top."

Management's Philosophy and Operating Style

- Managers' operating style supports the organization's values and desired culture — managers "walk the talk."
- Managers proactively communicate the organization's values.
- Managers have high expectations of employee performance.
- Management fosters pride in the organization, its work, and its achievements.
- Management fosters teamwork and an atmosphere of mutual trust.
- Management fosters open communication (e.g., encourages employee suggestions and concerns, responds appropriately).
- Management has sufficient interaction with lower levels to maintain open communication and lead by example.
- Management has sufficient respect for control functions like accounting, data processing, and compliance (e.g., accounting is viewed as a vehicle for controlling the business, not as a necessary evil).
- Management is not obsessively focused on short-term results.
- Accuracy is valued over "looking good" in reporting financial and operating results.

Organizational Structure

- The structure facilitates the flow of information upwards, downwards, and across organizational lines.
- Reporting relationships are appropriate (e.g., control functions have sufficient independence of the activities they are intended to control — compliance functions do not report to sales functions).

Assignment of Authority and Responsibility

- Authority is commensurate with responsibility.
- Accountabilities are clearly defined.
- Responsibilities and accountabilities are clearly communicated and understood.
- Managers and supervisors have sufficient time and resources to carry out their responsibilities effectively.

Human Resources Policies and Practices

- HR policies and practices reflect concern for control (e.g., control responsibilities included in job descriptions, ethical considerations included in hiring, training, and performance appraisal).
- Appropriate action is taken in response to improper behavior by employees.
- Quality of performance appraisals (e.g., frank and constructive discussion of performance issues versus "going through the motions").
- Communication of HR department with user departments.

RISK ASSESSMENT

Entitywide Objectives

- Quality of mission/vision statements and entitywide objectives (i.e., Are they vague and generic, or do they give clear direction for the entity and its employees? Are they consistent with current market conditions?).
- Entitywide mission/vision and objectives are clearly communicated to and understood by employees at all levels.
- The strategic plan supports the entitywide objectives.
- Business plans and budgets are consistent with entitywide objectives and strategic plan.
- All appropriate parties are involved in setting entitywide objectives.

Activity-level Objectives

- Quality of activity-level objectives (i.e., Are they appropriately general/specific? Do they provide real direction? Are they both challenging and obtainable?).
- Objectives are consistent with those of related activities and with entitywide objectives.
- Objectives are clearly communicated to and understood by employees.
- All appropriate parties are involved in setting activity-level objectives.
- Objectives include control objectives (e.g., safeguarding of assets, reliability of reports) where appropriate.
- Where possible, objectives include measurements to assess achievement.

Risks

- Management understands the risks they face (i.e., Do effective mechanisms exist to identify risks arising from both external and internal sources for all major objectives and/or activities? Has management assessed the likelihood and impact of each risk?).
- Risks have been communicated and are understood by the employees involved.

Managing Change

- Management is able to anticipate and respond to changes in the environment (i.e., Do effective mechanisms exist to anticipate such changes? Is management "plugged into" industry events?).
- Management is consciously and effectively managing current organizational changes (e.g., desired change in the corporate culture, corporate restructuring, new systems, rapid growth, new technology).
- Changes in one area of the organization are communicated to other areas that might be affected.
- Employees understand the controlling process (i.e., the risk assessment thought process) and are able to respond to changes as they occur.
- The assumptions behind the organization's objectives are periodically challenged.

CONTROL ACTIVITIES

- Control responsibilities have been clearly communicated to and are understood by employees.
- Employees feel accountable for their assigned control activities.
- Management override of established controls is not tolerated. Exceptions to established policy are approved and documented appropriately.

INFORMATION AND COMMUNICATION

Information

- Quality of information provided (e.g., relevant, useful, user friendly).
- Information system development plans are consistent with entitywide and activity-level objectives and plans.
- Users are effectively involved in information system development.

Communication

- Employees' duties and control responsibilities are clearly communicated to them.
- Management is receptive to employee suggestions, concerns and complaints.
- Communications across the organization are open and effective.
- Communications with external parties (customers, suppliers, etc.) are open and effective.
- Outside parties are informed of the entity's standards of business conduct.
- Customer complaints are communicated to the appropriate levels of management and are responded to appropriately.

MONITORING

Ongoing Monitoring

- Supervisory personnel feel accountable for monitoring the effective performance of duties.
- Employees at all levels feel accountable for monitoring the results of their activities.
- Monitoring is not limited to "hard" activities (e.g., reconciliations, supervisory reviews) but includes monitoring of the control environment by talking to employees.
- Supervisors understand and are watchful for the behavioral "red flags" of fraud (e.g., sudden changes in an employee's behavior or lifestyle).

Separate Evaluations

- Independent evaluations of control systems are performed by personnel with the necessary skills and business knowledge.
- The scope, frequency, and depth of coverage are sufficient.
- The methodology is logical and appropriate.
- The methodology addresses all control objectives and components.
- The methodology involves an appropriate mix of self-assessment and independence.
- Those responsible for corrective action are involved in developing the corrective action plans.
- Evaluations are performed in an atmosphere of cooperation, with the focus on identifying opportunities to improve the achievement of objectives.

Reporting Deficiencies

- Deficiencies are reported to the appropriate parties.
- Reports (formal and/or informal) put the deficiencies into appropriate perspective.
- Management feels accountable for implementing corrective action plans.

Chapter Summary

In this chapter, I tried to provide an understanding of what soft controls are, why they are important, and why internal auditors should evaluate them. I provided some basic principles and examples. The next five chapters offer a variety of tools and techniques that are working in the real world, as well as guidelines for applying these techniques.

CHAPTER 2

SURVEYS USED DURING AUDIT PROJECTS

This chapter begins with the simplest and, for many audit departments, most practical tool for evaluating soft controls on audit projects. It presents five organizations using surveys in a variety of ways:

- **University of Minnesota** uses a short standard survey on every audit and includes the results in audit reports.

- **Precision Drilling** uses a short standard survey, but administers it through interviews rather than in writing, and only reports the results verbally to local management.

- At **Boeing**, a former auditor who is now an internal consultant uses surveys customized for each engagement, administers them verbally, and includes the results in written reports.

- **Lowes** develops customized surveys addressing both hard and soft controls on some audits. They include the results in audit reports only when supported by evidence from testing.

- **New York State Comptroller's Office**, which is external to the agencies it audits, uses a lengthy standard survey and issues the results in a separate written report.

The chapter concludes with Guidelines for Using Soft Control Surveys During Audit Projects.

University of Minnesota

Internal auditors at the University of Minnesota use an employee survey to evaluate soft controls on every audit. They were fortunate in having a Center for Survey Research at the University. The Center reviewed their survey to be sure the statements were valid and not ambiguous. This assurance, plus the simplicity of the survey and practicality of its use, makes it a good model.

The survey form (Exhibit 2A on page 124) has 12 standard statements. For example, after the instructions clearly define who the word "management" refers to, the first three statements are:

1. Management demonstrates the importance of integrity and ethical behavior to their employees.

2. Management is open to employee suggestions to improve productivity and quality.

3. Management sometimes overrides university policies, procedures, or workplace rules (e.g., takes shortcuts that are contrary to policy).

As with many such surveys, employees are asked to respond to each statement on a Likert scale:

Strongly Agree	Agree	Disagree	Strongly Disagree	N/A
SA	A	D	SD	N/A

Unlike many such surveys, some statements (e.g., #3 above) are phrased so that agreement indicates a problem and disagreement is good. This helps to ensure that employees are reading each statement carefully rather than just responding in the same way to everything.

In addition to the 12 standard statements, area management can add statements on issues of concern if they like. The last item on the form asks employees if there is anything else they would like to tell the auditors about the area's operations. Employees can sign the form if they like, but this is optional, and the auditors keep the responses strictly confidential. The surveys go out under the signatures of both the chief audit executive (CAE) and the head of the unit — unless the head of the unit thinks her signature might inhibit employees from responding because of labor relations problems.

The auditors realize that surveys measure employee perceptions, which are not always accurate. They follow up on issues raised by the survey and only report a weakness as an audit finding if they have solid evidence that employees' opinions are correct.

If they cannot find evidence to support negative employee perceptions, or even if the evidence they find runs counter to perceptions, they still report the issue to management. Negative employee perceptions are always a problem, even if they are misperceptions. In these cases, though, they report the survey results as a self-assessment, and their comment in the report is that management should consider the survey results and respond accordingly.

When survey results are positive, the auditors report this as well. In effect, every report says one of three things:

- Control environment is sound, as supported by the survey.
- Survey indicated…and our testing corroborated this.
- Survey indicated…but our testing did not corroborate this.

Here are two examples from the conclusion section of audit reports, one generally positive and one negative. The body of the reports elaborates on these conclusions.

- We believe that XXX has developed a control environment and a system of internal control that addresses many of the processes that represent its major business and compliance risks. The results of an employee survey indicated that employees share a generally positive view of the management of XXX. Employees gave high marks for management's emphasis on integrity and ethical behavior; its openness to employee suggestions to improve productivity and quality; and its effective monitoring and oversight of the activities within their unit. We did, however, identify the following issues for which resolution is considered essential to minimizing existing operational, compliance, and financial risks.

- The results of our audit lead us to the conclusion that XXX faces significant challenges in its control environment. Over the past several years, XXX has devoted considerable resources toward enhancing educational opportunities and international experiences, and increasing public visibility. While this effort has produced notable successes, our employee survey indicated that further effort needs to be made toward achieving a unity of vision within XXX itself. The survey revealed a comparatively high level of disagreement with XXX's management's goals and actions and a fairly negative perception of the work environment in XXX.

When there are negative survey results on questions about reporting of misconduct, they also report the results to the university's compliance officer, who relates it to the university hotline.

To administer the survey, internal auditing uses an inexpensive online survey tool, Zoomerang (zoomerang.com). With an online tool they can survey 100 percent of faculty and staff, and the response rate is usually between 60 percent and 70 percent (the Center for Survey Research considers a 20 percent response rate representative of the population). Before using the online tool, they could only survey a sample manually and sometimes got the complaint from management that they only selected the complainers.

Besides improving the coverage, online survey tools save a lot of time in compiling and analyzing the results. The auditors are able to easily stratify the results in whatever way they or management choose. They will not, however, show management the stratified results if doing so compromises confidentiality.

Precision Drilling

The internal auditors at Precision Drilling have an even simpler tool to help identify potential soft control weaknesses. They refer to it humorously as their "happiness survey," and it consists of eight to 10 questions (see Exhibit 2B on page 126). They wait until a few days into the audit when they have developed a level of trust with employees. Then they interview a variety of people in different positions and levels in the area using these questions to generate discussion. They keep the interviews informal and guarantee confidentiality. When employees bring up what appear to be genuine soft control weaknesses, the auditors discuss them with the manager responsible. They present these verbally only and not as audit issues, more as employee perceptions that the manager should be aware of. Presented this way, managers do not feel threatened and welcome the feedback. Good managers work to correct these weaknesses on their own, and the work environment and control environment are improved.

Boeing

Ted Wills has been with Boeing for more than 30 years, and served in Internal Audit from 1995 to 2004. He was a leader in promoting the COSO view of internal control within Boeing.

In 2005, Wills was asked by one of his executive clients to join his team as an independent reviewer of business activities. The nature of his work is evaluating critical processes and other activities, and recommending improvements on short notice. Although he is no longer an internal auditor, his technique is instructive for auditors and could be applied in some routine audits and most high-level special assurance projects.

A significant focus of most of Wills' projects is the effectiveness of soft controls. Working alone it would not be practical to do extensive detailed testing, nor does detailed testing provide the level of insight into soft controls that is desired. Wills recognized that he could leverage self-assessment concepts. However, having tried CSA workshops in the past and e-mail surveys as well, Wills has found that he gets better results with a series of structured interviews.

A typical project involves 20 to 40 interviews. This can be time-consuming, but Wills is concerned about social norms influencing how people respond to surveys. In an interview, he can personally encourage people to be candid and objective. In addition, the interviews are strictly confidential with limited exceptions (e.g., violation of legal and ethical standards). He can also explore their responses with follow-up questions, read their body language, and probe for more information when needed. A helpful by-product of interviewing executive clients of the project is that it builds their confidence in assessment results because they personally experience the assessment methodology.

Wills does not use a standard questionnaire form but develops one for each project based on project objectives and research. He reviews the soft control points of focus in the COSO report to help him develop the questions.

His questionnaires typically have two sections, each taking about half the interview to complete. The first section has statements such as "I have a clear understanding of my responsibilities." The interviewee responds on a five-point Likert scale from Agree to Disagree, with a "Don't Know" option as well. The second, equally valuable, section has open-ended questions.

After the interviews are complete, Wills summarizes the key themes and reports the results to management. He prepares a written report but feels the discussion with management is more valuable than the report itself.

The reports typically start with the purpose, scope, approach, and an executive summary of the key themes. Then a one-page chart of the questionnaire ratings is presented, stratified by demographic group. The difference in perceptions among demographic groups can be valuable information (e.g., three levels: leadership of the activities under review; the direct reports of leadership; and others [a column for each level]). The chart helps focus management's attention on areas of relative strength and weakness.

The body of the report consists of one page for each key theme, typically focusing on areas of weakness identified by the questionnaire-rating chart. It features paraphrases of interviewees' key comments as well as an assessment prepared by Wills. This section of the report provides deep insight and generates the most valuable discussion. Wills has to be very careful in paraphrasing the comments to be sure confidentiality is preserved.

The recommendation section of the report is often developed in collaboration with the client. Implementation of recommendations is optional, but few clients choose not to address the issues. Typically, the report is presented to the leader(s) of reviewed activities along with other affected managers.

The nature of the projects varies from "micro" projects at a lower level to "macro" projects addressing leadership issues. Some typical subjects have been:

- Identification and deployment of strategic objectives.
- Efficiency initiatives.
- Implementation of capital projects.
- Department-level processes.

Exhibit 2C on page 128 illustrates the questionnaire for a "macro" project.

Lowe's

Internal auditors at Lowe's do not have a standard survey form, nor do they use surveys on every audit. They use surveys for the same purpose as interviews and tailor each one to the needs of that audit. In fact, they often prefer interviews when auditing a corporate office department because of the face-to-face contact and ability to ask follow-up questions. When auditing a process affecting more than 1,600 retail home improvement stores, surveys are more practical. They can reach a much broader base and produce quantifiable results. Like interviews, their surveys deal with soft controls, hard controls, or both, depending on the nature and objectives of the audit.

A good example of a survey dealing directly with soft controls is from an audit of IT project management. The IT auditors sent out two surveys, one to IT personnel and one to end users of IT services. Both surveys used the following rating scale:

Strongly Agree	Somewhat Agree	Unable to Rate or Not Applicable	Somewhat Disagree	Strongly Disagree
5	4	3	2	1

The end-users' survey had 17 statements, for example:

- "My input and feedback are actively solicited and considered throughout the project."
- "There is open communication across all levels of the project teams."

The IT personnel survey had 25 questions, for example:

- "Project managers have the flexibility to be creative in leading a project to provide a solution."
- "My department incorporates lessons learned from past projects into its project management methodology."

Exhibit 2D on page 130 presents the statements from both surveys.

For this survey, they developed the content from the *Control Objectives for Information Technology* framework (COBIT) and *Standards for IT Project Management*. These are excellent sources, but they are phrased in technical language. The auditors rephrased the issues in layman's terms. Then, before sending it out, they had internal reviews by members of IT, compliance, an audit director, and the CAE to resolve ambiguities and remove the remaining IT jargon from the survey statements.

For this and other audits on which they administer surveys entirely by themselves, internal auditing uses SurveyMonkey (surveymonkey.com). When they do a survey related to the stores, they work with the Store Communications group, which uses a Web-based tool called EMS (Execution Management System). Store Communications helps them phrase the questions, and they also work with some store personnel to make sure the phrasing fits that environment. This is partly because Store Communications requires all corporate office communications to the stores to go through them, but also because they have expertise in doing store-level surveys. For these audits, internal auditing selects desired participants by job code, and the survey goes to everyone with that job code. Store Communications sends the results to internal auditing in Microsoft Word and Excel formats.

Internal auditing usually uses surveys on operational type audits during the planning phase to get employees' perspectives, which they then attempt to validate during the testing phase. They have also used surveys later in the audit when they felt the responses would help to confirm or disprove their testing results.

They include survey results in the final audit report when they have more tangible evidence from testing to support their conclusions. The IT survey results, for example, were included in an appendix. If they have no supporting evidence, they discuss the results with management of the audited area and share the data with them if requested.

New York State Comptroller's Office

The Division of State Government Accountability in the New York State Comptroller's Office evaluates all state agencies, many of which have their own internal audit departments. With a staff of 250 auditors who stay informed of the agencies' policies and procedures, they are able to select audits using a risk-based approach that addresses likely residual risks. That is, they have indications that there are likely to be real problems in the agencies they select to audit. When they go into the agency, they audit just the area(s) responsible for the activities of concern.

In this environment, the managers whose areas they audit are understandably defensive. The soft control evaluation techniques that rely on a participative relationship with the manager will not usually work. Also, with 250 auditors, the aptitude for evaluating soft controls varies widely.

In this challenging environment, they use a standard questionnaire to address soft controls. The questionnaire is a series of statements to which employees choose one of five responses: Strongly Agree, Agree, Disagree, Strongly Disagree, or Don't Know. If they disagree or strongly disagree with any statement, they are required to explain why they disagree (e.g., what their manager did that makes them disagree).

The auditors guarantee confidentiality and reinforce this guarantee in the way they administer the survey. They bring the employees of the operating unit being audited — but no managers — into one room at one time. They begin with a brief training session on internal control. Then they have the employees complete the questionnaire. The questionnaires are hard copy and all handed in at once, so the auditors have no way of knowing who completed each questionnaire. With this approach, they get a very high response rate and encourage the employees to be honest.

The internal control training session uses an interesting technique. Rather than a prepared slide presentation, the facilitating auditor follows the instructions from the department's "Internal Controls Survey Guidelines" (see Exhibit 2E — on CD only — for the complete Guidelines):

> The auditor should:
> - Begin by asking the staff whether they know why they are at the meeting, then either confirm what the employees said or tell them the meeting is to gather information to assess agency internal controls.
> - Ask the employees what they think of when they hear the term "internal controls."
> - Listen to how the employees define internal controls and make a note of the components the employees are not talking about. Acknowledge answers that are right or partially right. Positive feedback helps to further the trusting relationship between you and the staff.
>
> When the staff finishes explaining their understanding of internal controls, summarize their input and then fill in the blanks for them. Describe each component of internal control as defined in the state comptroller's document *Standards for Internal Controls in New York State Government*, leaving the control environment as the last element described. This helps emphasize the importance of this element and sets the stage for the purpose of the survey. Describe how all staff members have a role in these controls.

The *Standards for Internal Controls* referred to above is based on COSO, including the five components.

The specific information that employees write onto the questionnaire provides valuable evidence for the auditors. It does not, of course, stand by itself. It must be corroborated. There are times when employees give what looks like extremely valuable information, but not enough of it to fully understand or corroborate. And there are times when employees use it as an excuse to complain about irrelevant or trivial matters. Most often, though, the information they give enriches the audit results tremendously.

Their use of the questionnaire is tailored somewhat to each situation. For example, on one audit they wanted to measure employees' perceptions of the ethical behavior of four levels of management, ranging from the immediate supervisors to the head of the agency. To avoid confusion they wanted to specify job titles, but these titles varied from one work unit to another. They consulted organization charts and created 11 versions of the questionnaire, each with job titles specific to a work unit. Because these titles referred to the same four levels of management, they were able to consolidate the results. The report on this survey's results is illustrated in Exhibit 2F (on CD only). It includes the questionnaire as Appendix D, with job titles left blank.

The report on survey results also has a standard format, but is tailored to the situation. The report in Exhibit 2F, for example, gives the background, methodology, and goal of the survey in a little over a page and then has four appendices:

- A — Scattergram
- B — Numerical summary of results
- C — Employee comments
- D — The questionnaire

An earlier report on the same area also included the auditors' conclusions, opinion, and recommendations for improvement. Perhaps because this was a follow-up audit and the results were definitely better this time, or perhaps because the auditors felt it would be more effective with this management team, they chose just to present the objective results with no commentary.

It is worth noting that the earlier audit of this area was one of the first times they used the survey. Agency management did not like the idea at first, but once they saw the results, they found it very meaningful and asked the auditors to give training on internal control to their senior staff.

The director of audits found the scattergram (Appendix A of Exhibit 2F) to be a powerful reporting tool because there is a clear line between statements for which the average response was positive (3.0 and above) and those for which it was negative. Statements are also grouped by the five COSO components with vertical lines, clearly showing the relative strength of the components.

Guidelines for Using Soft Control Surveys During Audit Projects

These five examples show the wide variety of ways auditors and consultants can use surveys as an effective soft control evaluation tool. Soft control surveys can be:

- Administered verbally or in writing, hard copy, or online.
- A standard survey form or developed ad hoc for each engagement.
- For soft controls only or for both soft and hard controls.
- Used to identify potential issues that can be tested later in the engagement or used to support hypotheses formed during testing.

However soft control surveys are used, the following guidelines generally apply:

- **Survey statements or questions should be unambiguous and phrased in simple, easy-to-understand language.** You can get help with this by using good models like those in the exhibits to this chapter, consulting an in-house function with expertise in doing surveys, and using the real "experts" in the language employees will understand — some of the employees themselves — to develop and then review the statements.

- **Field-test the survey.** Once you have developed your survey instrument, give it to a number of willing employees as a test, then sit down with each of them and ask what they thought each survey statement meant. This exercise will help you identify any confusing or ambiguous statements.

- **Soft control issues are rarely yes/no issues. Better results can be gained by asking for level of agreement or disagreement on some scale.** In most cases it is better not to have an option of "neutral," because people tend to gravitate toward the middle. It is better to force respondents to agree or disagree. The most common scale we have observed is a four-point scale from "Strongly Disagree" to "Strongly Agree," with an additional option for "Don't Know" or "Not Applicable."

- **Asking people to explain their negative responses often yields valuable information.** They will often identify the specific soft control weakness that makes them disagree.

- **People have to feel safe from retribution for giving honest answers.** Confidentiality is the key here, but the degree of confidentiality depends on the circumstances. At the University of Minnesota, for example, the surveys go out under the signatures of both the CAE and the head of the unit, and people can sign their names to the survey if they choose. For the State of New York Comptroller's Office, on the other hand, managers are excluded from the room and the paper-based survey is handed in so that even the auditors cannot tell who wrote what. When reporting results, specific comments should generally be paraphrased rather than stated verbatim to safeguard the employee.

- **Surveys can accurately measure employee perceptions, but perceptions are not always accurate. Results should not be reported as audit issues unless they have been validated with more tangible evidence.** They should, however, be reported to the responsible managers because managers need to know how employees are feeling.

- **Online survey tools allow you to survey 100 percent of the population and easily compile and analyze the results.** Using an outside vendor that guarantees confidentiality can also be an advantage. Some frequently used free or inexpensive tools are SurveyMonkey and Zoomerang. There are many others available on the Internet.

These guidelines apply to all engagement-level soft control surveys. Some additional practices to consider are:

- **Allow managers the option of adding items they want to know about to your survey.** They will have more buy-in to the results, and their additions may yield the most valuable information.

- **In addition to other surveys, you might find content for your survey in sources like the first COSO report, COBIT, or authoritative sources for the function under review**, as Lowes did with COBIT and *Standards for IT Project Management*. The partial inventory of soft controls at the end of Chapter 1 might also be a source.

- **Having some statements phrased so that agreement indicates a problem and disagreement is positive helps to ensure that people are reading each statement carefully** rather than just responding in the same way to everything.

- **It is often meaningful to stratify responses by level (e.g., senior management, middle management, staff) and compare the differing perceptions** — as long as doing so does not compromise confidentiality.

- **Consider having legal counsel review the survey instrument.** If you ask sensitive questions that could potentially cause legal liability, you should have your legal department or outside legal counsel review the survey tool before you use it with employees.

For additional guidelines and things to consider for soft control surveys, see Chapter 5, "Entitywide Surveys." For more extensive guidelines, tips, and examples of surveys used for various purposes, see Hernan Murdock, *Using Surveys in Internal Audits,* The Institute of Internal Auditors Research Foundation, 2009.

CHAPTER 3

PARTICIPATIVE, RISK-BASED AUDIT PROJECTS

Surveys are easy to administer — once they are developed — and produce quantified results. It is more difficult to evaluate and report meaningfully on soft controls without a formal evaluation tool designed for this purpose. As a general rule, young and inexperienced auditors cannot succeed in this realm, and neither can audit departments that have an adversarial relationship with their clients. Experienced auditors operating in an atmosphere of mutual trust, however, can accomplish a great deal.

This chapter profiles four such audit departments:

- **Allina,** with 10 experienced internal auditors, exemplifies the key ingredients of people and culture needed to be successful.

- **Securian** is similarly small (13 auditors) and experienced. Its story is similar and reinforces the key ingredients.

- **ING** has 700 auditors stationed around the world. To achieve much the same thing, they have developed a sophisticated formal structure that emphasizes soft controls at all levels, from annual audit planning to audit execution.

- **TD AMERITRADE** has 26 auditors. Their evolution shows how a participative, risk-based audit approach can grow into a companywide ERM program. It also shows how the audit approach changes when management does its own risk assessments and control testing.

The chapter concludes with Guidelines for Evaluating Soft Controls on Participative, Risk-based Audit Projects.

Allina Hospitals and Clinics

The Internal Audit Department of Allina Hospitals and Clinics is an excellent example of how a 10-person audit department can effectively evaluate soft controls on every audit without formal soft control evaluation tools. The key to doing this is the credibility and trust they have developed with management at all levels of Allina.

Three factors contribute to the "culture of collaboration" between internal auditing and management:

- The audit staff is very experienced, averaging 22 years in business. Seven have health-care experience, four are internal transfers, and three, including the CAE, are registered nurses. At the same time, three of five project leads bring a wealth of audit experience outside health care. They bring an "outside" perspective that is invaluable when breaking down the traditional "We've always done it this way" phenomenon. Their combined maturity and business knowledge help make them credible as business partners.

- They have a very participative audit approach, involving management of the area being audited in planning and conducting the audit to the extent possible. The ideal is to think through the steps of the audit with the manager of the area so they come to the same conclusions together. The extent to which they achieve the ideal, of course, depends on the manager, and they always have to think critically about what is being said. There are certainly times when they "agree to disagree," but it is with mutual understanding and respect for their business partner's point of view.

- The participative audit approach is supported by a practice called "relationship managers." The CAE meets regularly with vice presidents and some directors. Lead auditors meet with other directors and department managers. The frequency of these meetings varies from monthly to annual, depending on the best frequency with each manager. In each of these meetings they discuss changes in the business unit, areas of focus, concerns, and the manager's perception of current and future risks. Exhibit 3A on page 135 illustrates the interview guide they use for their annual risk assessment meetings. The other meetings are similar, with questions modified to address more timely issues.

The audit process itself is a fairly typical risk-based process, but with several features that facilitate a focus on soft controls.

Allina has a standard planning document that focuses on management's goals, risks, and controls. The document itself (Exhibit 3B on page 138) is noteworthy for two things. First, the clear way it distinguishes objectives from goals and standards. These are often confused, leading to a lack of clear direction and inconsistent audit results. Second, the instructions for listing controls say "List out the potential controls that would generally be in place to mitigate the adverse effects of the risks identified." That is, the auditors draw on their experience to develop a list of the generic controls that would typically be in place over the risks that have been identified. This helps them identify missing or poorly designed controls when they see the controls actually in place.

More important than the form itself is the way they use it. They do not complete it on their own or in collaboration with just one manager. They ask several managers and see if they get different answers. When there is a disconnect among managers, the lack of common understanding is itself a soft control issue, and the cause is often a deeper soft control issue.

In their information-gathering interviews of managers and staff, the auditors ask questions like: "What are the barriers you encounter when you do your work?" "How supportive is management?" "Does management set the right tone?" If they do not feel they are getting what they want from an interview, they discuss it with another auditor to see if there might be a better approach.

During the testing phase of the audit, they dig into any disconnects they found among managers during risk assessment and any potential soft control issues they identified during interviews. The testing itself is primarily of hard controls, but it includes hard controls that, if deficient, point to a weakness in soft controls as the cause.

To develop their audit findings, they use a standard five-attribute form (Condition, Criteria, Effect, Cause, Recommendation) and focus especially on identifying the underlying root cause of each deficiency. The focus they have had up to this point positions them well to identify the soft control weaknesses that cause hard control errors.

Two elements of supervision also contribute to evaluating soft controls:

- During the audit, the audit team has a "project status" meeting with the CAE, who raises questions about soft controls to ensure they have been considered. The CAE also asks, "Do we have enough evidence?" to support conclusions about soft controls.

- Workpaper review includes a focus on soft controls, asking questions like "Have you thought about...." and "Could this be happening because...," as well as on the sufficiency of root cause analysis.

When the auditors identify soft control weaknesses, they report them to management. Depending on the situation, the reporting may be verbal only or in the formal audit report — whichever vehicle is most likely to get corrective action taken without unintended negative repercussions.

This audit process applies to routine audits. Some audits are specifically focused on soft controls. Exhibit 3C on page 140 has portions of three audit programs, one for an audit of IT governance and two for readiness reviews. For the soft control portion of these programs, fieldwork consisted of interviewing, observing at meetings, and assessing plans and/or minutes. In the readiness reviews, interviews consisted of questions to help confirm management's reported status of implementation plans. The criteria for this kind of audit work is consistency (e.g., of business objectives with the corporate IT strategy and of statements during interviews of various managers with the reported status of implementation). Management took serious interest in the results of these reviews.

In addition to soft control auditing, internal auditing sometimes offers to facilitate a CSA workshop to help correct known soft control weaknesses, and on rare occasions an audit has turned into a CSA workshop. For example, an audit of utilization management (i.e., obtaining sufficient authorization from the insurance company to ensure full payment is achieved) turned into a CSA workshop to help management standardize the process for all locations. The auditors believed that standardizing this process would help management resolve the multiple issues, including soft control issues, more quickly and effectively than an audit report delineating these issues. The tool internal auditing created and the CSA methodology used was so successful that area management continued to hold workshops on their own for additional business processes associated with utilization management.

Many internal auditors hesitate to evaluate soft controls for fear of offending managers and therefore actually accomplishing less from the audit. This is certainly a risk, but done with business knowledge, credibility, and a collaborative relationship it can be received very well. On Allina's post-audit customer satisfaction survey, the managers whose areas were audited regularly rate the overall value of the audit as high and circle "Yes" when asked, "In the future, would you ask Audit Services for help in a situation that may warrant our attention?"

Securian

Securian Financial Group's Auditing Department is another good example of an internal audit function dealing effectively with soft controls without rigid use of soft control evaluation tools. As with Allina, the key to doing this is the credibility and trust they have developed with management at all levels. Their keys to success in building this trust are also similar to those of Allina.

The most important source of trust is the competence and mindset of audit management and staff. Experience contributes to competence. Securian's CAE and three audit directors/managers all have more than 20 years of internal audit experience, and five of the nine staff auditors have more than 10 years of experience. But experience is not enough. For example, 10 years of routine compliance auditing can be a barrier to having the right mindset.

Securian expresses the mindset they want in their Auditing Department Core Values (Exhibit 3D on page 143). These values are not just aspirational. As we will see, they put them into practice every day.

Securian works hard during the hiring process, screening applicants for the right mindset and passing on all applicants if they do not find the right person. While hiring is always an imperfect process, they have had good success in finding experienced auditors seeking to add real value in their audit work. To attract these people, Securian gives them concrete examples of high-level improvements their work has produced. They also make it clear that internal auditing at Securian is a career, not a training ground. This is important because experience builds strong client relationships, which increases the chance that an auditor will identify soft controls.

Securian has been successful at retaining good people. They credit an audit approach that enables them to exercise their creativity and add demonstrable value, the quality of the company, and a work environment that allows flexible work schedules.

Auditing Director Mark Sievers believes that building client trust throughout the company takes time and must be done bottom-up. Some managers were quite open to internal audit services when he joined the company 20 years ago, but others were not. One executive, for example, was not convinced auditing would add value to his area, saying things like "Your staff doesn't know my business, how can they help me?" He remained skeptical until Mark worked with him on a taskforce for about a year. This experience helped the executive see Mark as a valuable partner, and he has since become one of Mark's best clients.

Securian's internal auditors regularly participate on committees and taskforces. Working in partnership with clients to solve problems, especially during a crisis, helps them earn trust and break down barriers some managers have toward auditors.

Although the time spent on consulting could have been spent doing audits, this work pays substantial dividends from an assurance standpoint. About half of the most substantive soft control issues were brought to the auditors by clients who trusted them to help resolve the issues. Sometimes these discussions with clients were during formal audits or planned meetings. Other times they occurred during informal conversations between meetings.

Securian's internal auditors frequently ask clients about their concerns and challenges, not just during audits. When they hear of a soft control issue, they work with clients toward a solution rather than just report the issue to others. They also take great pains not to embarrass anyone.

Taken together, these ingredients make the auditors effective at identifying significant soft control issues outside of audits. How they report these issues varies widely and is often verbal, but they are appreciated throughout Securian for their contributions.

Securian's audit approach generates substantial soft control issues. There are four keys to their success: participative auditing at all levels, a focus on the design of controls, a rigorous investigation of the cause of control weaknesses, and a thoughtful and streamlined approach to reporting the issues.

Participative Audit Approach

Like Allina's, Securian's approach is highly participative. They work closely with their audit clients, helping them to see the audit as an opportunity to improve operations. They also use an audit planning checklist to encourage discussion with the employees throughout the company with expertise in the area under review.

Focus on Design of Controls

Most audit departments spend most of their time testing to determine whether controls are working as intended. They investigate the cause of exceptions but usually stop at a fairly superficial level for one of two reasons: either they do not feel they have the time to dig deeper or they sense that the deeper cause is sensitive (e.g., lack of competence, poor communications, or management style).

Securian auditors spend most of their time evaluating the design of controls, unless the design is already well documented and has changed little since the prior audit. With this approach, they find fewer minor exceptions but more significant issues.

They document the process flow in detail, not just to identify control points, but to really understand the business and the risks. Key to this understanding is hands-on supervision and training by the experienced auditors or managers. They do not just review workpapers at the end of the audit; they are involved throughout. It is not uncommon for a manager to have a two-hour meeting with the audit team, walking through flowcharts and other system documentation, to make sure they really understand the underlying business process and its risks and controls.

Throughout the audit, they ask probing questions of each other and their clients to learn:

- Are clients really doing what they say they are doing?
- Do clients understand what they are doing?
- What could go wrong? Where could the process break down? Where are errors likely to occur?
- Is the right information getting to the right people?
- Do areas of the company collaborate where necessary?
- What drives/motivates clients?

Complimenting this on-the-job training, they have monthly staff meetings during which they share their value-added experiences and lessons learned.

A key to Securian auditors spending enough time reviewing design is the way their time is charged to each division. Auditors do not track hours spent on each project. Business units are charged the same whether they use internal auditing or not. This eliminates fixed time budgets for each audit, freeing up the auditor to dig deeper if necessary. Managers are able to effectively monitor staff performance and audit calendar planning/completion by taking a higher level, more results-based approach.

Investigation of Root Cause

Investigating the root cause is a major source of soft control issues. Many audit departments focused on testing identify an exception and stop before they get to the true root cause. The best auditors go further.

At Securian, when an error or problem is found, they continue to probe for the root cause. With each answer, they ask, "Why was that?" and keep going, often several levels deep until they can go no further. The real underlying root cause is often a weakness in soft controls like unclear communication, training, or comprehension. Once they get to the root, they see if the root branches into other areas of the company. This allows them to uncover soft issues with companywide ramifications.

Reporting of Soft Control Issues

Soft control issues, by definition, are sensitive. Reporting them as directly as hard control issues is likely to embarrass people and destroy the trust that enables auditors to identify them in the first place.

At Securian, they handle the reporting very much on a case-by-case basis. Following are some things they are likely to consider.

- Not all issues are audit issues. If the auditor believes a client problem or concern would best be handled by HR (e.g., a specific job performance issue), the auditor may advise the person to approach HR with the issue.

- For determining corrective action plans for soft control audit issues, they use the following approaches, depending on the circumstances:

    - Work with the client to agree on a solution and then report that action plan.
    - Choose to report the issue without suggesting a solution.
    - Recommend forming a group to solve the problem.

- Is it best reported verbally? If so, they monitor the resolution by staying in touch with people. Verbal reporting is sometimes preferable because it allows much more candid conversations.

- If the issue is reported in an audit report, they attempt to avoid embarrassment as much as possible. If softer language is used in the report, the auditor meets with the client in person to talk candidly about the issue.

- Who is in the best position to address the issue? It may be the person accountable. It may be that person's immediate superior. In some cases, the employee who brings a concern about their supervisor's management style to the auditors may actually be in the best position to address it. With major issues, they may need to enlist the help of an executive who has greater influence and/or a broader perspective.

Securian provided two examples of their audit reporting. The first illustrates how to report a soft control issue indirectly in writing to defuse the issue by using a report format that leaves out the details to avoid placing blame. The second example shows how big issues may take time and tactfulness to report successfully.

A typical example of Securian's indirect audit report format resulted from an auditor's work on a potential concern about the effectiveness of a key Sarbanes-Oxley control. The control in question was the certification of a periodic reconciliation between administration systems and the general ledger. A corporate unit performed the Sarbanes-Oxley test of this control by reviewing the certification. An internal audit was done to determine whether the control and the Sarbanes-Oxley test were being done correctly.

The auditors found that the certification control and the Sarbanes-Oxley testing had been performed to the satisfaction of an external auditor, but they sensed people involved were not doing the certification correctly because they did not understand the process and were not clear about their responsibilities. The auditors had full verbal discussions with their clients on the root cause and reached agreement on how to address the situation. The auditors did not consider these issues to be significant enough to report to executive management or the board of directors.

In order not to embarrass the clients, the report addressed the issue only in terms of policies and procedures; however, correct implementation of the action plans would address the issue. Following is the results section of the report.

Results

The certifications are being performed. However, some of the certification forms were not completed appropriately, and not all reconciling items were supported or explained. The improvement agreements below were developed with the assistance of area management to strengthen controls. We believe the implementation of these improvement agreements will create adequate controls for the above objective(s).

Improvement Agreements

1. Create and document formal policies and procedures surrounding the quarterly and monthly certification process.

    The policies and procedures document should include:

    - Expectations of the corporate unit and the account owners.
    - An explicit definition of what qualifies as a complete certification form, including required supporting documentation.

- A monthly and quarterly certification schedule with due dates.
- A formal escalation process for unreturned or incomplete forms.

   Owner: xxxx — Manager   Due date: XX/XX/XXXX

2. Establish a process to distribute the policies and procedures to account owners annually.
   Owner: xxxx — Manager   Due date: XX/XX/XXXX

3. Revise the certification form to clearly identify the amounts being reconciled.
   Owner: xxxx — Manager   Due date: XX/XX/XXXX

4. Work with SBUs and financial reporting to develop certification for six reconciliations that are not part of the certification process.
   Owner: xxxx — Manager   Due date: XX/XX/XXXX

On the surface, this report is a typical procedures-oriented audit report about minor issues — noteworthy only in its extreme brevity. In addition to being indirect in how it states the issue, though, it illustrates two other very meaningful aspects of their reporting format.

- They do not state the condition (i.e., the client's failure) and they do not make recommendations (i.e., the auditors' better idea). Nor do they attempt to "sell" the issue in the report. They simply state the improvements that they and management agreed will be made as a result of the audit.

- They do not give details about how some of the action plans will be performed. The details are fully discussed and agreed with responsible management, and internal auditing tracks the implementation to ensure they are done timely and well. Elaboration in the report is unnecessary.

While the primary benefit of their report format is to maintain the trust they have with clients, it has another very practical benefit: it takes very little time to write. The Background, Objectives, and Test Plan sections of the report (not reproduced here) are taken straight from the memo that announced the audit, and the Results section takes only minutes to draft. Most of the time typically spent writing reports, after all, is figuring out how to explain a complex situation concisely in a way that alerts upper management to the seriousness of the situation without being too harsh on the audit clients. By handling this communication (the "sale") verbally, Securian is able to streamline their report writing process.

Securian's internal auditors categorize audit findings into three categories:

1) "Take-it-or-Leave-it:" These are items that the auditors believe do not impact the overall conclusion on the adequacy of internal controls for the area under review. These items are mentioned to the client in the closing meeting, but are not included in the audit report.

2) "Improvement Agreements:" These are items that impact the audit conclusion. The auditors verbally discuss the conditions and reach a mutually agreeable solution with clients, which is

included in the audit report. Internal auditing tracks implementation of these action plans (called "Improvement Agreements") to ensure accountability.

3) "Significant Audit Findings:" These are issues from the previous section that pose significant companywide risk. These are documented in the audit report and also are summarized in a report of significant audit findings to executive management and the audit committee with more background explaining the issue.

The second example illustrates how to succeed with a politically sensitive companywide issue.

Project management at Securian had been done in silos with no standard methodology. Some areas did very well; many did not. When the auditors first suspected an issue, people did not buy into solving the problem because the divisions did not want a standard methodology imposed on them. The auditors monitored the situation until they had enough examples to substantiate the existence of an issue. They partnered with a manager who was very experienced at project management to identify potential solutions that could work within the company culture. They agreed to recommend keeping a decentralized approach to project management while adding a central "competency center" for sharing tools and knowledge. This solution would have to be agreed on by senior management from each division. Rather than issue a report to the entire senior management team, internal auditing issued a report to two executives: the head of HR, who would lead the new competency center, and the chief financial officer (CFO), who agreed to champion this issue. These executives took the audit report to the senior management team, which ultimately endorsed a solution.

ING

It took years for Allina and Securian to develop the staff and client relations that enable them to evaluate soft controls. ING wanted to accomplish the same result with a huge global audit staff and in a short period of time. Clearly a different, more formalized approach would be needed.

ING's internal auditors went through a major transformation process over a two-year period, involving extensive benchmarking, best practice research, consultation with management, etc. Up to this time, audit work was often limited to transaction testing, with root cause analysis often stopping at the "control not working" level.

Audit management was keenly aware of the central importance of soft controls and self-assessment techniques. Two factors, however, created challenges to full use of soft controls self-assessment:

- The audit staff would not be comfortable evaluating intangible, inherently subjective controls directly. Even with a small staff, getting experienced auditors comfortable and competent in this realm is a major challenge. With over 700 auditors dispersed around the globe, it would not be practical in the short term.

- Central to audit's transformation is positioning themselves as the "third line of defense" against business risk. In this conception, management is the first line of defense; ING's risk management functions (credit, market, operational, insurance, and information risk management functions, as well as control & finance and legal & compliance) are the second line of defense; and internal auditing is the third. Thus, wherever possible, internal auditing will verify that the second line of defense is working as intended rather than duplicating their work. This approach should not only be far more efficient, but it promotes clarity regarding ownership of risk management and control.

To support this approach, internal auditing structured itself into (a) business line audit divisions (BLADs) that audit business lines and (b) risk audit divisions (RADs) that audit risk management functions and provide support to BLADs.

Rather than use techniques designed to focus directly on soft controls, ING weaves an emphasis on soft controls throughout their audit process, from annual planning through audit execution and reporting. Rather than evaluating soft controls as such, ING focuses its audit planning at all levels on the alignment of business unit objectives, value drivers, and activities with the overall corporate strategy, evaluates this alignment during audits, and drives root cause analysis deeper. The resulting audit work is more strategically focused, and it reveals soft control weaknesses when they are present.

RAAP

To understand the ING approach to soft controls, we must start with the annual risk assessment and audit planning (RAAP) process. This process is highly collaborative. It is done through Corporate Audit Services (CAS) management team meetings, extensive interviews and management workshops at the group, business line (e.g., insurance, banking), and organizational unit (e.g., a subsidiary in the leasing business) level. Through this process, CAS gains a solid understanding of the executive board's and business line's strategic priorities and views on key risks. It articulates group-wide and business line high-level risk themes. From this strategically risk-based viewpoint, it gathers the additional information needed for detailed risk assessment and audit planning at the organizational level.

At each level, CAS identifies the strategic objectives and value drivers. Value drivers may be traditionally financial/operational (e.g., penetrate certain markets, contain costs, automate certain processes), or they may be more directly focused on soft control issues (e.g., maintain a culture of compliance). Even the more traditional value drivers generate risks that require effective soft controls. A push to penetrate certain markets, for example, creates a temptation to push beyond what is strictly ethical; containing costs can put pressure on employees to cut corners. (Note: these value driver examples are not from ING, but are mentioned to illustrate the range of value drivers that can be present in companies such as ING.)

ING management focuses intensely on the alignment of value drivers and other business priorities at all three levels of the organization. The internal audit process, from high-level risk assessment through audit execution, also focuses on this alignment. This focus drives them to evaluate soft controls, and misalignment can become the basis for audit findings.

The RAAP process begins the process of evaluating soft controls in two ways:

1. By starting from objectives and value drivers rather than predefined risk factors, risk assessment focuses on factors that are important to the business at present and going forward. Asking what could go wrong in this context can surface qualitative risks that involve soft controls.

2. One of the major challenges in evaluating soft controls is finding agreed-upon standards to audit against. Inconsistency of management's focus and activities with higher-level objectives and value drivers is a practical standard to audit against. This inconsistency is an important criterion for CAS when making audit comments involving soft control weaknesses.

To ensure proper alignment with group-level objectives and value drivers, a "Group Audit Strategy Memorandum" (GASM — see Exhibit 3E on page 144) is developed. The GASM is then distributed to the business line chief auditors to be used as a starting point for developing business line ASMs (BLASM — see Exhibit 3F on CD only) and organizational unit ASMs (OUASM — see Exhibit 3G on CD only). During the development of ASMs at all levels, interviews and workshops are held with business management to gain insight into the "tone at the top" and risk management maturity. This understanding helps the audit teams to put the more tangible elements of their risk assessment into perspective and to know how to communicate soft control issues when they later get to audit execution. In addition to the workshops/meetings with business management, "challenge sessions" between the BLAD and RAD chief auditors occur.

Subsequent to the development of the organizational unit ASMs, the BLAD and RAD management teams rate each potential auditable unit using three factors:

- Importance to Value Drivers
- Risk Type Significance
- Quality of Internal Controls (based on prior audit work, etc.)

Based on the results of this rating process, along with other information gathered during the RAAP process, the draft audit plan for the organizational unit is developed. The business line audit management team then meets to share, digest, analyze, and challenge the various risk-based organizational units' plans; the result is a consolidated business line audit plan. During the course of the analysis/challenge, changes can be made to the individual organizational unit plans in order to help ensure that the business line is focusing on the right priorities.

The audits resulting from this approach may be traditional organization unit audits — but informed by an understanding of qualitative risks — or it may be of a risk theme throughout ING (so-called "thematic audits"). Examples of the latter are an audit of "compliance monitoring" (i.e., exceptions to policy) and an audit of "winning performance culture" strategy and results. The nontraditional audit topics clearly bring auditors into the realm of soft controls, while the business focus of the traditional audit topics enable meaningful work in this realm.

Throughout the RAAP process, audit management ensures that all audit work is aligned (as much as possible) to the group-level strategic business and risk priorities. As one would assume, there is much discussion of the control environment at each level during these discussions.

Once each business line has developed its audit plan for the coming year, with its list of audits in the BLASM, the management team (including the general manager [global head of audit], business line and RAD chief auditors) discuss and agree upon group-level audit priorities. The challenges from the RADs is key to providing independent oversight to help ensure that the BLAD's plans do address the full range of risks, and that the key focus areas within the proposed audits include a focus on soft as well as hard controls.

Audit Strategy Memos

The planning focus that drives auditors into the realm of soft controls is clearly seen in the Organizational Unit Strategy Memo (Exhibit 3G — on CD only).

The ASMs follow a logical flow of the risk-based approach and include such information as:

- Business mission and objectives, critical success factors, and key performance indicators.
- Business management issues and concerns (including technology and HR issues).
- Ongoing projects and planned business changes.
- Initial view of risk management functions maturity of the organizational unit (or the next higher level, if applicable). Because these functions form the second line of defense against risk, their maturity will fundamentally influence CAS' response (i.e., the amount and type of audit work needed).

CAS rates the risk maturity of each of five risk functions (control & finance is embedded in the other risk functions):

- Compliance.
- Credit risk.
- Market risk.
- Operational, information, and security risk.
- Insurance risk.

The risk management maturity rating is one of five levels: Risk Naïve, Risk Aware, Risk Defined, Risk Managed, or Risk Enabled. An appendix to the Audit Strategy Memo provides the following information for each maturity level:

- Key features of the risk maturity level.
- Additional features of the risk maturity level.
- Suggested CAS response for each maturity level.
- Other considerations.

The more mature the risk management function, the more reliance CAS can place on risk management functions, thereby supporting efficient and optimal use of resources.

The RAAP process is intense. It is time-consuming, but not unreasonably so for an organization this size. It produces not just a list of audits but the key focus areas for each audit that are clearly aligned with group strategy and cannot be addressed adequately with traditional procedural/compliance auditing. In addition, the ASMs provide a rich source of information regarding the ING businesses.

Audit Execution

The central audit tool CAS uses is a risk control matrix (RCM) that guides the auditors through a risk-based audit project. Using the RCM, the auditors:

- List the relevant value drivers for this process.
- Identify the specific risks and control objectives regarding the value drivers within each process area.
- Assess the inherent impact and likelihood of each risk.
- Identify the control process(es) for each risk.
- Evaluate the design and operating effectiveness of the important controls.
- Identify any control deficiencies.
- Assess the residual risk impact and likelihood.

The use of the RCM ensures that a consistent risk-based approach is used on every audit. The inclusion of value drivers within the matrix ensures that the auditors focus on the bigger picture (relative importance to the business line and/or group of the risks and controls being tested).

An optional part of the audit process is a meeting once the auditors have assessed the inherent likelihood and impact of key risks. This meeting is attended by the auditors, the organization's management, and the "second line of defense" functions for that organization. Because inherent risk assessment is largely subjective, divergence of opinions can often occur initially. However, by bringing together the different perspectives, this meeting can produce a more realistic assessment of the risks. This approach helps auditors to avoid wasting time on insignificant matters, and also helps to ensure that when they find a control weakness, managers cannot argue that it is trivial.

In practice, the auditors find that they can usually raise management's assessment of a risk to match their own when they bring up reputation risk (e.g., "What would happen if this occurred and it showed up in *The Wall Street Journal*?").

After the inherent risk assessment, the auditors identify the controls over the significant risks. Within the context of all the discussions that have taken place up to this point, these include the important soft controls. This phase is done largely through walkthroughs, review of relevant documentation, and discussions with management asking constructively challenging questions (e.g., "How does X tie back to the business priorities and value drivers?" and "What do you have in place to be sure you achieve the value driver?").

The auditors then evaluate the design of the controls, discussing weaknesses with management to confirm the results of their evaluation. Again, this can involve asking constructively challenging questions and using alignment (or misalignment) with value drivers as the criterion to audit against.

After reaching their conclusion on design, they test the effectiveness of controls (hard and soft) that are key to managing risks that could negatively impact achievement of business objectives. When hard control testing discloses a weakness, the auditors focus intensely on identifying the root cause. Very often, the root cause is a soft control weakness. Material/significant weaknesses are reported immediately to business management — not just at the end of the audit. Taken as a whole, ING's audit process inevitably leads the auditors into the realm of soft controls, particularly human resources issues, without using "soft controls" terminology or having to rely on CSA workshops or questionnaires.

At the end of the testing phase, another meeting is held to go over the results. The issues discussed can be complex, involve objective evidence and subjective judgment, and have a meaningful impact on business results. Ideally, this meeting includes all three "lines of defense," although that is up to management. Having the second line of defense in the meeting helps to avoid the "us/them" dynamic that can arise in a meeting with defensive management. More important, it brings in their valuable perspective on the best resolution of the issues.

Discussion with some CAS auditors who have individually had long experience in evaluating soft controls with more direct techniques indicates that the CAS approach is highly effective. These auditors have seen dramatic improvements in soft control auditing throughout ING because of this approach.

Benefits and Challenges

It is not just the auditors who value this approach. They have gotten excellent feedback from senior and executive managers who have told them their audit reports are now addressing meaningful issues that help the executives decide where to focus their own efforts.

The external audit firm that helped CAS develop this approach told them that other large audit departments have tried it and failed. Two of the major challenges and how they are overcoming them are:

- **The inherent subjectivity of soft control issues.** The auditors must have audit evidence that convinces a reasonable person that the weakness is real. While the CAS approach toward soft controls is much more than "conversational auditing," it does rely heavily on interviews.

    One key to success in meeting this challenge is support from the top. At the time the approach was developed, the CEO was a strong advocate, and other executives have seen the far greater value it produces.

    Another key is communication. By working with management throughout and bringing the second line of defense into the key meetings, CAS reaches conclusions that are genuinely good for the business.

    The third key is the focus on the alignment of value drivers. This focus matches that of ING as a whole, and it gives CAS standards to audit against. There are still times when audit and management "agree to disagree," but they are minimized.

- **Getting a 700-person staff to adapt to the new approach.** For auditors used to hard control testing and completely objective audit evidence, higher level auditing can be difficult to embrace. At ING there was indeed a learning curve.

    One key to overcoming this "mindset" issue is the "challenge sessions," in which the Risk Audit Division chief auditors challenge the business line chief auditors regarding the robustness and completeness of their audit plans and key areas of focus. This helps to ensure that audit plans have the strategic/comprehensive focus that, by definition, leads to some soft control auditing.

    Another key is the quality assurance reviews that the CAS professional practices division performs on each of the audit groups. If audit execution fails to carry through on the planned focus and approach, this will be an issue that needs to be corrected.

The CAS Risk Audit Division recently hired a specialist to focus on developing a methodology and work programs for HR-specific areas. This is an important development and will help to further strengthen the focus on soft controls.

TD AMERITRADE

I said in the first chapter that the use of CSA workshops has evolved in many organizations from being audit-facilitated into being part of an ERM program. Exhibit 1A on page 119 showed how this occurred at BellSouth. A similar evolution has occurred in some organizations with a participative, risk-based audit approach. TD AMERITRADE is one such organization.

The company has grown tremendously through acquisitions and internal growth, from around 400,000 or 500,000 accounts in 1999-2000 to 6.9 million at the time of this writing. The number of internal auditors has grown from four to 26 during this period.

As the company has grown, risk management has become much more formalized, soft controls have become more formalized and better documented, and internal auditing's approach to soft controls has changed.

Internal auditing has facilitated CSA workshops, participated in workshops facilitated by others, and done custom surveys. However, their most successful and effective tool for evaluating both hard and soft controls throughout this period has been the risk/control matrix. Their use of the matrix has evolved as the organization has changed.

During the early part of this period the matrix was primarily an internal audit tool and served as the work program for the audit. The auditors would prepare the matrix based on input from management. The matrix was maintained and retained by internal auditors within their working papers. However, appropriate management representatives would certify (provide management representation) as to the accuracy and completeness of the matrix at the end of each audit. The matrix served as a tool to guide management of the area subject to audit through a risk assessment of the area, discussing and reaching agreement on the assessment of risks and importance of controls. Using this participative approach and reminding management that they were not just interested in policies and procedures but in what management really relied on to deal with each risk, internal auditing was able to effectively identify and then test soft controls.

Today, TD AMERITRADE has advanced from strong but informal risk management to a robust, highly formalized risk management program. The risk/control matrix is still central, but area managers are now the owners, not internal auditing.

To understand how internal auditing now uses the risk/control matrix to evaluate soft controls, it will be helpful to get a brief overview of the ERM program at TD AMERITRADE. The ERM program incorporates all strategic, operational, financial, and compliance objectives and risks. The company's corporate risk structure spans all risk-focused functions like internal auditing, compliance, safety and health, business continuity planning, information protection, and Sarbanes-Oxley compliance. It includes an Executive Risk Committee that serves as the oversight steering committee supported by several other high-level risk subcommittees like the Brokerage Risk Committee, Business Continuity Planning Committee, and the Asset/Liability Management Committee.

At the operational level, process managers own the internal controls and are responsible for documenting and testing (verifying) the effectiveness of the controls. Managers use the risk/control matrix to document the business objectives, related risks, and internal controls relied upon to ensure risks are mitigated and objectives are achieved. Management updates a risk/control matrix as changes occur, identifies which controls are primary and secondary, and tests the effectiveness of controls. This program is known as the internal control assessment program (ICAP). Every quarter, the manager certifies that the risk/control matrix is accurate and the controls are operating effectively. These matrices include all categories of objectives and risks (financial, operational, and compliance), and both hard and soft controls designed to mitigate significant risks. All matrices use the same format and are kept in a central repository subject to formal change management procedures. With all this in place, TD AMERITRADE is able to aggregate the detailed risk assessments into a true portfolio view of risk, understand the total risk of the organization, compare it to their risk appetite, and make risk-informed decisions.

Internal auditing has played a crucial role in the evolution of this robust ERM program. By using the risk/control matrix and involving managers in the risk assessments, they introduced managers to the risk assessment thought process. By including all categories of risk and both soft and hard controls, they brought managers to a broader understanding of control. And by gradually involving managers more and more into the assessment process, they prepared management to take over the ownership and responsibility for the design and ongoing evaluation and certification of internal controls.

Today, whenever a manager updates a matrix, internal auditing is notified and reviews the changes. Their review is for reasonableness. They ask themselves questions like: "Can we think of risks the manager has not identified related to the change? Has the manager assessed the risks correctly? Does the design of the controls appear adequate?" The manager addresses any concerns they raise at this point but is not required to make any changes on the submitted matrix. The manager remains the owner and accountable for the adequate design and effective operation of internal controls.

When planning an audit, internal auditing reviews the current version of the risk/control matrix of the area to be subject to audit. They compare the current risk/control matrix to the matrix they saw during the previous audit to be sure all changes have been captured and analyzed correctly. They also meet with the manager during planning to ask what has changed, what keeps him awake at night right now, and other high-level risk questions.

Also during planning, they evaluate how robust the manager's self-testing procedures have been since the last internal audit. If self-testing and supporting documentation has been robust, they reduce their testing to the level of sub-testing they need to justify reliance on the self-testing.

Throughout the audit, the auditors' goal is to determine whether the control design and control effectiveness, as certified by management, is accurate and correctly stated in the risk/control matrix. Using this approach, the auditors not only give an independent assessment of the adequate design and effective operation of internal controls, but also give assurance that management's self-assessment is reliable.

Guidelines for Evaluating Soft Controls on Participative, Risk-based Audit Projects

The four examples in this chapter show how the same thing can be accomplished in very different ways in relatively small and very large audit departments. The keys to success, however, are the same regardless of size.

- **Use a participative, risk-based audit approach.** When an auditor disagrees with a manager, the auditor rarely wins without tangible proof, and this is hard to find with soft control issues. To be successful, the auditor must engage the manager whose area is under review in the audit process. This means working together with the manager to:

    - Identify the business objectives (not control objectives like safeguarding, but what the area is really there to accomplish).
    - Identify the risks that could prevent the manager from accomplishing these objectives. (This might be better phrased as "threats," "barriers," or "what could go wrong.")
    - Assess the likelihood and impact of each significant risk.
    - Identify the controls, both hard and soft. (This might be better phrased as risk management practices, and the auditor might have to remind the manager from time to time that he is not just asking for procedures but whatever the manager really relies on to manage that risk.)
    - Determine together how best to give the manager independent assurance about the significant soft controls.

    A fully participative audit is a form of self-assessment. When the manager and the auditor think through these steps together, the manager often sees the weakness through her own eyes, drawing the same conclusion from the same evidence that leads the auditor to that conclusion. When this happens, the manager wants to correct the situation and is usually thankful she found out about it, even if the weakness is initially painful to recognize.

    Consider what happens, on the other hand, when an auditor arrives at the same conclusion without involving the manager and then reports the weakness. Most managers become defensive and argue against it. Because soft controls involve subjectivity, the auditor is unlikely to convince the manager and nothing is accomplished.

- **Be participative at higher levels as well.** How do senior managers perceive the objectives and risks of this area? Do they have concerns about soft controls in the area? Is there alignment of objectives at various levels? These discussions provide valuable information and elevate the focus of the audit to higher-level issues. When pursuing these issues, of course, the auditor must work with, not against, the responsible manager to the extent possible.

- **Focus on the design of controls.** Testing compliance with procedures usually yields exceptions, which may or may not point to a design weakness. Evaluating the design first can yield much higher-level, more significant findings, often involving soft controls.

- **Investigate the cause of findings rigorously.** The underlying root cause, even of minor procedural exceptions, is often a soft control issue. This point compliments the focus on design. When an auditor starts from exceptions and identifies the design weakness that caused the exceptions to occur, it is easy to consider the job done. When an auditor starts from a design weakness, on the other hand, the root cause will be more important and often a weakness in soft controls.

  Even when auditors start from exceptions, though, investigation of root cause can lead to a soft control issue. Assume, for example, that a control is well designed but not performed consistently. Auditors may think they are done when they have identified the immediate cause of the exceptions: the inconsistent performance. But full investigation of the cause requires the auditor to ask the question "Why?" several levels deep. For example:

  "Why did these exceptions occur?"
  — The control was not performed consistently.

  "Why wasn't the control performed consistently?"
  — The employees didn't think it was important to do so.

  "Why didn't the employees think it was important?"
  — Their supervisor never explained its purpose to them.

  "Why didn't their supervisor explain its purpose to them?"
  — He spends all his time performing his own tasks rather than supervising them.

  "Why does he do this?"
  — He was promoted to supervisor because he was the best worker, but never received supervisory training (or he is unwilling to change his role, or because his manager gives him so many tasks he has no time to supervise).

  We now have three possible causes, each of which could have a still deeper cause. But going this far is enough to see that if we correct the deeper cause, we not only prevent future instances of the same exceptions, but many other potential problems as well.

  In a sense, this is basic internal auditing. The five-attribute approach to developing audit findings (Condition, Criteria, Effect, Cause, Recommendation) has been in the *Standards* for decades, and training in this approach is (or should be) in every training program for new internal auditors. But it is not usually taken deeply enough to disclose a soft control weakness.

- **Use experienced auditors with strong interpersonal skills** for soft control evaluation. Auditors fresh from college lack the credibility, confidence, and savvy to engage a manager in a meaningful discussion of soft controls. Experienced business people who are new to auditing, on the other hand, can be very successful in this realm.

These five guidelines apply to a department's overall audit process, and two are technical (focus on design and investigate cause). The interpersonal skills needed and how to apply them in the participative relationship are never-ending challenges worth elaborating on.

Four anecdotes shared by participants in the study illustrate these skills, exemplify some of the guidelines above, and lead to additional guidelines. The first story involves an experienced auditor who met with an extremely analytical C-level executive to discuss an important governance issue. With this person, the auditor recognized that he had to proceed slowly and intellectually. Over the course of 10 meetings, he was eventually able to tactfully box the executive into a logical corner. By this point, because of the careful buildup to that point, the executive saw the need for change.

In the second story, the same auditor dealt with another executive whose style was challenging. He realized that with this person, he would have to stand his ground to establish credibility. After three or four meetings, this executive also came around to see the need for change. The additional guideline that emerges from these experiences is:

- **Tailor your approach to the individual.** You need to know a manager's intellectual and emotional style and adapt your approach accordingly. With some managers, you have to go slow and let the realization come to them gradually over time.

The third story involves a routine audit of the capital expenditure process. During the planning stage, the auditor came across the following situation.

A road construction project blocked both entrances to a company-owned gas station. A competitor's gas station across the street faced the same problem. Putting in a new entrance just past the construction would solve this problem. The competitor did so quickly, but by the time the auditor's company approved the capital expenditure, the road construction was completed and the company had lost business and customers.

The cause of the delay was the approval process. The subsidiary company's CEO had to approve every capital expenditure over an unusually small dollar amount. The CEO considered capital expenditure proposals once a month at a meeting with all his direct reports. On the day before that meeting, his direct reports met to discuss and prioritize their proposed projects. This meeting was often contentious and had a negative effect on their relationships.

But why did the CEO have to approve small expenditures? The lead auditor met with the CEO. She did not ask this question directly, which would have implied that the CEO was guilty of micromanagement. Instead, she presented the facts in a way that guided the CEO's thinking and tactfully probed until "the light bulb went off." The CEO realized for himself that the real cause was his unwillingness to trust his direct reports. With this self-realization he not only changed the approval process, but very likely improved his relationship with them in other ways as well.

A similar but different example from the same CAE suggests two important caveats when investigating root cause. An accounting function performed valuation and billing which sometimes involved complex calculations. During an audit of the function, the auditor learned of a US $6 billion error that management had discovered. Investigating how this error had occurred, the auditor found that the manager made the error himself. Rather than blame the manager, the auditor worked with him to determine why it happened and how to prevent or detect such errors in the future. He said he had to do all the calculations himself because his staff was not capable of doing them. The auditor could see that he seemed overworked and stressful.

Rather than take the manager's word for it, the auditor maintained his healthy skepticism and asked the staff about their background and experience. He found that the staff was very experienced and many had performed similar calculations in the past.

The auditor tried to work with the manager to get him to realize that he was unnecessarily micromanaging his staff. In this case, he was unable to do so. The CAE had to elevate the issue. The manager was reassigned, had the same issues in his new position, and eventually left the company. The two additional guidelines or caveats that emerge from these examples are:

- **"Trust, but verify."** The best internal auditors work with managers to evoke positive self-discoveries, but we should always verify what managers tell us.

- **Elevate when necessary.** When the self-discovery does not happen, we may need to elevate the issue. Whether and how high we elevate it depends on the level of risk. If the risk is not great, it is usually better to let the matter rest than to make an enemy of the manager.

A fifth anecdote about elevating soft control issues is worth sharing. During a presentation of the author's training program on evaluating soft controls, a CAE said, "Everybody should realize that when you report a soft control weakness, you'd better be ready for a fight!" She had raised the issue of a C-level executive's management style to the CEO and audit committee. He fought back viciously. She had ample evidence, but in the realm of soft controls the best evidence can be disputed. It was very painful for her to go through, but it was eventually resolved in her favor. Afterward, the CEO said to her, "Thank you very much! We've all felt that was true, but none of us dared say it." Her credibility was greatly enhanced.

Finally, it might be worth sharing the following "Five Principles for Evaluating Soft Controls" from the author's soft control seminar. The second and fifth principles elaborate on two of the guidelines above. The other three were probably applied in the examples and stories above, although the participating auditors did not specifically say so.

- **Ask "constructively challenging" questions of management and confirming questions of employees.** For example, a CAE interviewed executives about soft controls. The company had a code of ethics, but this is a hard control that may or may not accomplish anything. The real question is, "Do our employees really understand and practice our corporate values?"

    But the CAE did not phrase the question this way. Instead, he asked the executives, "*How do we know* that our employees really understand and practice our corporate values?" He asked it in a constructive way, but it challenged the executives to ask themselves how they know this was true. When they could not think of a good answer, they felt uncomfortable. They wanted better assurance that this is true, and they developed action plans to give them this assurance.

    One of their action plans was to enhance an existing employee survey. Again, the phrasing of questions was critical. Instead of asking, "Do you understand and practice our corporate values?" the survey asked, "Do *other employees* in your area understand and practice our corporate values?" This phrasing could yield more reliable answers, and comparing the ratings from one area to another could yield interesting results.

- **Identify and obtain management's agreement on the criteria for evaluation and what will constitute legitimate audit evidence.** During a participative, risk-based audit, auditors should prompt managers to identify soft controls among their risk management practices. Good managers want to know whether the soft controls they rely on are effective. They have their own observations, but the auditor can give them assurance that is independent and at least somewhat more objective.

    It is very important that the auditor work with the manager to design tests of soft controls. These tests will rarely be as objective as tests of hard controls, but if the manager participates in the design of the test, she will usually accept negative results as legitimate and want to address the situation. She will not be happy with the results, but she will be grateful to the auditor once the situation is resolved.

    It is worth emphasizing this guideline, because it is exactly opposite of the normal rule of audit reporting. When testing hard controls, the rule is to complete the test, be certain your evidence is solid, and then report the weakness. As stated above, if auditors proceed this way with soft control weaknesses, they will usually have a fight on their hands that they cannot win.

- **Get "hard" evidence about the results of the soft control when possible.** For example, if you want to determine whether employees understand compliance rules, you can quiz them and produce quantitative results. You can also test to determine whether there have been any violations of the rules.

- **Focus on the underlying management process.** If it is not possible to test the existence of a soft control directly, there is usually a management process designed to create the soft control within people. That process might be training, communication, performance measures, or various other formal processes. The auditor can at least evaluate the design of the process and whether it is applied consistently. This would not determine whether it is effective (i.e., producing the desired result), but it would be valuable as far as it went.

- **Develop and report results in partnership with those accountable. Use appropriate (perhaps informal) means of reporting.** The first sentence is central to almost everything in this book. The second sentence is worth elaborating upon. Through the author's 16 years of working with auditors who evaluate soft controls, he has found that soft control weaknesses are usually reported verbally and not written up in audit reports. There are at least two reasons for this.

    - Even with hard control weaknesses, managers may agree verbally but get defensive when they see it in an audit report. This will be more often the case with soft control weaknesses, which can be quite personal. Stating the weakness in an audit report can destroy the partnership, perhaps prevent the corrective action from being taken, and make it more difficult to evaluate soft controls in that manager's area in the future.

    - It can be very difficult to put a soft control weakness into full perspective in a concise written statement. The manager's superiors might misunderstand and unfairly think less of the manager.

That said, I did find some audit departments that report soft control weaknesses in written audit reports. Securian does so only indirectly. New York State Comptroller's Office (Exhibit 2F on CD only) and WorkSafeBC (Exhibit 6D on CD only) do so directly. Chapter 7 presents many sanitized examples of direct reporting. The wording there might be helpful to readers interested in doing this. The guideline that applies is that auditors must have valid proof of a soft control weakness to take it from verbal to written reporting.

CHAPTER 4

STRUCTURED ENTITY-LEVEL INTERVIEWS

As mentioned in Chapter 1, the root cause of major frauds and business failures is almost always a weakness in the corporate culture; in other words, a weakness in soft controls. Chapters 2 and 3 presented techniques for evaluating soft controls during audit projects. The focus at this level is on the subculture created by management over the area being audited (although the same weakness found in many areas is likely to be a symptom of an entitywide weakness). Chapters 4 and 5 present techniques that focus on entitywide controls directly, in a single review.

The COSO report posited two levels of control: activity level (i.e., within a functional area or process) and entity level. Regulations like Sarbanes-Oxley, using COSO as the criteria for evaluating control, require an evaluation of entity-level controls. Entity-level hard controls like those in the financial reporting process can be tested with traditional transaction-testing techniques. Entity-level soft controls are more problematic and are often not evaluated very effectively.

Many organizations use lengthy COSO-based questionnaires developed by their public accounting firms to review entity-level soft controls. These questionnaires often have Yes/No answer choices. In my view, such questionnaires have limited value because soft controls are not Yes/No issues.

For example, two of the most common and important issues addressed are whether management demonstrates high ethical standards and whether undue pressure is put on employees to achieve performance targets. These questions cannot be answered with a complete yes or no. It is a matter of the degree to which these are true. Realistically, someone asked to respond yes or no will almost answer yes, because it would be extremely difficult to justify an absolute no answer.

This chapter shows how three audit departments dig beneath the surface with structured interviews:

- **Precision Drilling** uses a lengthy questionnaire from their public accounting firm, but completes it through interviews and does several things in their interview technique and follow-up to dig beneath the surface.

- **Kaiser Permanente** does a "tone at the top" interview project with executives. They have just 11 questions, but the way they phrase the questions and probe into the answers generates hour-long interviews with meaningful results.

- **Anonymous** does a corporate compliance review through structured interviews to evaluate the effectiveness of the formal compliance program (i.e., do people really understand the requirements and are they fully committed to compliance?). The phrasing of the questions is again key to success.

- **Aquila Inc.** expands on the concept of structured interviews by conducting workshops (which might be thought of as group interviews) and bridges into the next chapter by surveying managers who could not attend the workshop.

Best Practices: Evaluating the Corporate Culture

The chapter ends with Guidelines for Entity-level Interviews.

Note: The reader might find a disconnect in how questionnaires administered through interviews are treated. In Chapter 2, they are included with audit project surveys, but here they are distinguished from entity-level surveys, which are covered in the next chapter. The reason is the difference in the people interviewed. During audit projects, the responses come from line employees, so whether they give those responses in writing or verbally is not a significant difference. At the entity level, interviews tend to be with upper management, while the bulk of surveys go to line employees. The source of information is different, and the information gathered can be substantially different because of the different perspective executives and employees often have about the same issues. This difference is significant enough to treat entity-level interviews and surveys in separate chapters.

Precision Drilling Corporation

Although Precision Drilling is a Canadian company, it complies with Sarbanes-Oxley. Internal auditing is using this compliance exercise as an opening to deal effectively with entity-level soft controls.

The formal tool they use for entity-level controls is a questionnaire they got from their external audit firm and tailored somewhat to Precision Drilling. This questionnaire is longer than it would be if internal auditing developed it, but the external audit firm required all the issues to be addressed. In many organizations, completing this sort of questionnaire is a checklist exercise. As long as the objectively verifiable hard controls are in place and no one who is interviewed volunteers that there are soft control weaknesses, the evaluators are satisfied. At Precision Drilling, the internal auditors probe deeper.

Probing deeper is a matter of asking the right follow-up questions and thinking creatively about how to get beneath the surface. Most of the questions on the questionnaire can be answered yes or no, but when the interviewee is uncertain or the answer is a weak yes (as indicated by tone of voice, body language, or hesitancy), the auditors ask why.

One way they sometimes dig beneath the surface after the interviews is by sorting information in different ways. An example is the issue of turnover. HR provided them with data on the number of positions turned over sorted by job classification. On the surface this data looked reasonable, but the auditors wondered whether some areas were experiencing excessive turnover. They went to payroll to identify employees who had left, sorted by area, and calculated percentage of turnover in each area. They then went back to HR and reviewed exit interview documents to determine the cause of terminations in areas of the company with a high percentage of turnover. This led them to identify reportable soft control issues.

Another element of Sarbanes-Oxley entity-level evaluation not done in many organizations is how they choose whom to interview. In many organizations, the same executives and managers are interviewed every year and it becomes a mostly repetitive exercise. At Precision Drilling, internal auditing works with the CFO to identify specific areas of the company for interviews at lower levels (different areas each year) in addition to the usual required interviews. This sometimes yields new information about soft controls. Exhibit 4A on page 150 is a spreadsheet showing the entire questionnaire and identifying which level of the organization, from board members to employees, will be asked each question.

Two other Sarbanes-Oxley-related activities deal with both entity-level and activity-level soft controls. The whistleblower hotline required by Sarbanes-Oxley is also a good source for identifying soft control weaknesses. A third-party vendor administers the Precision Drilling hotline and sends the reports directly to internal auditing, the audit committee, and legal. The internal auditors think of these reports as "arthroscopic surgery" that penetrates the surface to reveal what is really going on inside. They look for patterns that might indicate a weakness in the ethical climate or related soft controls that allow or may even encourage violations to occur. They also look for patterns in how these violations are dealt with, especially whether they are handled consistently. Consistency is an attribute that can be measured somewhat objectively, and inconsistent treatment of violators (e.g., not taking action against the "best salesman" because he is too valuable) sends a powerful negative message to all employees about the real values of the organization.

To help management create a positive ethical environment, internal auditing presents ethics training. In 2006, they trained about 220 managers, from supervisors and managers up to C-level executives. This training program (see Exhibit 4B on page 157) included real-world scenarios of ethical dilemmas that required a difficult judgment as to the correct course of action. They will conduct further ethics training sessions in 2009.

Two interesting and somewhat unexpected results of this training were managers bringing up their own ethical dilemmas during the training and later calling the auditors for advice when they encounter an ethical dilemma. When such issues are raised during the training sessions, internal auditing asks the appropriate higher-level managers, "Have you heard of this?" to be sure they are aware of and will act to address them. When asked for advice, the CAE makes it clear that he cannot simply tell them what to do. He can help them clarify the issues they need to consider in deciding what to do, and they should then have the same discussion within their chain of command to get the decision made with the appropriate accountability.

The issues raised during the training sessions and in the calls for advice have educated the auditors in specific things that could go wrong that they never would have thought of on their own. This has enriched the quality of their routine audit work in that they know better what to look for and how to probe into potential issues.

Kaiser Permanente

Internal auditing at Kaiser Permanente also reviews entity-level soft controls for Sarbanes-Oxley compliance. For their "Tone at the Top Interview Project," the CAE and Sarbanes-Oxley leader met with approximately 35 business leaders for one hour each. They worked from 11 broad questions such as whether the leaders saw changes in the organization's ethical climate over time and how leaders reinforce "transparency" and "integrity of information" with their teams. To dig below the surface, they asked for concrete examples and how the business leader addressed them. These interviews were very productive, and when the CEO suggested they conduct similar interviews with the board members, they did so. The results were reported to senior leadership, finance, and other leadership groups, and to the board.

Based partly on this tone at the top work, internal auditing was able to give the audit committee an assessment on internal control for the organization as a whole in its annual report. The other major sources of this assessment were their audit work and discussions among internal audit management, the Sarbanes-Oxley group, compliance, and other governance-related groups. Internal auditing found that everyone's picture of the organization was consistent, which helped give them confidence in the essential correctness of their assessment.

In the assessment report to the audit committee, they stated the sources of their opinion and made it clear that they do not audit everything. They structured their report according to COSO. For each component of control, they presented both strengths and opportunities for improvement. There were no major surprises for the executives or audit committee, but everyone felt it was helpful to see the overall picture clearly. Exhibit 4C on page 171 illustrates the slideshow they used for this report. The specific results, of course, have been deleted; but the format might be useful for readers.

A second segment of work at the entitywide level began when the CAE co-presented a session on internal auditing's role in corporate governance at an IIA conference, including the work that she was doing in her organization. She decided to review that presentation with the audit committee chair and the CEO and discuss what else internal auditing could do. She pointed out that internal auditing was already involved in most of the activities suggested in the IIA Position Paper on Organizational Governance, except for audits of the board activities.

As a result, internal auditing was asked to review the key board committees. The Governance Committee was selected for the pilot audit, and other committees are now being audited. A senior audit manager developed criteria for this review from the committee charters and external sources such as the Conference Board Commission on Public Trust. See Exhibit 4D on page 175 for the criteria used for the Governance Committee. Much of it focuses on formal controls (charters, etc.), but the elements of "best practice" and observing committee meetings involve soft controls.

Anonymous

A third example of entitywide interviews is from an organization that wishes to remain anonymous. There is no regulatory requirement involved, but compliance is a significant exposure for the organization.

This organization has a good formal compliance program. All new hires receive classroom training on compliance. Later, all employees take an online refresher course, which includes a quiz that asks what decision they will make in given situations. Thus, it determines whether they really understand the essence of compliance, not just the rules. They are expected to score 90 percent or more on the quiz.

Rather than rely on the formal controls alone, internal auditing does a periodic audit to determine whether employees really understand and are committed to all aspects of the program, and whether management is creating a culture of compliance. For this review, an audit manager not associated with compliance interviews about 65 of the roughly 1,000 employees. The interview guide has four pages of open-ended questions. It starts with simple questions about hard controls to make the interviewee feel at ease. As it proceeds, the questions become more soft-control focused and sensitive. The interviews can become fairly lengthy, as the content and phrasing require reflection and in-depth discussion. When the audit manager detects discomfort with a question, she probes to determine why.

The interview guide ends with a 10-question "Quick Compliance Quiz." See Exhibit 4E on page 177 for the questionnaire.

Aquila Inc.

As first reported in *Four Approaches to Enterprise Risk Management…and Opportunities in Sarbanes-Oxley Compliance* (IIARF, 2007), Aquila's internal auditors evaluated entitywide controls for Sarbanes-Oxley compliance, and this review became an element of their ERM program as well. Rather than interviewing executives individually, they conducted two six-hour workshops. One workshop was with the Leadership Team (the CEO and his direct reports) and the other with the Extended Leadership Team (those people's direct reports). After the workshops, they surveyed those who could not attend. They presented both sets of results to the audit committee and discussed the differences between the two groups.

The workshops and survey were based on a maturity model that is being used with increasing frequency by internal auditors. The generic model (Figure 4A) has five levels of maturity.

Stage A	Stage B	Stage C	Stage D	Stage E
• Process ad hoc. • Results are often left to heroics of individuals.	• Informal processes. • Not well communicated or executed.	• Formal processes that are adequate. • Processes may not always be consistent or well communicated. • Areas of improvement in efficiency and effectiveness.	• Formal processes that are well executed. • Processes are consistent and well communicated. • Improvement area exists in relation to monitoring and KPIs.	• Processes are optimal. • Best practice methods and metrics.

Figure 4A: Generic Maturity Model

For their review, the auditors defined 13 entitywide capabilities based on the COSO control model. They also defined specific criteria for each maturity level as it applies to each capability — 65 criteria in all. Exhibit 4F on page 181 presents the capabilities and complete set of criteria.

For each capability, workshop participants evaluated two things: where this capability is today (current state) and where it should be considering current business conditions (desired state). They used voting technology and had in-depth discussions after each vote.

There are some unusual features of the voting and discussion that readers interested in doing something similar might consider. Aquila had developed these features doing capabilities maturity workshops at lower levels before they conducted this entity-level workshop.

Although they used five levels of maturity, participants voted on a nine-point scale, with 1 = Stage A, 3 = Stage B, etc. Participants could then vote an even number if they believe the maturity is between two stages. This feature saves time because participants do not spend time debating in their minds whether a capability is closer to 3 (Stage B) or 5 (Stage C). If they think it is in between, they vote 4.

Aquila's standard for an "adequate" rating is Stage C (or 5 on the 9-point scale). Any capabilities that fall more than a little short of this measure, as well as any capabilities with a significant gap between the actual and desired maturity level, is subject to further analysis. Further analysis is needed because the capabilities with the lowest ratings and/or largest gaps may have less impact on the business than others that are rated somewhat higher or have smaller gaps. Workshop participants take the ratings, gaps, and impacts into consideration as they prioritize the capabilities to decide which to focus on for improvement. They then develop action plans for the capabilities whose improvement will most benefit the organization.

Guidelines for Entity-level Interviews

For the most part, the same guidelines that apply to audit project interviews apply to entity-level interviews, especially:

- Use experienced auditors with strong interpersonal skills.
- Tailor your approach to the individual.
- Ask "constructively challenging" questions of management.

Two additional guidelines emerge from the examples in this chapter.

- **Ask questions that force people to think.** Phrase questions in a way that cannot be answered superficially or with generalities.

- **Read body language and tone of voice.** When you sense discomfort, probe tactfully into the reasons for this discomfort.

- **Ask for concrete examples.** Especially with senior managers who know all the "right" answers. For example, if you want to know whether they informally communicate the importance of ethics, ask for the most recent instance of doing this and what exactly did they do or say. If you want to know whether they exemplify the organization's values in how they treat vendors, ask for a recent example of conflict with a vendor and how they responded.

CHAPTER 5

ENTITYWIDE SURVEYS

In Chapter 4, I said that structured interviews are more effective than lengthy questionnaires with Yes/No answers. In my opinion though, a different kind of questionnaire is the most effective way of evaluating entity-level soft controls. There are two reasons for this belief.

- First, senior management can only tell us what they want and believe the soft control to be. Employees who live in the culture can tell us what it really is. For example, executives may say and believe that teamwork is one of the organization's central values. They may have done everything they can to instill it into the corporate culture. But if employees believe that the way to get ahead is by making their peers look bad, teamwork is not — or not yet — part of the culture.

    It is not practical to interview a large enough sample of employees to generate sufficient audit evidence about the corporate culture. Cultural surveys, on the other hand, are very practical tools. Such surveys are often administered through **HR** and address many, but not all, of the soft controls of interest to internal auditors.

- The second reason that entitywide surveys can be more effective than structured interviews is that survey results can be quantified. We can actually measure aspects of the culture with a well-constructed survey. We must, of course, recognize that the measurement will not be precise, and its reliability depends on how effectively we construct and administer the survey (the guidelines at the end of this chapter elaborate on this point). We must also put the measurement into a meaningful context. An average response of 3.2 on a four-point scale to a survey statement is not meaningful by itself. We have to compare it to the average response for other statements to identify relative strengths and weaknesses, or to previous years to track trends over time, or to industry averages if they exist.

Surveys are not a perfect tool for evaluating entitywide soft controls, but they are the best available at this time. They provide a reasonably accurate measure of the corporate culture. Properly constructed, administered, analyzed, and interpreted, they are more likely than any other technique to identify the kinds of weaknesses that result in business scandals and failures.

In this chapter, I present six such surveys:

- **Ameritech** — This is the first and still one of the best entitywide soft control surveys I have seen. Although it was included in a previous IIA study, it is worth repeating here because it best exemplifies the guidelines presented at the end of this chapter.

- **United Stationers** — This is a direct descendant of Ameritech's survey, expanded for Sarbanes-Oxley compliance, and administered somewhat differently. United Stationers' experience raises the issues presented when HR does a similar "cultural" or "engagement" survey.

Best Practices: Evaluating the Corporate Culture

- **BP PLC** — Shows how internal auditing can use the results of an engagement survey contracted for by the organization rather than create their own survey.

- **City of Austin** — Shows how internal auditing was able to enhance an HR-administered survey to include all the most relevant soft controls. Internal auditing also correlated the survey results to measures like absenteeism and complaints to demonstrate the concrete impact of soft controls.

- **Lennox International** — A survey developed by internal auditing, then turned over to the Business Practices Division, which contracts with an external vendor to administer the survey.

- **Robeco** — A survey based on external research and adapted by internal auditing to the organization. This case study presents a highly disciplined technique for developing a survey tailored to a specific organization.

The chapter concludes with Guidelines for Entitywide Soft Control Surveys.

Ameritech

The first and still one of the best entitywide soft control surveys I have seen was developed by Ameritech and included in the 1997 IIARF study, *Control Model Implementation: Best Practices*. Although I was unable to determine whether it is still used, it was effective for more than a decade and has been the model for many organizations to create their own, including the State of New York Comptroller's Office presented in Chapter 2. I will describe how it was used in 1996 because it illustrates some of the guidelines at the end of this chapter particularly well.

The history of this survey began in 1989 when the audit committee asked the CAE to review entity-level controls as a response to the Treadway Commission's 1987 *Report of the National Commission on Fraudulent Financial Reporting*. He developed a survey and sent it to Ameritech's 15 business unit presidents to complete. This turned out to be a mistake. Asking managers to evaluate things they are personally responsible for is rarely effective. Even if they have the integrity to admit their own failings, they are probably not aware of them.

When the presidents' responses indicated nothing could be improved, the CAE realized his mistake. The next year he did not send the survey to the presidents, nor to their direct reports. He sent it to a random sample of lower-level managers. The response was very different and very meaningful.

The reader might wonder why the CAE only surveyed midlevel managers and only a sample of them. The reason is that in 1996, the survey was paper-based, and Ameritech had 24,000 midlevel managers. A 10 percent sample was all they could realistically deal with. Their response rate had grown through seven years to 50 percent, a remarkable response rate for a paper-based survey. This response rate testifies to the credibility the survey had developed. Today, of course, auditors use Internet tools to survey 100 percent of employees, and Internet surveys typically get a much higher response rate than paper-based surveys.

Ameritech's survey (see Exhibit 5A on page 188) contained 45 statements (e.g., "Senior management of my business unit demonstrates high ethical standards" and "My business unit learns from its mistakes"). The survey uses a Likert scale (SD = Strongly Disagree, D = Agree, A = Agree, SA = Strongly Agree, DK = Don't Know).

The survey is structured into five sections corresponding to the five COSO components. This structure was added and some of the statements changed after the COSO report came out in 1992. The CAE found that some managers were put off by the COSO terminology they did not understand, so he changed the section titles as follows:

COSO Component	Ameritech Section Heading
Control Environment	Company Culture
Risk Assessment	Goals and Obstacles
Control Activities	Policies and Procedures
Information and Communication	Information and Communication
Monitoring	Evaluation and Feedback

Each section ends with a question, "If you disagree/strongly disagree with any of the above questions on _____, why do you feel this way?" The comments written in, which they referred to as "verbatims," often provided very meaningful feedback.

Because the survey probes into sensitive issues, and candid "verbatims" were crucial to success, confidentiality was essential. To preserve confidentiality, managers were asked to send the survey directly to an independent market research firm. This firm compiled the statistical data, transcribed the written comments, and sent the results to internal auditing. Thus, even internal auditing did not know how individuals responded. As a final safeguard of confidentiality, internal auditing did not show or read the "verbatims" to upper management, even if they were asked to do so, so that no one would be able to identify the source by the way a comment was phrased.

The market research firm compiled the statistical results by business unit and for Ameritech as a whole. They also compared each year's results to the previous year. After analyzing the results, internal auditing sent them to selected officers (direct reports of the presidents) within each business unit for review. These officers include the CFO, the HR vice president, and the other vice presidents who are key from a control perspective. The entire Ameritech results were shared with 12 officers at the corporate level.

Internal auditors met with each of the selected officers one-on-one to discuss the results and get the officer's perspective on potential action plans for improvement. These discussions were conducted very much in a self-assessment mode, with the auditor facilitating the officer's analysis.

After these facilitated sessions, the general auditor met with each of the 15 business unit presidents to discuss and finalize the potential action plans. The presidents then sent the finalized action plans in writing to internal auditing. Finally, the general auditor met personally with the chairman of the board and the three executive vice presidents who are responsible for managing sectors of Ameritech.

It is important to note that this process focused less on individual problems than on trends — and especially on creating positive trends. It is treated throughout as a learning experience, not an exercise in faultfinding. See the last page of Exhibit 5A on page 188 for the format used to present comparative results over the previous four years (actual data deleted to preserve confidentiality).

United Stationers

United Stationers' Internal Audit Department started using an entitywide survey when Bruce Adamec was its CAE. The current version has been expanded to address issues needed for it to serve as support for Sarbanes-Oxley compliance, and the current CAE, Sandy Kruse, has continued to adapt it to a changing environment.

Internal auditing surveys three groups: senior leadership, financial leadership, and all other exempt associates (i.e., salaried employees). They do not survey nonexempt (i.e., hourly) employees because the survey is intended to be *management*'s self-assessment of risk. The core questions are the same for all three groups, but there are a few differences depending on that group's knowledge. For example, only senior leadership was asked a question relating to the board.

Exhibit 5B on page 194 is the invitation letter for all other exempt associates to take the online survey. Exhibit 5C on page 196 shows the survey statements and structure for this group. Exhibit 5D (on CD only) shows the differences in survey statements among the three groups.

Like Ameritech, United Stationers uses an external firm to increase the perception of confidentiality. Their response rate in 2008 was 76 percent.

Unlike Ameritech and earlier versions of the survey at United Stationers, the 2008 survey asked for comments just once, at the end of the survey, rather than at the end of each of the five sections. This was because of the sheer volume of the comments they had received in the past. Kruse feels they get basically the same information more efficiently this way. Even with this streamlining, they had more than 5,000 comments.

Kruse reviewed departmental results with senior leaders and followed up on comments when she saw a pattern that may have indicated a soft control weakness. It was useful to compare and contrast the scores of the three shared services functions versus the three business units. The presentation to the audit committee focused on overall year-to-year trends.

Entitywide surveys can be especially useful when there is an acquisition. In 2007-2008, United Stationers acquired a new subsidiary, and comparing survey results from this subsidiary to the organization as a whole was quite meaningful. One of the main causes of failures in mergers and acquisitions is a clash of corporate cultures. Identifying differences at an early stage can help management deal effectively with them.

As valuable as the survey has been, internal auditing did not conduct one in 2009. There were three reasons: 2008 results were consistent with prior years and did not result in significant new action plans; the audit committee wanted to know how the numerical ratings compare to other organizations; and HR used an external vendor, Strativity Research, to do an "Associate Engagement Survey," which is a form of cultural survey. There was a lot of overlap between the HR and internal auditing surveys, so Kruse decided to take a year off and reassess for 2010.

Cultural surveys are becoming more frequent in large organizations, and they do cover most of the important soft control issues. They also make it possible to compare ratings with other organizations that use the same survey. The next two case studies show how internal auditing can use the results of such surveys.

BP PLC

BP, a company known as a leader in corporate governance, has an 84-page code of conduct (available at www.bp.com). This document provides detailed behavioral guidance in areas like health and safety, the environment, treatment of employees, dealing with business partners, relations with governments and communities, and company assets and financial integrity. The code includes several methods for reporting violations or concerns. It is communicated via online training and through line managers to their staff. Employees must certify that they have taken the training, read the code, and are in compliance.

These are all best practice examples of ways to communicate and reinforce the stated values of the company. But some of the largest and best-known cases of management fraud (e.g., Enron) had similarly excellent formal practices. The real values of those companies, as evidenced by executive and employee behavior, were almost diametrically opposed to the stated values.

For assurance that the real values match the stated values, BP has a robust entitywide survey process called the People Assurance Survey. A third-party vendor, Sirota Survey Intelligence (sirota.com), administers the survey. The full survey, with about 100 questions, is administered online to every BP employee once every two years. The response rate is about 50 percent.

The survey includes standard questions that BP can use to benchmark with industry in general, questions standard to BP that can be trended over time, and questions that address issues that "keep management awake at night" at the time. The actual survey form and questions cannot be published, but Sirota shared enough to understand how it works.

The BP survey addresses 10 dimensions of employee engagement, with statements for each dimension. Following are the statements for the "leadership" dimension used by another Sirota client:

- The leadership regularly communicates plans, vision, and strategy of the company.
- The leadership is highly visible and accessible.
- The leadership of the organization acts as an integrated team.
- I understand the direction that XYZ Company is taking.
- Senior managers are good role models of our values.
- Senior managers have passion for our brands and our consumers.
- I have confidence that senior managers are leading the company in the right direction.

Some of the other dimensions this client uses are: "Immediate Manager," "Customer Focus," and "Employee Development."

Best Practices: Evaluating the Corporate Culture

Employees respond to each statement using a Likert scale ("Strongly Agree," "Agree," "Neither Agree nor Disagree," "Disagree," "Strongly Disagree," or "Not Applicable"). The survey begins and ends with a confidentiality statement, but BP employees can waive confidentiality if they want to speak directly with someone from Sirota.

Sirota sends the results to BP's Human Resources Department, which distributes them to about 400 people in group leadership with the expectation that they be shared further. Results are broken down by major business unit, so each management team can compare their results with those of their peers and BP as a whole. Executives can target areas whose employees are less engaged and strongly suggest that managers in these areas learn from managers of areas with highly engaged employees. In this way, best practices in people management are shared within BP. Figure 5A shows the format of a typical Sirota report. Results are trended over time and stratified by grade level of employee or in whatever other way BP requests.

Variance Reduction: A Powerful Way to Drive Attitudinal Improvements

Distribution of Engagement Across XYZ company

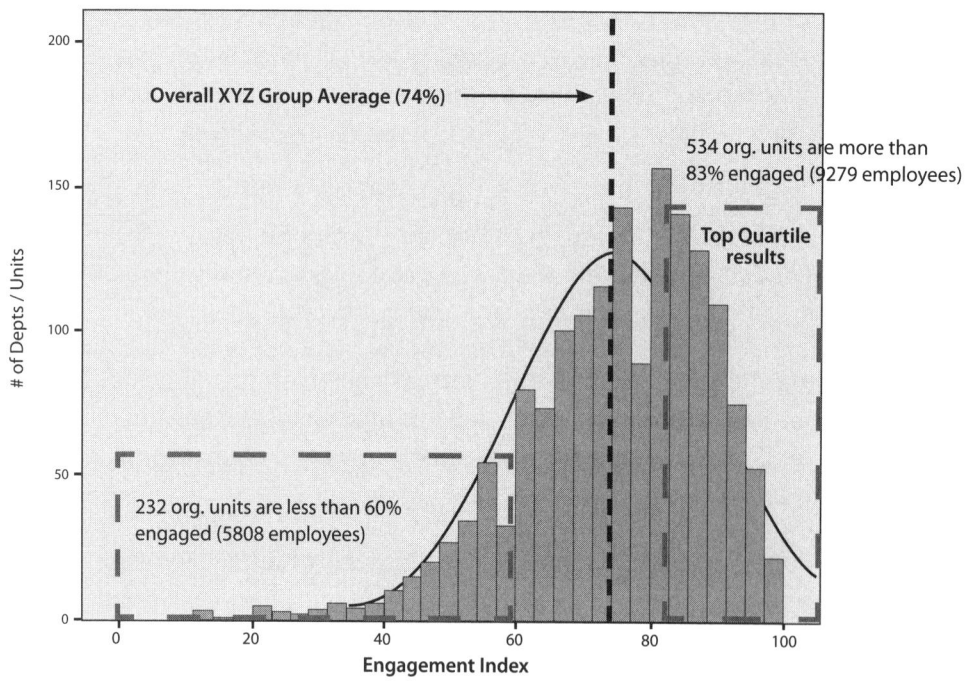

- Overall XYZ Group Average (74%)
- 534 org. units are more than 83% engaged (9279 employees)
- Top Quartile results
- 232 org. units are less than 60% engaged (5808 employees)

X-axis: Engagement Index (0 to 100)
Y-axis: # of Depts / Units

Engagement distribution represents 1637 (n = 10 or above) org. units across XYZ

Figure 5A

In addition, BP conducts focused surveys called "Pulse" or "PING" with a sample of employees, also through Sirota. These may be done to drill down into issues raised by the People Assurance Survey, or they may be requested by management to address concerns about a specific area. For example, if a business unit is undergoing downsizing or was recently acquired, management might want specific information about the inevitable morale issues.

Business unit leaders are expected to respond with constructive action plans to issues raised by the surveys and communicate these plans to their employees. How they do this is their choice. One successful approach, the auditors find, is to form an action committee representing the area(s) most affected by the issues. This committee of employees develops action plans. The leaders endorse them and communicate the plans to employees throughout the business unit. Some leaders prefer to develop action plans on their own, but this is usually not as effective.

Throughout BP, business unit owners report to their superiors in periodic performance reviews, which internal auditing sometimes attends. A typical topic during these reviews is the owners' response to survey results for their unit. A former BP HR director interviewed for this project said that executive management takes the data produced by these surveys as seriously as it takes financial or operational data.

With such a robust process to evaluate soft controls in place, internal auditing does not use surveys, workshops, or other formal tools to evaluate soft controls. Instead, they use the survey results as audit evidence at all levels.

At the most general level, they use the results for perspective on the entitywide and business unit control environments. The results are one factor they consider in selecting audits for their annual audit plan, and they use the results directly during audit projects.

During the planning stage of an audit, the results help them focus on possible problem areas. During fieldwork, they test the effectiveness of management's response to survey results by typically asking between five and 50 people if they have heard of any actions taken in response and how effective the actions have been. This in itself can be an important indicator of the strength of the control environment.

When the auditors think there is a weakness in soft controls, the survey results provide evidence to pursue the issue. When the auditors find exceptions in their hard control testing, the survey results might point them to the root cause.

In their audit reports, they sometimes report soft control strengths, as long as the survey results and their own observations support this conclusion. They sometimes report weaknesses, although they always need corroborating evidence to support the conclusion. More often, they report soft control weaknesses verbally. To ensure that soft control weaknesses are corrected, internal auditing includes them in their issue tracking system, where each issue is risk-ranked using BP ERM risk ranking categories.

At the time of this writing, BP internal auditing's approach to evaluating soft controls continues to evolve and be enhanced. The approach described here has provided a strong foundation for them to build upon.

The City of Austin

As reported in the "Risk Watch" column of *Internal Auditor* (December 2004), the Office of the City Auditor (OCA) used an existing citywide survey to good effect. The city had been doing an annual Listening to the Workforce Survey. The auditors compared the 300+ points of focus in COSO to this survey and found that it included almost all of the points important to city government, although in very different language. There was one exception. The existing survey had nothing on ethics. OCA suggested nine ethics-related questions, and the city included them in the survey. With these questions added, OCA uses the survey much like BP's internal auditing.

This in itself is a good tip for any audit department whose organization has an existing cultural survey. Cross-map the points of focus in COSO to the existing survey and see if there are any important soft controls not covered. Work with the survey administrator to develop questions on these controls. If the administrator is willing to include them, use the existing survey rather than developing a survey of your own. Not only will this save time, but, more importantly, you will not have to ask busy employees to respond to another survey.

Besides using the survey results for audit planning, support for findings, and root cause analysis, OCA used them for a very meaningful project. They took three years' data from this survey, together with the results of management interviews OCA had done and the Integrity Unit's database (investigations conducted and planned), to perform a citywide ethics audit.

These sources provided good evidence of a positive or problematic ethical climate in the city's various departments. But what difference does a good or not-so-good ethical climate make to the departments' outcomes? OCA set out to answer this question by drawing correlations among the following measures (the source of the measure in parentheses).

Indicators of a positive ethical climate:

- A high level of employee agreement that managers in their workgroup set a good ethical example (workforce survey).
- A high level of employee perceptions of a departmental commitment to enforcing high ethical standards (workforce survey).
- Managers advocate frequently reminding employees of ethical considerations related to their work (OCA manager interviews).

Indicators of a problematic ethical climate:

- A high level of employee agreement that they are personally aware of unethical or illegal behavior by city employees (workforce survey).
- Whether the department had any integrity investigations initiated (OCA integrity unit database).
- Managers express fatalistic attitudes toward unethical conduct (OCA manager interviews).

Measures of the financial and administrative impact of departmental differences in ethical climate:

- The number and cost of successful claims filed by Austin residents and businesses for damage caused by city employees (Law Department claims data).
- Injuries to employees involving time lost from work (workers' compensation claims data).
- Complaints made by customers (Public Information Office data).
- Employee assessments of the value their departments provide to customers (workforce survey).

- Sick leave usage (HRD Banner data).
- High employee turnover (HRD Banner data).
- Employee intentions to continue working for the city (workforce survey).

OCA's purpose was to draw conclusions useful for the city as a whole, rather than to rate individual departments. For this purpose, they could simply divide the departments into two groups for each ethical climate indicator — those who scored in the top half and those who scored in the bottom half. In addition, for some analyses they controlled statistically for relevant differences between departments, such as size and the nature of their work, which might have skewed the results.

Some of the correlations between ethical climate and real-world outcomes were dramatic. OCA's report convinced city management to take a more proactive approach toward promoting an ethical climate. Exhibit 5E on page 202 is the "Risk Watch" article that appeared in the December 2004 issue of *Internal Auditor* magazine. It gives a more detailed description of OCA's approach and results. A still more detailed description can be found at http://www.ci.austin.tx.us/auditor/downloads/indicators.pdf.

Lennox International

BP and the City of Austin show how internal auditing can enhance an existing entitywide survey and use the results to enhance audit work. Internal auditors at Lennox International developed their own soft controls survey to perform a tone at the top review and then turned it over to a newly formed Business Practice Office.

To develop their survey, the audit staff did some research and found similar surveys they could use as models. They administered it for two years using in-house tools and resources. The Business Practice Office contracts with an external vendor, The Foresight Group, for survey administration.

The survey form is an excellent example of using very simple language, which is easy to understand for employees at all levels. Exhibit 5F on page 208 is the text of the survey. The online version has respondents reply to statements 1-37 on a Likert scale ("Strongly Agree," "Agree," "Neutral," "Disagree," "Strongly Disagree").

Like the other surveys in this chapter, the instructions guarantee confidentiality. The third section does ask employees to rate the behavior of their immediate supervisor/manager, but only aggregate results by business unit and location are given to Lennox. With this information, Lennox can analyze and interpret the results at the level of, for example, a manufacturing plant, but at no lower level.

The overall results are communicated in summary form to the executive staff and board of directors. Individual business unit results are presented to the respective unit's top management and, if requested, to lower levels of the business unit. In addition, several of the issues that were raised during the survey are subjects of articles in the Lennox quarterly Business Conduct newsletter. Employees who complete the survey know that their opinions are respected and acted upon. Like others in this chapter, internal auditing uses the survey results as part of the risk assessment to develop their annual audit plan, as well as during audit projects.

Best Practices: Evaluating the Corporate Culture

Robeco

Developing an entitywide soft control survey is challenging. The soft-control "points of focus" in the COSO report and the "Examples of Soft Controls" in Chapter 1 have good content (the wording must, of course, be simplified). The surveys presented as exhibits in this chapter and Chapter 2 are good models. But from such a wealth of possibilities, how can you select the soft controls most relevant to your own organization? Some readers will feel they know their organization well enough to do this intuitively, but others might want to use a more disciplined approach. This might be especially true of readers whose CEO or audit committee might see a proposed survey and ask, "Where did you get this stuff from?"

Rick Mulders of Robeco, an asset management firm headquartered in the Netherlands, used an interesting and highly disciplined approach in 2007. His approach is illustrated in Figure 5B.

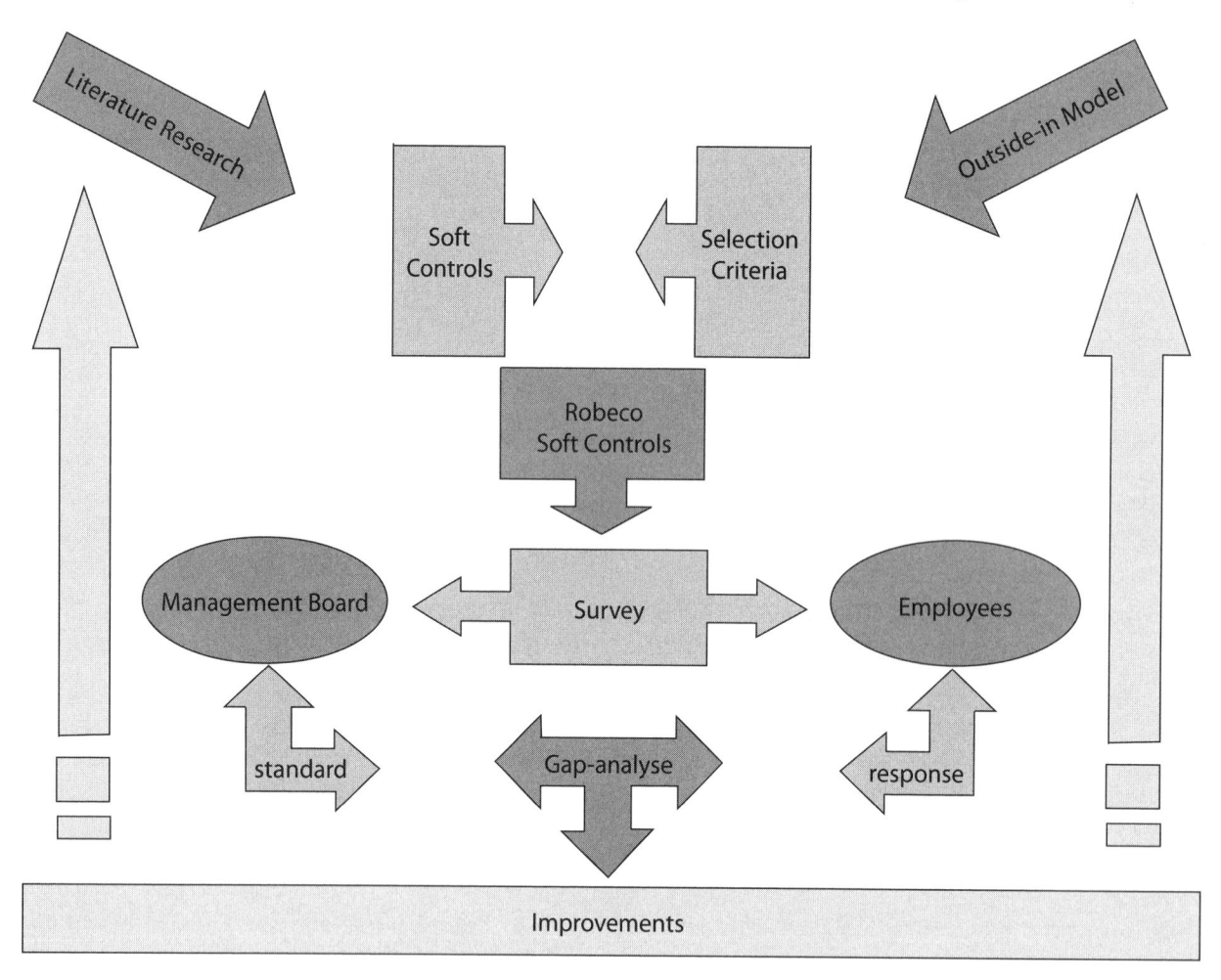

Figure 5B: Research Approach

First, he did an extensive literature search (see his bibliography at the end of this section). From this research, he compiled a list of 30 soft controls that are applicable to organizations in general (see Figure 5C).

> Management of an organization should periodically determine whether its employees:
>
> 1. Are aware of the targets of the organization and acknowledge them;
> 2. Know what the targets of the organization mean for their individual activities;
> 3. Are motivated to come up with new ideas that contribute to the realization of the targets of the organization;
> 4. Are able to get trainings that contribute to their development;
> 5. Are aware of the code of conduct and act in accordance with it;
> 6. Experience group rewarding indeed as a shared responsibility;
> 7. Are stimulated to have a horizontal or vertical career within the organization;
> 8. See that their superiors communicate inside as well as outside the company in a positive manner about the core values of the company;
> 9. Act integer and in line with the core values of the company;
> 10. Perform their tasks as good as they can;
> 11. Acknowledge the vision of their superiors and consider their management style constructive;
> 12. Are aware of the internal (employment) policies and act in accordance with them;
> 13. Work together in a constructive way;
> 14. Feel comfortable with the culture of the organization;
> 15. Are informed about important developments within the organization;
> 16. Know their responsibilities and are accounted for them;
> 17. Are involved with important developments within the organization;
> 18. See changes within the company as opportunities instead of threats;
> 19. See that management has a well thought risk appetite;
> 20. See each other as equals;
> 21. Have the possibility to develop inside as well as outside the company;
> 22. Are satisfied with their job;
> 23. Have personal targets that align with the company targets;
> 24. Are rewarded by their superiors for their performances;
> 25. Have an inner drive to work for the company;
> 26. Perform tasks for which they are capable;
> 27. Perform tasks from cradle to grave that lead to a visible result;
> 28. Perform tasks that have an impact inside or outside the company on other people;
> 29. Have the freedom to perform tasks independently according a personal plan and vision; and
> 30. Receive feedback from their superiors regarding the effectiveness of their efforts.

Figure 5C: Generally Applicable Soft Controls

Best Practices: Evaluating the Corporate Culture

At the same time, he developed criteria for selecting soft controls that are most relevant to Robeco. For this purpose, he used the "outside-in" model (Vlotman, 2001; illustrated in Figure 5D). This model is based on four components that are called systems: the environment system, the management system, the organizational system, and the management accounting system. The model works from the external environment through the strategy and culture created by management, to the organization structure and process, and finally to the management accounting structure and process.

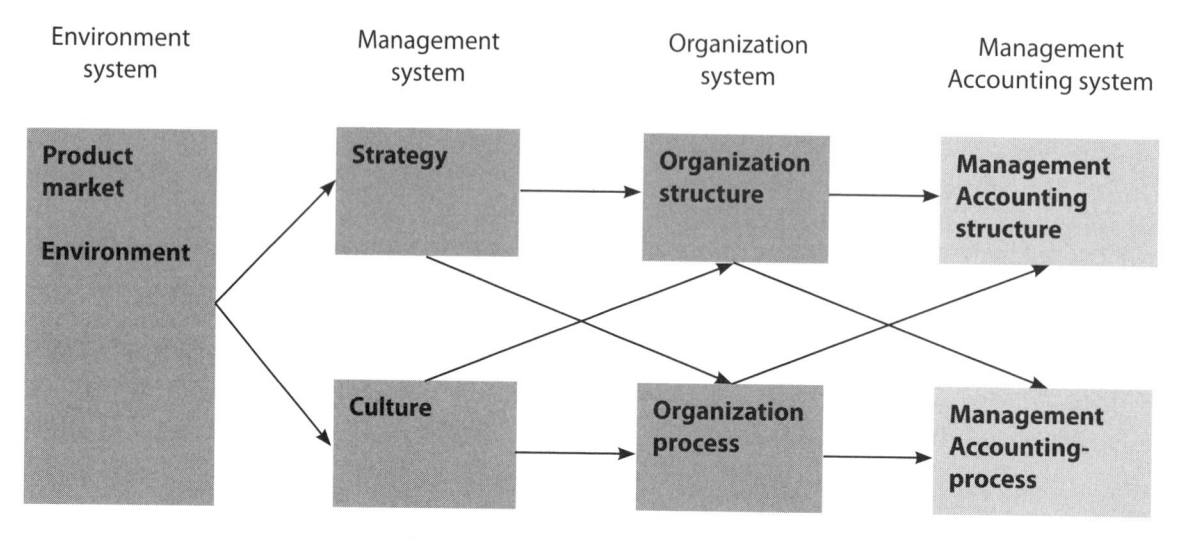

Figure 5D: Outside-in Model

Applying this model to Robeco, Mulders developed selection criteria for the most relevant soft controls. His thought process here was not linear. It involved thinking through from a variety of perspectives what he knew to be important to Robeco. The model helped him do so in a logical fashion and give him some assurance that he was not missing a major element. The five selection criteria he developed were:

- *Growth targets*: Robeco has ambitious growth targets that should be realized. A system of soft controls should contribute to this.
- *Compliance*: at all times Robeco must comply with relevant laws and regulations.
- *Core values*: the soft controls of Robeco should fit with its core values.
- *Client trust*: clients trust their assets to Robeco. This trust should never be damaged.
- *Sustainability*: the soft controls should, if possible, contribute to the sustainability of Robeco.

He next applied these selection criteria to the list of 30 generally applicable soft controls. To simplify his analysis he combined some of the 30 into a shorter list of 16 elements. Figure 5E shows the results of his analysis. The first column has the 16 elements, the second column references the original 30 soft controls, and the remaining five columns include his rating of the relevance of each element to each of the five criteria. For his rating, he used a five-tiered scale ranging from least relevant (-/-) through three intermediate ratings (-, +/-, and +) to most relevant (+/+).

Chapter 5: Entitywide Surveys

		Selection Criteria				
Element of Soft Control	*Soft Control Number*	**Growth targets**	**Compliance**	**Core Values**	**Client Trust**	**Sustainability**
Communication	*1,15*	+/-	+/-	+/+	+/-	+/-
Dedication	*2,10*	+	-/-	+	+/-	-/-
Innovation	*3*	+	-/-	+	+	+/-
Group rewarding	*6*	+/+	-/-	+/-	-/-	-/-
Integrity	*9*	+	+/+	+/+	+/+	+/+
Management vision and style	*8,11,14,19*	+/+	-/-	+/+	+	-/-
Internal policies	*5,12*	+/-	+/+	+	+/+	+
Cooperation	*13,20*	+/-	+/-	+/-	+/-	+/-
Responsibility	*16*	+	+	+	+	+
Involvement	*17*	+	+/-	+/-	+/-	-/-
Flexibility	*7,18*	+/-	-/-	+/-	-/-	-/-
Personal development	*4,21*	+	-/-	+	-/-	-/-
Employee satisfaction	*22,24,25, 29,30*	+/-	+/-	+/-	+/-	+/-
Goal congruence	*23*	+	+/-	+/-	+/-	+/-
Skills	*26*	+/+	-/-	+/-	+/-	-/-
Task identification	*27,28*	+/-	+/-	+/-	+/-	+/-

Figure 5E: Elements of Soft Control

The following elements score relatively high and are therefore considered especially relevant for Robeco:

- Communication
- Integrity
- Management vision and management style
- Internal policies
- Responsibility

These five elements include 10 of the soft controls in Figure 5C. These 10, with the number from Figure 5C in parenthesis, are:

Management of an organization should periodically determine whether its employees:

- Are aware of the targets of the organization and acknowledge them (1).
- See that their superiors communicate inside as well as outside the company in a positive manner about the core values of the company (8).
- Act integer and in line with the core values of the company (9).
- Acknowledge the vision of their superiors and consider their management style constructive (11).
- Are aware of the internal (employment) policies and act in accordance with them (12).
- Feel comfortable with the culture of the organization (14).
- Are informed about important developments within the organization (15).
- Know their responsibilities and are accounted for them (16).
- See that management has a well thought risk appetite (19).
- Work together in a constructive way (13).

With this shorter list of 10 soft controls in mind, Mulders developed his survey statements. Again, this was not a linear thought process. It involved creatively developing statements that provide meaningful information about these controls expressed in language that would be clear to Robeco employees. Figure 5F shows which of the statements apply to each soft control. As seen in other surveys, this one asks for responses on a five-point scale from "Fully Agree" to "Fully Disagree" with each statement.

	Soft Control	Survey statement
1.	Are aware of the targets of the organization and acknowledge them	1, 2
2.	See that their superiors communicate inside as well as outside the company in a positive manner about the core values of the company	4, 5
3.	Act integer and in line with the core values of the company	6, 7, 8
4.	Acknowledge the vision of their superiors and consider their management style constructive	9
5.	Are aware of the internal (employment) policies and act in accordance with them	10, 11, 12, 13, 14, 15, 16, 17, 18, 19, 20
6.	Feel comfortable with the culture of the organization	21, 22, 23, 24, 25, 26
7.	Are informed about important developments within the organization	27, 28, 29, 30
8.	Know their responsibilities and are accounted for them	3, 31, 32
9.	See that management has a well thought risk appetite	33
10.	Work together in a constructive way	34, 35, 36, 37

Figure 5F: Relation of Soft Controls and Statements in Robeco Survey

The survey instrument (see Exhibit 5G on page 213) was now ready to use. Mulders applied it in an interesting and meaningful way. He administered the survey first to Robeco's Management Board, asking them to fill it out not for themselves, but for how they expect their employees to respond. He then administered the survey to 50 percent of Robeco employees through an Internet site he built for this purpose with the use of an external service provider (www.enqueteviainternet.nl). Mulders realized a response rate of 20 percent.

Comparing the Management Board's expectations to employee perceptions provided valuable information for the Management Board. Mulders talked through the gaps with the Management Board, and they developed action plans to address those gaps greater than 1.5.

Mulders also wanted to compare perceptions among employees in different business units and at different levels of employees and management. To enable this more discrete comparison without compromising confidentiality, the survey asks respondents to identify which of five business units they work in, but it does not ask their job title. With business units ranging from roughly 150 to 500 employees, a job title would in some cases identify the individual. Instead, the survey uses three tiers for level of employee:

- No one (in)directly reports to me.
- Less than 20 people (in)directly report to me.
- More than 20 people (in)directly report to me.

Each of these three tiers will have enough employees in a business unit that confidentiality is preserved.

Comparisons among business units and levels of employee/management also yielded valuable information and action plans. The survey has been very successful and well worth the effort put into its development.

Following are publications Mulder consulted in developing his approach. Readers who want to do further research might be interested in at least the English language publications.

> Anthony, R.N., and V. Govindarajan, *Management Control Systems, 9th Edition* (McGraw-Hill, 1998).
> Bouwens, J.F.M.G., *Voorwaarden voor meten is weten* (Tijdschrift Bedrijfskunde, 2003).
> Goldberg, D., "The Soft Approach to Auditing," *Internal Auditor*, 2007.
> Société Generale, Explanatory note about the exceptional fraud, 27 januari 2008.
> Hartmann, F.G.H., Hard and soft management controls, MCA, nummer 2, maart 2008.
> Hartmann, F.G.H. & S. Slapnicar, How formal performance evaluation affects trust between superior and subordinate mangers (working paper presented at IFAC conference, Amsterdam, 28 maart 2007.
> Heus, De, R.S., and M.T.L. Stremmelaar, Auditen van Soft Controls, Auditing in de praktijk nummer 8, 2000.
> Hopwood, A., *Accounting and Human Behaviour* (London: Accountancy Age Books, 1974).
> Kerklaan, V., Integriteit beheersbaar maken, Finance & Control, augustus 2006.
> Kiewiet, M., de & J.M. Pleunes-Caljouw, Monitoren en auditen van Soft Controls als sluitstuk van de compliancecyclus, Tijdschrift voor Compliance, volume 2, 2006.
> McGregor, D., *The Human Side of Enterprise* (New York: McGraw-Hill, 1960).
> Merchant, K.A., "Control in Business Organizations," *Pitman*, 1985.
> Merchant, K.A., and W.A. van der Stede, Management Control Systems: Performance measurement, evaluation and incentives (Harlow, England: Prentice Hall, 2007).
> Roth, J., *Control Model Implementation: Best Practices* (Altamonte Springs, FL: The Institute of Internal Auditors Research Foundation, 1997).

Simons, R., Performance Measurement & Control Systems for Implementing Strategy (New Jersey: Prentice Hall, 2000).

Velasquez, M.G., *Business Ethics* (Englewood Cliffs, New Jersey: Prentice Hall, 1992).

Vlotman, F.W., Doeleinden van Management Accounting, artikel A1100, Handboek Management Accounting, Kluwer Financieel Management, april 2001.

Guidelines for Entitywide Soft Control Surveys

A well-designed and administered survey can give senior management and the audit committee a good measure of the strength of the corporate culture and its trend through time. A survey that is not well designed and administered, on the other hand, can give false assurance — which is worse than no assurance at all. I have seen this especially with surveys used for Sarbanes-Oxley compliance. Such surveys often make one or both of the following mistakes:

- They ask managers to rate their own areas. Managers cannot evaluate their own performance any better than clerical staff can review their own work.
- They ask for yes/no responses. Issues of corporate culture are rarely black or white.

The guidelines in Chapter 2 for audit project surveys apply equally to entitywide soft control surveys, especially:

- Survey statements or questions should be unambiguous and phrased in simple, easy-to-understand language.
- Field-test the survey.
- Soft control issues are rarely yes/no issues. Better results can be gained by asking for level of agreement or disagreement on some scale.
- Ask people to explain their negative responses.
- People have to feel safe from retribution.
- Consider having legal review the survey instrument.

The following guidelines also apply.

- **Get proactive support from the top.** Surveys can actually be harmful if senior management fails to act on the results. Its inaction sends the message that it does not care what employees think or feel. To be sure executives will take action, get their commitment to support it and act upon it before sending it to employees. Some "selling points" might include:

  - **It is an excellent feedback tool for senior management.** For example, a colleague tells of a CEO he once worked for whose personal integrity was exceptionally strong. But the CEO felt the pressure all CEOs feel to keep quarterly financial results steadily improving. When results were not promising, he would phone subsidiaries and ask if there was anything they could do to help out this quarter. He did not think he needed to specify "ethically." He thought that everyone would assume this as he did. Most did, but some did not. The result was a financial reporting scandal.

Good executives do their best to send the right message, but they are human. Sometimes they neglect to include a key part of the message and the message is misunderstood. Other times they send the completely right message but something interferes. Controls cannot prevent this from happening. A good monitoring tool — a well-designed entitywide survey — might detect when it is happening in time to correct it.

- **There is a strong likelihood that an effective survey will detect any serious problems in the control environment.** This statement is supported by something Sharon Watkins, the Enron whistleblower, said in a presentation. About six months before the scandal broke, HR sponsored a survey similar to those I have discussed. Watkins and several other people she knew wrote comments specifying their concerns about financial reporting. Unfortunately, the only criteria HR used for summarizing the results for management was the number of similar responses, so their concerns were never reported.

  Watkins told this story to make the point that someone like an internal auditor who can do a qualitative review of comments should be involved in summarizing and reporting the results. Another point we can take from the story is that surveys done correctly are indeed likely to detect serious problems in the control environment.

- **It demonstrates that management has created a basically sound control environment and is continually working to improve it.** No control environment is ever perfect, but a monitoring control that is highly likely to detect anything seriously wrong provides the best assurance possible that nothing is seriously wrong. Thus, an entitywide survey that follows these guidelines is the most effective thing a company can do for Sarbanes-Oxley compliance or similar purposes.

- **It improves the control environment.** When employees see that management really cares what they think and takes action in response, they feel valued and motivation improves. When the survey and resulting action plans include ethical issues, employees see that management is serious about promoting ethical behavior.

• **Use the survey as an "upward" or peer evaluation.** As stated before, the results of a survey in which managers evaluate their own areas cannot be relied upon. On the other hand, people can assess the environment created for them by higher-level management quite accurately. Similarly, people can evaluate their peers more reliably than themselves. I gave the example in Chapter 3 that the question "Do you understand and practice our corporate values?" would not yield reliable answers. The question "Do *other employees* in your area understand and practice our corporate values?" is much better.

Some additional things to consider in developing an entitywide survey:

- **Balance confidentiality against the ability to follow up.** Eliminating the fear of retribution is essential, but this does not always require absolute confidentiality. It is fairly common, for example, to have respondents specify their level in the organization. The results can then be stratified and differences in perception among the levels identified. It is also fairly common to have respondents specify their business unit or functional area, as long as there are enough employees in it to preserve the appearance and the reality of confidentiality. This can be very useful in identifying problem areas and best practice models.

  At Ameritech, the auditors would not show or read any of the "verbatim" comments to upper management, so no one would be able to identify the source by the way a comment was phrased. At another organization, they send the comments together with the numerical ratings to the manager responsible, but with the following limitations:

  - A manager or supervisor with six to 15 direct reports gets the ratings but no comments.
  - A manager or supervisor with five or fewer direct reports gets nothing.

  Every organization must determine for itself the level of confidentiality needed to eliminate the fear of retribution. Size and level of trust in management are the key determinants.

- **Balance the number of issues addressed against the length of the survey.** I have referred to COSO's 300+ "points of focus." Every one of these points could be used as a survey statement. I have, in fact, seen this done but never with good results. Long surveys tend to be overwhelming and completed with little thought or not completed at all. Short surveys, on the other hand, may not provide all the information desired. Here again, every organization must decide for itself what the optimum length will be and which issues to include.

- **Consider enhancing an existing survey** as the City of Austin's auditors did. This may be preferable to asking people to respond to a separate survey. However, the point that Sharon Watkins made is worth considering. Someone who can make qualitative judgments about individual comments should be involved in summarizing and reporting the results.

CHAPTER 6

COMBINATION OF TECHNIQUES

The soft control evaluation techniques presented in the previous chapters can be used alone or in combination. This chapter presents three audit departments that use a combination of techniques.

- **A Fortune 500 company** uses phone interviews, a survey, and focus group discussions during operational audits.

- **WorkSafeBC** uses executive interviews and CSA workshops at three levels for an entitywide review.

- **Sarasota County** uses a survey and interviews for an entitywide review that also serves as the risk assessment to develop their annual audit plan. They may use interviews, surveys, or CSA workshops during audit projects, depending on which technique(s) will work best in the environment to meet their audit objectives.

There are no guidelines at the end of this chapter because guidelines for each technique have already been discussed.

A Fortune 500 Company

This company, which wishes to remain anonymous, uses a combination of interviews, tailored surveys, and focus groups to evaluate soft controls on every operational audit. Although they only have reportable findings on soft controls for about five to 10 percent of their audits, these are the issues that upper-level management have been most interested in and have generated the most positive feedback on the auditors' post-audit customer satisfaction surveys. This is true both for executives and upper-level management of the area audited (e.g., the general manager who oversees an administrative office). For perspective, their operational audits are conducted on a geographic region with one administrative office and some number of field offices.

Evolution of Soft Control Evaluation

The first efforts at soft control auditing, approximately 10 years before this writing, were not as effective as desired. The lessons learned may be instructive for others.

Initially, the auditors conducted structured phone interviews during pre-fieldwork and focus groups in the field, which involved (at most) 10 percent of the employees. From the beginning, they were looking only for trends and patterns rather than individual complaints, but the general managers sometimes complained that they just happened to pick the bad apples.

To address this concern, they now review performance ratings in picking their samples and do not include the highest performers or underperformers. They also added an electronic e-mailed survey so they now include 30 percent to 40 percent of the employees in a subsidiary.

The second issue they had to deal with was their audit staff. About 95 percent of their auditors were hired from outside the company and had an average of about two to three years' experience. The CAE recognized right away that operational experience is needed to put soft control issues into perspective. He brought in a manager from operations to be director of North American Audit (about 75 percent of the audit universe).

This new director was often hesitant about the findings being created by the staff. He asked many follow-up questions and provided significant perspective before any finding would go into an audit report. He knew that there will always be a certain percentage of employees who are negative by nature, have a bone to pick, or recently received a poor performance review, and will naturally provide negative responses. Less experienced auditors have a tendency to overreact to some of the expected negative responses and create unnecessary findings. The key is to know from experience when the number and substance of negative responses has gone beyond what might be considered normal.

Today, the audit department hires about 95 percent of their auditors from field operations, including employees ranging from accountants, supervisors, and managers, up to former field controllers. Given this experience and perspective within the audit team, the director is much more comfortable in the findings created today. Also, management is much more receptive to the feedback knowing the auditors providing the feedback have been in field operations before and have a similar perspective.

Evaluation Technique

The core of their approach to soft controls is the survey. The phone interviews are based on the survey, and the focus groups are based on the survey results. They conduct the survey and phone interviews during the planning stage of each audit, and hold the focus groups during fieldwork to dig into the issues raised.

I was not able to reproduce the survey, but I can describe it. It is structured into the following sections:

- Training and Career Development
- Promotional Process
- Retention and Turnover
- Communication and Cooperation
- Core Areas
- Integrity and Ethics
- Miscellaneous

The survey has a total of 41 questions. Each section has two to six questions, except for Integrity and Ethics, which has 12. Most of the questions ask for a response on one of a variety of rating scales (e.g., Yes/No; Excellent/Satisfactory/Needs Improvement). For each of these questions, responders are asked to elaborate if their response is negative. Each section ends with a question asking for any other thoughts the responder has on this topic.

To administer the survey, they use the online survey tool SurveyMonkey. The tool allows them to gather perceptions from a much larger sample of employees than would be feasible with interviews, and to easily aggregate and analyze the responses. They typically have about a 90 percent response rate.

The survey is not anonymous, because the auditors want to be able to follow up with responders if they want more explanation. It is, however, confidential. The survey form states that the auditors are only looking for overall trends and promises that all responses will be kept confidential — and this promise is kept.

The auditors do not rely solely on the survey. Many people will open up more when talking to someone than they will in writing, and the auditor can ask follow-up questions on the spot during an interview. During the phone interviews, the auditor fills out a survey on SurveyMonkey. The results can go into the tabulation of surveys.

They use a standard script for the phone interviews. This script is derived from the survey, but the questions are phrased in a more conversational way. Where the survey asks, "Please rate....," the script asks, "How do you feel about..." or "How well do..." This phrasing generates a more open-ended response. The auditor takes notes on the response, asks follow-up questions, if appropriate, and translates the response into the survey rating scale.

Although the script is written in conversational language, auditors are encouraged to put it into their own words once they feel comfortable doing so. If they are not getting a meaningful response to a question, they are told to go back to the script for guidance.

The focus groups do not have a standard script or set of questions. The auditors use the focus groups to dig into some of the issues raised by the interviews and survey. They typically work with four focus groups. Each focus group has six people from one of the four levels in the field offices: Staff, Senior Staff, Supervisor, and Manager. (They do not include administrative office employees because they work in different functions, so they do not relate to each other's concerns as well.) By having people from just one of the four levels in each focus group, the auditors are able to identify and analyze differences in perceptions among the four levels.

The attendees typically come from within a two-hour drive of the administrative office where the sessions are held, because of travel costs. There are sometimes exceptions when the auditors get very pertinent information from someone in a more distant location. They want to know if this is isolated or a real issue. They will first expand the sample of phone interviews and, if called for, involve a couple of people from that person's area.

The value of their inclusion of soft control issues in what they call their "COSO-based approach" is apparent in the comments made by managers on their post-audit survey. The following are only a few of the dozens of similar comments they have received.

> "I like the new audit approach much better than the old style. I felt like they really looked at each line of business and really gave us some good feedback. When we were audited in the past, it seemed like XXX was the main focus and it was all about looking at documents and questioning procedures. This one did that but it did not always seem like the main focus.

Best Practices: Evaluating the Corporate Culture

They looked more at the business and the people and how we were managing that with the focus groups, etc. and really gave us feedback based on those findings."

"In my opinion, the audit approach was highly effective in identifying all areas of major risk in our business. I cannot think of any areas of major risk that were not addressed."

"Love the idea of obtaining information from all levels. It is extremely important that we know that the message about our fiduciary actions is reaching all levels. Obtaining information from all levels shows cohesion in the team. I feel comfortable with the COSO approach and enjoy the process."

"For those of us that go back to the days when audits were not really a helpful tool, the newer process is greatly appreciated!"

"As many of our staff managers have little time to stop and look at the big picture of their piece of the company and whether or not there is a better way, I found this very valuable."

"The new process also makes the other department managers (non-BMs) seem much more accountable."

"This audit provided the best, useful feedback of any audit we have had."

"I felt the COSO approach was a much more encompassing audit and therefore the feedback was much more useful. The entity-level interviews were very insightful and help provide information on how well our message is getting to the intended parties."

"Much more in depth and I believe more relevant from the days prior to COSO."

"Lawsuits are our major risk. The COSO approach helped uncover possible problem areas."

"I believe the new audit approach was more in tune with determining the culture of our region than the previous audit approaches. I believe that this was the most important confirmation of the audit process from my perspective."

"We are very concerned with maintaining our brand in the public eye, as well as with our employee's perception of how we are living up to what we preach to them every day. I believe the auditors did a nice job in their focus groups drawing out employee opinions on how we are perceived internally and externally in regards to integrity and customer service."

WorkSafeBC

In 2004, the WorkSafeBC internal auditors recognized the importance of giving assurance on entity-wide soft controls. That year, they developed their approach and piloted it within their own department. In 2005, they rolled it out throughout the organization. Their technique involves both interviews and workshops. It has evolved over time — first to improve the technique and later to adapt to changes within the organization.

In 2005, they used 11 COSO-based questions for:

- Interviews with the vice presidents and directors of each division — a total of 54 executives. They sent a handout (see Exhibit 6A on page 218) ahead of time stating the purpose of the interview, the COSO control framework's components and factors, and the 11 questions, together with their rating scale. They also sent a brief PowerPoint presentation explaining their purpose and process (see Exhibit 6B on page 227) and another brief presentation on the COSO Framework. They asked the executives to scan these items so they could finish the interviews in the time allotted. During the hour and a half interviews, they probed to gather full information about the 11 issues before asking the executives to rate them. Afterward they sent their interview minutes and ratings for an accuracy check and to see if the executive had anything to add.

- Workshops with managers, using the same questions. These lasted three to four hours. The number and percent they invited varied by division. To get a representative sample, they felt they had to invite all of the managers from some small divisions but a much lower percentage from larger divisions. In total, about 50 percent of the managers attended.

    They introduced each workshop with a brief PowerPoint presentation similar to the one they used for interviews. During the workshop, they used confidential voting technology to assess the importance and confidence of each of the 11 COSO-based issues. After showing the results of the voting, they asked for comments and projected "minutes" summarizing the comments on a screen as they went.

From these interviews and workshops, they wrote a report on each division, giving the ratings (separate ratings for the executives and the managers) together with graphs and comments. Internal auditing did not make recommendations to address the issues raised in these reports. They let divisional management decide how to address the issues and whether to distribute the reports to their managers and/or staff. They strongly encouraged them to do so.

This review produced meaningful assurance and some good action plans, and the auditors feel they were successful in meeting two unspoken, secondary objectives as well: 1) to educate management about internal controls and the COSO framework, and 2) to raise the profile and change the image of internal auditing with managers and staff in the organization. Although some executives initially felt that this review was outside the scope of internal auditing, all the executives in the most recent round of interviews were receptive to the process.

In 2006, they repeated the interviews and workshops, and they added an interview with the CEO and workshops involving about 10 percent of the staff (24 staff workshops in all). They also modified the interview guide, condensing the information on COSO but putting the questions into five sections, one for each component. They added a question on control activities for completeness' sake, although they feel their regular audit work gives sufficient assurance for this component. And they improved some of the wording based on their 2005 experience (see Exhibit 6C on page 232).

Although some directors found it repetitious, most were very receptive to repeating the exercise. In an attempt to make it efficient, the auditors sent the prior year's minutes ahead and asked just for updates during the interviews and workshops. They found that the sessions lasted just as long, though, as the executives had much they wanted to discuss. In fact, they found that providing the previous year's minutes was confusing for many interviewees and did not do this again.

They also added an interesting slide (Figure 6A) into the workshops to interpret the voting results:

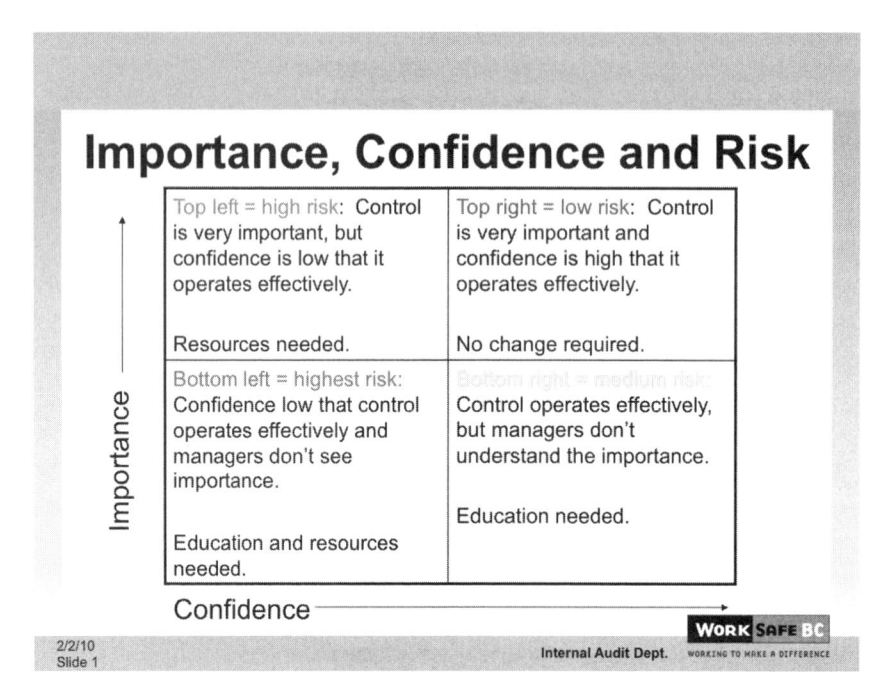

Figure 6A: Risk Rating Matrix

The risk rating system is unusual, because a control is rated higher risk if participants consider its importance to be low. This is because all the controls included in the workshop are important. A rating in the bottom left corner is considered the highest risk, because the participants do not recognize the importance of the control so presumably would have no motivation to improve it.

Exhibit 6D (CD only) is one of the divisional audit reports issued in 2006, sanitized to remove identifiers of the area. This 40-page report is longer than some organizations would want, but it shows the value of internal auditing's work in both the seriousness of management's response to the issues and the improvement in the ratings over 2005.

In 2007, HR worked with an outside firm to do a companywide staff survey to measure staff engagement. Internal auditing reviewed it and found that most of the issues from COSO are addressed in this survey. They did not want to duplicate work so they asked HR to include the COSO-based issues not already addressed by their survey. HR did not do so because they felt that, if they did, other functions would want to add their own issues and the survey would become unwieldy. Instead of doing any further survey work themselves, internal auditing obtained the HR survey results and mapped them back to the factors in COSO. They then did a brief report for management putting the results in terms of the COSO factors, but indicating which factors were not covered, and explaining why internal auditing did not do their own review.

In 2008, internal auditing was able to streamline their soft controls work because of the efforts made to address the issues raised previously and because some of the issues are addressed in HR's survey. This time they interviewed the CEO and all the vice presidents, but only half the directors. They surveyed one-third of the managers and 10 percent of the staff rather than using workshops. And they included just those COSO-based issues not included in HR's survey, with one exception: both surveys address the control environment factors because they are so important. Exhibit 6E on page 241 presents the cover memo, survey form, and ratings scale they used for the executive interviews. Exhibit 6F on page 247 is the online survey form they used for managers and employees.

Going forward, internal auditing will continue to reassess, streamline, and improve their approach where possible. Because of the time involved, they are unlikely to write divisional reports in the future, and they may feel they can do their review every other year and still provide adequate assurance. The HR survey, which will not be repeated until at least 2010, will also affect the extent and timing of internal auditing's work.

In addition to the assurance and action plans these reviews have generated, internal auditing has found them to be a valuable ongoing source of information. For the first time, they have an overview of the entire organization to put things into perspective. And when planning an audit project, they review the relevant director interviews and/or reports as background information. These results give them an excellent starting point for understanding the key objectives, risks, and activities.

Sarasota County

Sarasota County, Florida, has a complex, many-layered audit approach based on the COSO control framework. CAE Mark Simmons has a long history of COSO-based auditing, including soft controls. While at Rensselaer Polytechnic University in 1997, he published an article on "COSO Based Auditing" in *Internal Auditor* magazine. At that time, his approach involved a standard questionnaire for each of the basic business functions like accounts payable, addressing both hard and soft controls. Respondents completed the questionnaires through interviews or focus group sessions, and issues were identified and explored with them on the spot.

Simmons enhanced his approach while at Dartmouth and since 2004 as CAE for Sarasota County. At Sarasota County he is using COSO to reinvent internal auditing, develop his annual audit plan, and conduct audit projects.

Soft Control Focus in Annual Risk Assessment

Sarasota County uses a high performance organization (HPO) management framework with eight elements:

a. Vision
b. Values
c. Mission/Niche
d. Theory of Business
e. Leadership
f. Environment
g. Operational Plan
h. Results

Best Practices: Evaluating the Corporate Culture

To develop his approach for the county, Simmons combined this framework with COSO's five components of control. He also developed 10 strategic risks for the county and got county executives' concurrence that these were the top 10:

- A. Negative Publicity/Damage to Reputation
- B. Legal Liability
- C. Fraudulent Activities
- D. Inaccurate Budgets or Plans
- E. Insufficient Funding/Loss of Revenue
- F. Noncompliance with Laws/Regulations/Policies/Procedures
- G. Unreliable Reporting (Financial/ Managerial)
- H. Business Interruption
- I. Compromise of Sensitive Data/Information
- J. Loss or Waste of Resources/Assets

Considering these risks — COSO and HPO — he developed 25 strategic points of focus. Exhibit 6G on page 251 cross-references the five COSO components, the 10 strategic risks, the eight elements of the HPO framework, and the 25 strategic focus points. Figure 6B shows the header and two soft control focused rows of this exhibit.

	Business-risk Mitigation — Strategic Focus Point	**Relevant Risks**	**Management Control Component**	**Elements as Defined by the HPO Model**
1.	Managers reinforce the need for making ethical decisions.	A,B,C,E, F,G,I,J	Control Environment	b, c
10.	People routinely accomplish those outcomes most important to their mission and objectives.	A,B,C,D,E, F,G,H,I,J	Business Risk Assessment	a, c, d, g, h

Figure 6B: Format of Cross-referencing Exhibit 6G

The emphasis on soft controls is further shown by the fact that 16 of the 25 focus points were in the control environment and risk assessment components.

Simmons then conducted a risk assessment workshop with the 15 top county executives. Using voting technology, he had the executives risk assess the 25 focus points using a seven-point rating scale as follows:

- Inherent likelihood of each of the 10 strategic risks:
  1 = Might Never Happen
  6 = Occurs Once Per Week
  7 = Don't Know

80

- Consequences of each of the 10 strategic risks:
  1 = Little Impact
  6 = Catastrophic
  7 = Don't Know

- Mitigation effectiveness of each of the 10 strategic risks:
  1 = Doing Everything Right
  6 = Doing Nothing
  7 = Don't Know

- Consequences of each of the 25 focus points:
  1 = Little Impact
  6 = Catastrophic
  7 = Don't Know

- Mitigation of each of the 25 focus points:
  1 = Doing Everything Right
  6 = Doing Nothing
  7 = Don't Know

When rating scales like these are used, "Don't Know" responses are usually not included in the calculation of results. In this case, however, executives not knowing would have indicated the highest level of risk. This technique generated good discussion, especially when there was a divergence of opinion among the executives or a large gap between inherent risk and mitigation effectiveness.

This risk assessment workshop was the basis of the first year's audit plan. Using this method, internal auditing generated an audit plan that was:

- Based on COSO.
- Integrated into the organization's management framework.
- Focused on strategic risks.
- Focused on soft as well as hard control issues.

The next year, Simmons used the same questions and technique but not with the 15 top county executives. Instead, he conducted workshops with the executives of each of the county's nine business centers (about 90 executives in all). He and his staff analyzed the results for changes from the previous year and disconnects between the levels of management.

For the third year's audit plan, they again used the same questions and technique, but this time they went to the business centers and randomly selected 180 lower-level managers/supervisors.

Soft Control Focus during Audit Projects

During the **Planning** stage of an audit, the audit team gathers the usual background information, potential risks, best practices, etc. from internal and external sources. The CAE then meets with the executive director who oversees the area to be audited. During this meeting, the auditors use a slide of the 10 strategic business risks to keep the discussion strategically focused. They have a standard agenda (Exhibit 6H on page 252) that they send before the meeting. It asks the executive director to identify:

- The area's greatest operational risks, and a range of risk tolerance for each risk (e.g., a risk tolerance for business interruption might be how long a key system is down; a risk tolerance for reputational damage might be how long it takes for the fire department to respond to an alarm).
- The top three conditions that, should they occur, would warrant immediate attention.
- The top three conditions that, should they occur, would warrant attention within one year.
- The top three operational governance processes that mitigate mission critical business risk.
- Specific risk mitigation practices the executive feels are carried out well by the responsible manager.
- Any specific operational concerns.

The strategic focus of this meeting encourages the executive director to bring up issues that go beyond policies and procedures and deal with soft controls. The auditors send a summary of the discussion to the executive director to gain concurrence and establish these issues as an approved basis for the audit.

The senior auditor then meets with local area management to confirm, enhance, and gain concurrence on the audit approach. On the final audit plan, the senior auditor rates each of the 10 strategic risks as they apply to this unit (high/medium/low) and prioritizes the risks 1-10.

During the **Survey** phase, the audit team gathers detailed information on the operations and risks selected for review and then forms an opinion on the design of the controlling process. The heart of the audit program for the survey phase is steps 4 through 8. Each step instructs the audit team to gather evidence and draw conclusions about one of the five COSO components. Each step lists the factors to be addressed within each component (e.g., culture, integrity, and ethical values; commitment to employee competence; and managerial oversight are three of the seven factors within the control environment). The instructions say, "Steps 4 through 8 can be accomplished by using control assessment tools such as: electronic voting software, facilitated focus groups, interviews, questionnaires, or survey instruments."

The specific tools used vary widely and are usually developed for use on just one audit, due to the diversity of county operations. As an example, Exhibit 6I (CD only) has the management interview guide, employee interview guide, and results of an employee survey for an audit of procurement cards in the Public Works division.

The survey program is by no means limited to soft controls, but it forces the audit team to include soft as well as hard controls in their evaluation of control design. At the end of this phase, the senior auditor fills out the form "Overall Assessment of Management Control," which requires an opinion on each of the 17 factors listed in the audit program. This opinion is given on a five-point scale, with 1 and 2 being concerns, and 3 through 5 being strengths." See Exhibit 6J on page 254 for a sample of this form.

During the **Examination** phase, the audit team corroborates the opinion formed during the survey phase by testing whether the key controls (hard and soft) are operating effectively. At the end of this phase, the senior auditor fills out the form "Reassessment of Management Control," which is identical to the form completed at the end of the survey.

Throughout these phases, the auditors fill out a "fact sheet" for each issue of concern. These sheets use the traditional five-attribute approach to developing audit findings (Condition, Criteria, Effect, Cause, Recommendation). Forcing the audit team to identify the root cause of each deficiency, of course, often leads the auditors from hard control exceptions to soft control root causes.

During the **Reporting** phase, the auditors work closely with local management to reach concurrence on the issues and corrective action plans. Exhibit 6K on page 256 shows the three pages of their report format that explain the COSO criteria used in the audit.

CHAPTER 7

SOFT CONTROL AUDIT REPORT COMMENTS

Reporting soft control weaknesses poses a particular challenge. In the author's experience, most audit departments only do so verbally. There are several reasons for this:

- Soft controls involve subjectivity. It is more difficult to prove the existence of a soft control weakness beyond reasonable doubt.

- Soft control weaknesses are sensitive. The responsible managers may be offended and client relationships suffer.

- Soft control weaknesses are difficult to describe clearly and with the proper perspective. Responsible managers may be blamed unfairly if their superiors misinterpret the audit comment.

- The reporting of soft control weaknesses in some cases could expose the organization to legal liability.

- If verbal reporting leads to effective corrective action, the most important goal of audit reporting is accomplished.

The downside of verbal-only reporting is that it tends to diminish the perceived importance of the issue. Effective action is less likely to occur. Also, executives and audit committees highly value information on the control environment and work environment. Having this information in formal audit reports ensures they get and have a permanent record of that information.

This chapter presents a variety of audit report comments on soft control weaknesses. They are all from the real world but have been sanitized to preserve confidentiality for the organizations that provided them.

There is no "right" or best way to write audit report comments. As with any written communication, it depends on the audience, the writer's purpose, and the context of the communication. None of the examples in this chapter may be exactly right for you, but you might find some good ideas to develop or enhance your own approach to writing such comments.

The report comments here are from three audit departments. I have grouped the reports from each department together. You can review the first one from each audit department to see the general approach. If this approach looks promising for your own organization, you can then review others from the same department to see how it reports different results. If the approach does not look promising, you can move on to the next department:

- Report excerpts A-G are from one audit department.

- Reports H-J are from a second audit department. These are complete reports, although some portions that deal only with hard controls have been deleted.
- Report comments K are seven comments taken from various reports of a third audit department.

In addition to these reports, the following are audit reports that contributors to this project were willing to have associated with their audit department:

- Exhibit 2F from New York State Comptroller's Office
- Excerpts from a Securian audit report in Chapter 3
- Exhibit 6D from WorkSafeBC

The chapter ends with Guidelines for Formal Reporting of Soft Control Weaknesses and a Conclusion for this study.

REPORT EXCERPT A:
WORK ENVIRONMENT (XXX)

1. A survey of employees in XXX indicated a need to improve the work environment.

As a means of obtaining employees' perspectives on the nature and effectiveness of internal controls in XXX, we conducted an employee survey. Accordingly, we sent the survey to all employees working at the XXX. Seventy-five percent of all employees responded. Of the 12 questions on the survey, the following seven had an unfavorable response rate of 35 percent or greater:

- 43 percent of the respondents did not believe management demonstrates the importance of integrity and ethical behavior to their employees.
- 45 percent of the respondents did not feel that management is open to employee suggestions to improve productivity and quality.
- 38 percent of the respondents believe management sometimes overrides policies, procedures, or workplace rules (e.g., takes shortcuts that are contrary to policy).
- 43 percent of the respondents did not feel that management has the right knowledge, skills, and training needed to effectively perform their duties.
- 40 percent of the respondents do not believe management effectively monitors and provides oversight and direction for the activities in their unit.
- 50 percent of the respondents do not believe they would be free to report suspected or actual wrongdoing/misconduct without fear of retaliation.
- 55 percent of the respondents are not familiar with how to report violations of law or policy, including the organization's confidential reporting line.

In addition to replying to the standard questions, employees had the opportunity to make their own comments. These narrative comments generally reinforced the issues above. Staff commented favorably on their day-to-day supervision, yet described concerns about other aspects of the XXX operation. Some of the specific concerns raised include a need for better strategic and operational planning, a need for improved oversight and communication of budget decisions, a level of travel perceived as unjustified, and a need for increased attention to fundraising, exhibition planning, and other programming.

The organization's leadership has emphasized to employees that ethical behavior, knowledgeable performance of duties, and compliance with policies are a priority. The survey results indicate opportunities exist within XXX to improve their employees' perceptions in these areas.

By emphasizing ethical behavior and encouraging employees to make suggestions for improvements and report suspected wrongdoing, the control environment is enhanced and the goals of the organization are more likely to be achieved. The president's service quality initiative strongly encourages XXX departments to actively seek out operational improvements and solicit suggestions and feedback from customers and employees.

Recommendation:

1. XXX management should work to address the issues brought out by the employee survey results. This should include establishing an environment in which ethical behavior and compliance with policy are emphasized. This emphasis should be communicated to employees, reinforced through adequate training, and exemplified through management's actions.

REPORT EXCERPT B:
XXX

1. A survey of employees in small and mid-range projects indicated that the work environment can be improved.

As a means of obtaining employees' perspectives on the nature and effectiveness of internal controls in XXX, we conducted an employee survey. Accordingly, we sent the survey to all XXX employees working in small and mid-range projects. A low response rate of only 37 percent reduces the usefulness of this survey. With a low response rate, it could be argued that employees with complaints are more apt to have responded and the results may or may not be representative. It should also be noted that the survey took place during a time of change and reorganization in XXX. It is common for organizational change to raise concerns by affected employees. Nonetheless, the results of the survey still point out some areas where XXX management can work to improve employee relations. Of the 12 questions on the survey, the following seven had a negative response rate of 36 percent or greater from the employees who responded.

- Management of your unit demonstrates the importance of integrity and ethical behavior to their employees. (38 percent disagreement)
- Management is open to employee suggestions to improve productivity and quality. (57 percent disagreement)
- Management sometimes overrides organization policies, procedures, or workplace rules (e.g., takes shortcuts that are contrary to policy). (48 percent agreement)
- Management has the right knowledge, skills, and training to effectively perform their duties. (61 percent disagreement)
- Management effectively monitors and provides oversight and direction for the activities in my unit. (50 percent disagreement)
- Management would take appropriate corrective action if policy, procedure, or workplace rule violations were detected. (52 percent disagreement)
- I would feel free to report suspected or actual wrongdoing/misconduct without fear of retaliation. (36 percent disagreement)

(Organization) leadership has emphasized to employees that ethical behavior, knowledgeable performance of duties, and compliance with policies are a priority. The survey results indicate that opportunities exist within XXX to improve its employees' perceptions on a number of attributes related to the XXX control environment.

By emphasizing ethical behavior and welcoming employees to report wrongdoing or make suggestions for improvements, the control environment is enhanced and the goals of the organization are more likely to be achieved. President XXX service quality initiative strongly encourages (organization) departments to actively seek out operational improvements and solicit suggestions and feedback from customers and employees.

Recommendation:

1. XXX management should work to address the issues brought out by the employee survey results. This should include establishing an environment in which ethical behavior and compliance with policy are emphasized. This emphasis should be communicated to employees, reinforced through adequate training, and exemplified through management's actions.

    Rating: Significant

REPORT EXCERPT C:
CONTROL ENVIRONMENT (XXX)

1. The work environment in XXX is not conducive to employee feedback.

In an effort to elicit employees' perspectives on the nature and effectiveness of internal controls within XXX, we conducted a survey of all XXX employees (three managers and 13 staff members). The response rate was high, with 82 percent (14 of 17) of the surveys returned.

Responses to two survey items indicated a significant concern by employees with regard to their ability to provide feedback to XXX management. In response to the statement, "Your work environment would allow you to report suspected or actual wrongdoing without fear of retaliation," 64 percent of respondents disagreed or strongly disagreed. Another statement pertained to management's openness to employee suggestions for improvements in organizational structure, operational productivity, and service quality. In response, 50 percent of employees either disagreed or strongly disagreed with the statement that XXX management is open to such suggestions.

Modern theories of management view employees as basically honest and competent with a desire for their organization and themselves to succeed. Where an open and nonthreatening environment is created for employees, they are usually willing and able to identify the obstacles that prevent them from carrying out their work successfully. Similarly, employees often are in the best position to spot procedural errors or policy violations.

If an environment exists that encourages employees to make suggestions for improvements and to report errors and irregularities, traditional internal controls are enhanced and opportunities for efficiency and effectiveness are maximized. As a result, the organization as a whole has a better chance of achieving its objectives.

In written comments and follow-up interviews, employees indicated they perceive individual managers as having hidden and contradictory agendas. We also noted a high frequency of employees expressing concern over their comments remaining anonymous for fear of jeopardizing their employment. In addition, employees described management's view of employee feedback as an obstacle to overcome rather than an opportunity for improvement.

Recommendations:

1a. XXX management should seek input from employees and the XXX office as to how to establish an effective mechanism to encourage the reporting of procedural errors or irregularities. It should be emphasized that confidentiality will be protected and no form of retaliation will be tolerated. Confirmed wrongdoing should result in appropriate corrective action. As appropriate, assistance should be sought from HR and/or the office of XXX.

Rating: Essential

1b. XXX management should work with employees to develop a system for soliciting, evaluating, and implementing employees' ideas for improvements. A suggestion box, periodic surveys, or open discussions could be useful tools.

Rating: Significant

2. *Employees reported an ineffective control environment within XXX.*

As noted above, we conducted a survey of all XXX employees. While 85 percent of the respondents agreed that XXX management emphasizes the importance of integrity and ethical behavior to their employees, 45 percent of respondents also reported "XXX management sometimes overrides organization policies and procedures (i.e., takes shortcuts that are contrary to policy)." These contradictory or mixed messages do not foster an effective control environment, since compliance with established policies and procedures is not consistently practiced.

In addition, survey results revealed a perception among many XXX employees that the quality of management supervision for critical activities is not adequate. In response to employee survey statements, "XXX management monitors and provides effective direction for the critical activities of XXX" and "Management staff in your unit have the right knowledge, skills, and training to effectively perform their duties," 43 percent of respondents disagreed or strongly disagreed.

One of the primary elements of an effective control environment is an emphasis on ethical behavior throughout the organization. This attitude is best established through the actions of management that demonstrate a commitment to compliance.

Effective monitoring and oversight are also primary elements of internal control. They provide the linkage between the goals and objectives of the organization and the day-to-day work of employees in pursuit of those objectives. In order to facilitate change within the system of internal controls as conditions warrant, supervisors must have the knowledge, abilities, and training necessary to recognize and react to conditions within their environment.

Without a control environment that consistently maintains a high standard of ethical behavior and compliance with policies, other existing control mechanisms often become ineffective. In addition, internal controls cannot function effectively without adequate monitoring and supervision.

Several written comments and interviews pointed out management's tendency to circumvent certain policies that might adversely affect XXX initiatives. Other comments suggest a level of secrecy that raised suspicions of wrongdoing. With regard to supervisory skills and oversight, respondents specifically reported problems with budget and finance, human relations, and planning.

Recommendations:

2a. XXX management needs to emphasize the importance of compliance with XXX and all other applicable policies, and establish an environment where compliance is expected and practiced.

Rating: Essential

2b. The XXX office should review the skills and training of XXX management personnel in light of the concerns described above. If it is determined that those skills and training need to be enhanced, a plan for appropriate training or other action should be devised.

Rating: Essential

3. *There is a need for improved communication in XXX.*

Employee responses to two statements on the employee survey (described previously) indicate a concern related to the effectiveness of communication within XXX. Five of 13 respondents (38 percent) disagreed with the statement that information needed to do their job is communicated effectively. Also, five of 14 (36 percent) respondents indicated a lack of an effective resource within XXX for obtaining clarification of policies. We further noted that most departmental policies have not been placed in writing.

Employee comments included the statement that information is shared with them on what management determines as a "need-to-know basis," and other employees suggested management's level of secrecy undermines open communication. In addition, some employees felt excluded from planning processes where their input could have had a beneficial impact. Finally, employees expressed frustration with management in obtaining answers to their questions relating to policies and procedures. Some employees described receiving admonishment when seeking clarification or direction on policies and procedures, to the point where they say they no longer attempt to seek such clarifications.

Further, we noted that significant information was not always communicated to appropriate XXX. For example, the XXX director did not always communicate concerns timely to his supervisor, the XXX. While information was given when requested, pertinent information was not always volunteered. Also, XXX was not fully informed of relevant concerns regarding XXX sponsored contracts.

A lack of communication results in employees not understanding the objectives of an organization. This can cause effort to be expended in a less than optimum manner, which in turn hampers efforts to fulfill objectives. By not sharing information with appropriate XXX, an opportunity is lost to gain valuable input or perspective when making decisions.

Recommendations:

3a. Efforts should be made to improve the communication within the XXX department. This should include providing all necessary information to the staff, seeking input from appropriate staff when making decisions, and documenting departmental policies and procedures in writing. In particular, adequate information should be shared with the individuals responsible for budgetary and financial compliance.

Rating: Significant

3b. XXX management should communicate with appropriate central XXX units. This should include sharing information as appropriate with supervisors or other central units, and seeking input from those units that could be useful in decision-making or policy clarifications.

Rating: Significant

REPORT EXCERPT D: CONTROL ENVIRONMENT (XXX)

1. ***XXX administration needs to place a greater emphasis on ethical behavior and compliance with policies.***

In an effort to obtain employees' perspectives on the nature and effectiveness of operational controls within XXX, a survey of all employees was conducted. The response rate was quite high, with 65 percent of the surveys returned. One item on the survey asked if XXX's administration emphasizes the importance of integrity and ethical behavior to employees. Of those responding, 49 percent disagreed. In response to the statement, "XXX administration sometimes overrides policies and procedures (i.e., takes shortcuts that are contrary to policy)," 59 percent of respondents agreed.

Even if the perceptions noted above are not fully accurate, this would still be an area of concern because of the high percentage of employees who hold these opinions. If employees receive the message that ethical behavior and compliance with policy are not a priority, this perception becomes the employees' reality and could easily prevent this unit from operating at its optimal level.

One of the primary elements of an effective control environment is an emphasis on ethical behavior throughout the organization. This attitude is best established through the actions of management that demonstrate a commitment to complying with institutional expectations. If ethical behavior is not emphasized, or employees believe management circumvents policies, the control environment is seriously undermined and the goals of the organization are less likely to be achieved.

Recommendation:

1. XXX administration needs to establish an environment in which ethical behavior and compliance with policy and procedure are emphasized. This emphasis should be communicated to employees in writing, reinforced through the provision of adequate training to ensure employees fully understand policies and procedures, and be exemplified through management's actions.

2. ***The work environment in XXX does not encourage employees to suggest improvements or report wrongdoing.***

The responses to two items on our employee survey indicate that the work environment in XXX is not conducive to suggesting improvements or reporting violations. In response to the statement, "XXX administration is open to employee suggestions on improvements in productivity and quality," 60 percent of those responding disagreed. Likewise, 51 percent said their work environment would not allow them to report suspected or actual wrongdoing without fear of retaliation.

Modern theories of management view employees as basically honest and competent with a desire for their organizations and themselves to succeed. Where an open and supportive environment is created for employees, they are usually willing and able to identify obstacles that prevent them from carrying out their work successfully. This enhances traditional internal controls and gives the organization a better chance of achieving its objectives.

The president's service quality initiative strongly encourages units to actively seek out operational improvements and solicit suggestions and feedback from customers and employees. Promoting a culture that is responsive to such suggestions is fundamental to continuous improvement.

Recommendations:

2a. XXX administration should utilize the knowledge, skills, and talents of its employees to help identify XXX priorities and formulate effective methods for accomplishing those priorities. The department should work with HR to develop a system for promoting employee involvement and input. This could include the use of periodic surveys, suggestion boxes, or open discussions.

2b. XXX administration should seek input from employees and **HR** as to how to establish an effective mechanism to encourage the reporting of procedural or operational errors or irregularities. It should be emphasized that confidentiality will be protected and no form of retaliation will be tolerated. Employees should be reminded in writing of the policy "Dealing with Allegations of Financial or Operational Misconduct," and of the availability of the DKA (designated key administrator) as a resource to employees. It should be pointed out that this policy encourages employees to report known or suspected violations of policy to either the DKA or the audit department.

Best Practices: Evaluating the Corporate Culture

REPORT EXCERPT E:
WORK ENVIRONMENT/SAFETY (XXX)

1. *Employee survey results indicate the need for management action.*

As part of our audit, we conducted a survey of XXX employees. The survey solicited opinions on the operations of the XXX and focused on the work environment established by management. A total of 287 surveys were sent and 94 responses were received (a 33 percent response rate). While the overall response rate was low, there were still important trends from this survey that XXX management should address.

Overall, for the 13 questions on the survey, the following five questions had an unfavorable response rate of 35 percent or greater:

- *Question #2:* 39 percent of the responding employees did not feel that management is open to employee suggestions to improve productivity and quality.
- *Question #4:* 39 percent of the responding employees did not feel that management has the right knowledge, skills, and training needed to effectively perform their duties.
- *Question #6:* 42 percent of the responding employees did not feel management effectively monitors and provides oversight and direction for the activities in my unit.
- *Question #11:* 35 percent of the employees responding to the survey would not feel free to report suspected or actual wrongdoing/misconduct without fear of retaliation.
- *Question #12:* 37 percent of the responding employees did not feel familiar with how to report violations of law or policy, including the organization's confidential reporting line.

Development of a "culture" in which employees feel management adheres to organization policies and feel free to openly discuss and/or report concerns and other issues to management is critical to reducing institutional risks and promoting an effective control environment. Similarly, providing effective monitoring and oversight is a critical responsibility of management, and risks are increased when that does not occur. Finally, providing training and direction on how an employee may report possible violations of law or policy promotes an honest and ethical work environment and enables units to address important issues more promptly.

XXX recently reorganized its management structure with an increased emphasis on productivity and accountability. In addition, VMC has started 85 process improvement projects. In the view of XXX management, the changes associated with these projects, combined with reorganization, have raised employee stress levels and may have contributed to the employee survey results. This is consistent with our experience in other units.

Recommendation:

1. XXX management should review the specific issues mentioned above and develop a plan to address these work environment concerns. Particular attention should be given to providing effective oversight and direction of XXX operations. This should include creating a work environment in which employees are encouraged to come forward with both suggestions for improvement and report suspected wrongdoing or misconduct.

    Rating: Essential

REPORT EXCERPT F: XXX

1. *XXX employees perceive that the work environment can be improved.*

In an effort to elicit employees' perspectives on the nature and effectiveness of internal controls in XXX, we conducted an employee survey. Accordingly, we sent the survey to half of all XXX employees. A low response rate of only 36 percent reduces the usefulness of this survey. With a low response rate, it could be argued that employees with complaints are more apt to have responded and the results may or may not be representative. Nonetheless, the results of the survey still point out some areas where XXX management can work to improve employee relations. Of the 14 questions on the survey, the following eight had a negative response rate of 40 percent or greater from the 36 percent who responded.

- XXX leadership demonstrates the importance of integrity and ethical behavior to their employees. (44 percent)
- XXX management is open to employee suggestions to improve productivity and quality. (44 percent)
- XXX management/administrative staff have the right knowledge, skills, and training to effectively perform their duties. (45 percent)
- XXX management effectively monitors and provides oversight and direction for the activities in my department. (43 percent)
- XXX management takes appropriate corrective action if policy or workplace rule violations are detected. (47 percent)
- I would feel free to report suspected or actual wrongdoing/misconduct without fear of retaliation. (42 percent)
- XXX management recognizes and rewards good performance. (67 percent)
- XXX management takes appropriate and timely corrective action to address safety issues that arise. (40 percent)

(Organization) leadership wants all employees to understand that ethical behavior, knowledgeable performance of duties, and compliance with policies are a priority. The survey results indicate that opportunities exist within XXX to improve its employees' perceptions on a number of attributes related to the XXX control environment.

By emphasizing ethical behavior and welcoming employees to report wrongdoing or make suggestions for improvements, the control environment is enhanced and the goals of the organization are more likely to be achieved. President XXX service quality initiative strongly encourages organization departments to actively seek out operational improvements and solicit suggestions and feedback from customers and employees.

Recommendation:

1. XXX management should work to address the issues brought out by the employee survey results. This should include establishing an environment in which ethical behavior and compliance with policy are emphasized. This emphasis should be communicated to employees, reinforced through adequate training, and exemplified through management's actions.

    Rating: Significant

Best Practices: Evaluating the Corporate Culture

REPORT EXCERPT G: GENERAL CONTROL ENVIRONMENT (XXX)

1. An employee survey revealed concerns about the work environment at YYY.

In an effort to obtain employees' perspectives on the nature and effectiveness of operational controls within (XXX), we conducted a survey of all employees. Overall, the results of the survey were very positive. However, the results from YYY were distinctly negative. Although the response rate from YYY was relatively low (27 percent), the results do warrant the attention of XXX management. Specifically, the following survey items elicited negative response rates of between 38 percent and 71 percent:

- Your department emphasizes the importance of integrity and ethical behavior to their employees (three of eight respondents disagreed = 38 percent).
- Your department is open to employee suggestions on improvements in productivity and quality (four of eight disagreed = 50 percent).
- Your department sometimes overrides organization policies and procedures (i.e., takes shortcuts that are contrary to policy) (five of seven agreed = 71 percent).
- Your department would take appropriate corrective action if policy, procedure, or workplace rule violations were detected (four of eight disagreed = 50 percent).
- Your supervisor has effectively communicated your job duties and responsibilities to you (three of eight disagreed = 38 percent).
- Your work environment would allow you to report suspected or actual wrongdoing without fear of retaliation (four of eight disagreed = 50 percent).

As indicated, the number of respondents from YYY was quite small. Nonetheless, we saw no evidence that these results were not representative of the total population of YYY employees. Even with the small response rate, the negative perceptions held by these employees should still be a matter of concern to XXX management. It should be noted that for the other three sections within XXX, none of the survey questions elicited negative response rates exceeding 33 percent.

One of the most critical components of a successful organization is a positive work environment. Such an environment is characterized by an emphasis on ethical behavior throughout the organization and a demonstrated commitment to compliance with institutional expectations. In this environment, employees feel valued, respected, and safeguarded against retaliation.

A positive work environment fosters harmonious workplace relationships, employee retention, and productivity. In contrast, if an environment exists in which ethical behavior and compliance with policies are not emphasized and employees feel their contributions and suggestions are not valued, the control environment is seriously undermined. As a result, the goals of the organization are less likely to be achieved.

Recommendations:

1a. XXX management needs to emphasize the importance of compliance with organization and all other applicable policies and establish an environment at YYY where compliance is expected and practiced.

Rating: Significant

1b. XXX management should work with YYY employees to develop a system for soliciting, evaluating, and implementing employees' ideas for improvements. A suggestion box, periodic surveys, or open discussions could be useful tools.

Rating: Significant

1c. XXX management should seek input from YYY employees and HR on how to establish an effective mechanism to encourage the reporting of procedural errors or irregularities. It should be emphasized that confidentiality will be protected and no form of retaliation will be tolerated. Employees should be reminded in writing of the policy "Reporting and Addressing Concerns of Misconduct." It should be pointed out that this policy encourages employees to report known or suspected violations of policy to either their local unit, the Office of Internal Audit, or through the (organization's) confidential hot line service or Web site.

Rating: Significant

REPORT H.

Summary of Observations

Recent restructuring of authority, ongoing evaluation of processes, and development of more discreet performance measures are designed to provide reasonable assurance that significant business risks are mitigated. Effective mitigation can in turn enhance the high performance capabilities of this organization by improving the likelihood of quality outcomes and services. Opportunities exist to further mitigate risks by:

- Defining a change management process to assign authority, evaluate risk, track progress, and measure outcomes of changing conditions.

- Increasing the level of communication and interaction at each level of the organization.

- Seeking input and buy-in from staff members before policy or procedural changes.

- Establishing and communicating a procedure for employees to report ethical violations. This procedure should include assurance of non-retaliation.

The responsible manager has recognized these issues and is addressing them.

We also noted an opportunity to reduce potential health and safety risks and exposure to legal liability by using vehicle safety checklists.

(Please read Appendix A for details)

APPENDIX A

Organizational changes are driving an increased level of exposure to noncompliance, low productivity, and decreased quality of work.

Managers' Proactive Practices

Responsible managers have mitigated risks associated with organizational change through the following actions.

The Control Environment
- Emphasizing responsibility and due diligence
- Emphasizing accuracy in operations
- Providing continuous professional education
- Conducting a leadership retreat attended by all managers

Control Activities

- Partnering with the human resources staff to pursue reclassification of job descriptions
- Conducting regularly scheduled departmental meetings

Monitoring Activities

- Reviewing biweekly activity reports
- Evaluating performance measures to determine whether staffing levels are appropriate

Opportunities to Further Enhance Risk Mitigation

Risk Assessment

Our discussions with the responsible managers indicated that due to the large number of changes occurring across all levels of management, it has been difficult to focus attention or recognize all the relevant risks associated with changing conditions.

Recommendation:

1. The responsible managers should evaluate the specific risk factors associated with organizational change more closely and develop a plan to address the most important issues in the near term. One way to accomplish this would be to define a change management process to assign authority, evaluate risks, track progress toward mitigation, and measure the outcomes of changing conditions.

Information and Communications

Interviews and observations indicated a disconnect among the various levels of the organization.

The managers' perception and those of the staff differ concerning the impact of changing conditions. Managers believe that attitudes within the department continue to be an obstacle, and staff indicated that they feel uninvolved in the process of organizational changes.

Recommendations:

1. During this period of reorganization it is increasingly important to communicate clearly with all levels of the organization the department's mission, objectives, goals, risks, and plans to address changing conditions.

2. Responsible managers should seek the input and buy-in from staff before policy or procedural changes and enhance communication and improve interaction between levels of management and staff.

Management Action:

The responsible manager recognizes the importance of addressing the observed disconnect among the various levels of the department. The responsible manager further agrees that a change management process would be beneficial to assign authority, evaluate risk, track progress, and measure outcomes of changing conditions. The development of performance measures is in progress and these measures aim to evaluate and address the increased exposure to risk factors as well as the department's position in relation to its goals.

Chapter 7: Soft Control Audit Report Comments

REPORT I.

Summary

Managers have a number of processes in place over revenue collections and reporting designed to provide reasonable assurance that significant business risks are mitigated. However, we observed several critical issues associated with reporting of statistics to federal agencies, management of grant revenues and ticket sales, and compliance with the Purchasing Card Program that need to be addressed as soon as possible. Mitigation of the related business risks could be accomplished by:

- Strengthening communication and information reporting across the organization.

- Implementing a risk management process and monitoring risks proactively.

- Aligning critical job roles, responsibilities, and duties with organizational risk mitigation strategies and revising job descriptions accordingly.

- Implementing more comprehensive managerial monitoring and follow-up techniques and reporting results upward routinely to the executive director level.

The responsible general manager agrees that there are opportunities to improve risk mitigation and has developed action plans to do so.

Status of Business Risk Mitigation

The following conditions impact all of the identified risks:

1. Federal reports had not been submitted timely and/or accurately.

2. Information needed for effective management of grant revenues is not readily available for use by upper management.

3. Monitoring of ticket sales revenue is not occurring.

4. Individual purchase-card holders routinely neglect to submit purchase receipts to the responsible coordinator.

While each of these conditions has unique factors as to causes, we believe they are symptomatic of systemic control issues that could be addressed by:

- Clarifying roles and responsibilities of staff.

- Communicating the importance of National Transit Database (NTD) reporting.

- Implementing an internal reporting schedule within each department to improve employee efficiency, data accuracy, reporting confidence, and management oversight.

- Continuing to meet with department managers and receive electronic progress reports monthly.

- Managing and submitting federal reports from within the responsible organization rather than relying on outside support.

The responsible manager concurs, has taken or plans to take appropriate action, and will report the status of these actions regularly to the executive director.

APPENDIX A

Scope and Methodology

To achieve our objective, we evaluated key elements of the five components of management control as of XXX.

The Control Environment

- Conducted interviews with both managers and staff to determine the existence, consistency, and awareness of core values and objectives.
- Observed management and staff interactions and demeanor when visiting facilities.
- Toured facilities to gain an understanding of operations.
- Evaluated staff knowledge and awareness of statutory and regulatory requirements.

Risk Assessment Practices

- Completed risk assessment questionnaires and conducted interviews with both managers and staff.
- Researched revenue collections and reporting practices, business risks, and vulnerabilities, and discussed risk mitigation strategies with both managers and staff.

Control Activities

- Performed testing on purchasing card transactions and revenues.
- Evaluated compliance with policies and federal law requirements.
- Established, through interviews with managers and staff, the presence of revenue collections and reporting controls.
- Discussed departmental procedures.

Information and Communications

- Evaluated, through interviews with managers and staff, whether information and communications were appropriate, timely, current, accurate, and accessible.

- Established, through interviews and interactions with managers and staff, the adequacy and effectiveness of information and communication processes.

Monitoring Activities

- Reviewed monitoring for compliance with policy and federal law requirements.
- Reviewed the existence and adequacy of reporting practices.

APPENDIX B

Detailed Results: FEDERAL REPORTING

Inherent Risk #1: Loss of Revenue/Funding

Inherent Risk #2: Noncompliance

Through inquiry and observation, we learned of past challenges the organization faced in submitting federal reports timely and accurately. Some of these include:

- Changing of leadership.
- Insufficient resources to report required data.
- Labor intensive data collection process.
- Training of three new staff members.
- Newly imposed recordkeeping requirements.
- Broken or aged equipment.

These factors resulted in the following conditions:

1. Department of Transportation (DOT)

   - Grant information had not been submitted to the DOT for the second quarter of XXXX. This was an oversight and not considered a reoccurring issue.

2. National Transit Database (NTD)
   NTD requires monthly and annual reporting.

   - Monthly ridership information had not been collected and submitted to NTD from November XXXX through June 11, XXXX.

   - Between October XXXX and July XXXX, only three safety and security reports had been submitted to NTD on time.

   - The annual report for FY XXXX had not been accepted after at least four attempts as of July XXXX. NTD continued to request explanations for significant changes in the organization's reported statistics.

Opportunity for Change:

To ensure continued grant funding, the responsible general manager could:

- Strengthen communication and information reporting across the organization.

- Implement a risk management process and monitor risks proactively.

- Align critical job roles, responsibilities, and duties with organizational risk mitigation strategies and revise job descriptions accordingly.

- Institute more comprehensive checks and balances in day-to-day operations.

- Implement more comprehensive managerial monitoring and follow-up techniques, and report results upward routinely to the executive director level.

The responsible manager plans to address these issues immediately by:

- Clarifying roles and responsibilities of staff.

- Communicating the importance of NTD reporting.

- Implementing an internal reporting schedule within each department for the purpose of improving employee efficiency, data accuracy, reporting confidence, and management oversight.

- Continuing to meet with department managers and receive electronic progress reports monthly.

- Managing grants and submitting federal reports from within the organization.

- In addition, a consultant will be retained to perform a comprehensive operations analysis to help evaluate staff performance and efficiencies of operations. The responsible general manager expects the staff analysis will be completed by January XXXX, and the operations efficiency analysis by June XXXX.

Note: Appendices C and D are not included because one is similar to the above and the other deals with hard control issues only.

Chapter 7: Soft Control Audit Report Comments

REPORT J.

Summary

The executive director requested this review of management controls over business center P-card administration.

Due to changes in organizational structure, processes, and procedures, management controls in XXX did not provide reasonable assurance to the responsible general manager that significant business risks related to P-card usage were mitigated. While senior management had been in the process of strengthening P-card controls within the business center, improved processes and procedures had not been fully realized at the time of our review.

The responsible general manager agreed there are opportunities to improve risk mitigation related to P-card usage and has developed an action plan to be completed no later than May 30, XXXX.

Status of Business Risk Mitigation

Management controls did not provide reasonable assurance to the responsible general manager that significant business risks related to P-card usage were mitigated.

Mitigation of the business risks could be improved by:

- Modifying reporting mechanisms.
- Requiring supervisor and/or manager review of original P-card purchase documents for approval of purchases; routine monitoring of charges using online sources.
- Communicating with the Office of Financial Planning's (OFP's) Purchasing Card Administrator (PCA) to coordinate and strengthen controls.
- Addressing specific areas identified by a P-card holder survey conducted by internal auditing as part of this review.
- Tracking P-card purchases and merchandise usage and retention in inventory.

During the course of our review, the responsible general manager implemented a process whereby division managers started to develop a practical P-card control policy. The project is scheduled to be completed by April 30, XXXX. Supervisors and managers will be trained by May 15 and the new policy will be in effect by May 30, XXXX.

In addition, all cardholders have been notified to complete the new online P-card training that the "Procure to Pay" team (Office of Financial Planning) has developed. Cardholders must pass the exam by April 25, XXXX, and on an annual basis thereafter or their P-cards will be cancelled. A contact person for cardholder questions and concerns was designated.

For issues related to loss of assets/resources, please read Appendix B.

APPENDIX A

Scope and Methodology

To achieve our objective, we evaluated key elements of the five components of management control as of December XXXX. This included a P-card holder survey of 80 percent of cardholders. The survey focused on items pertaining to each of the components shown below.

The Control Environment

- Conducted interviews with both managers and staff to determine the existence, consistency, and awareness of core values and objectives.

- Observed management and staff interactions and demeanor when visiting facilities.

- Reviewed responses to inquiries regarding the assignment of authority and responsibility.

Risk Assessment Practices

- Conducted interviews with both managers and staff to determine the objective-setting processes, risk identification, and risk analysis processes.

- Researched business risks, vulnerabilities, and best practices; discussed risk mitigation strategies and possible opportunities for improvement with the executive director, responsible general manager, and staff.

Control Activities

- Reviewed departmental policies and procedures.

- Performed testing on P-card transactions for compliance with operational and fiscal requirements.

- Discussed upcoming changes in policies and procedures with the OFP's procure to pay team members; reviewed documents in the revision process.

Information and Communications

- Evaluated, through interviews with managers and staff, whether information and communications were appropriate, timely, current, accurate, and accessible.

- Established, through interviews and interactions with managers and staff, the adequacy and effectiveness of communication processes.

Monitoring Activities

- Through inquiry, observation, and analysis, assessed management's monitoring, oversight and reporting practices.

Chapter 7: Soft Control Audit Report Comments

APPENDIX B

Detailed Results

Inherent Risk #1: Loss of Assets/Resources

The following conditions were observed:

1. *(Conditions 1 through 4 dealt only with hard controls and tangible errors.)*

5. A cardholder survey we conducted indicated specific areas that could be addressed by management to improve controls over P-card usage.

Responsible managers have planned to take the following actions to mitigate the likelihood or impact of loss of assets or resources:

Control Environment:

- Division managers will discuss the contents of the audit report and participate in the development of a practical management control policy in light of the audit findings. The policy will be developed by April 30, XXXX, and all supervisors and managers will be trained by May 15, XXXX. The policy will be in effect by May 30, XXXX.

Control Activities:

- *(Deal with hard controls only)*

Monitoring Activities:

- *(Deal with hard controls only)*

Information and Communications:

- Managers will assist their cardholders to get the best value for the dollar and reduce risk by coordinating and providing an educational information session to cardholders, including the issue of Internet security and stored card numbers when purchasing online.

- Responsible managers will partner with the PCA to provide clarification on the extent of control provided by merchant category code blocks.

- The responsible general manager has notified cardholders of the revised P-card policy. Cardholders will be required to complete the new P-card holder training and pass an online purchasing card test by April 25, XXXX, and annually thereafter. New P-card procedures will be distributed to staff after the initial training is completed.

Results of Interviews:

We conducted one-on-one interviews with the purchasing card administrator, the OFP's financial supervisor, five (of six) OFP account managers, and the responsible general manager in the business center. Interviews indicated that, although account managers reconciled a variety of documents with the charges on cardholder statements, questioned any items that appeared to be out of order or incomplete, and checked that each charge appeared to be a legitimate charge, they did not approve purchases or payments.

The responsible general manager indicated that P-card usage had created a "virtual warehouse." For purchased items that were supposed to be shipped, it could not always be determined from available documentation whether or not the merchandise had been received. Also, even though the specific business purpose of the purchase may be referenced on the document (such as by a work order number and annual agreement number, when applicable), there was no tracking mechanism for leftover items that had not been used on the specified job.

Numerous changes in P-card processes and procedures occurred and were still occurring during the time period being examined and extending through March 2008. The Purchasing Card Policy and Procedures Manual and P-card training were both being revised. Previously, payment request approvals had been signed in operating divisions, but at the time of our review they were being signed in OFP. Also, account managers had been located in the operating divisions, but as of October XXXX were relocated in OFP, resulting in a significant change in P-card analysis and reporting.

Cardholder Survey:

For cardholder input, we conducted a survey of 80 percent of P-card holders (92 participants) using voting technology to rate 23 items covering the five components of management control. Results indicated several specific areas that could be addressed by management to improve controls over P-card usage, including:

- Stating objectives and strategy for the program within the business unit.
- Providing instructions.
- Providing information on changes.
- Assisting cardholders to receive the best value for the county.
- Providing a mechanism to report misuse or abuse.
- Soliciting recommendations.
- Reviewing the purchases that employees make using their P-cards.
- Addressing any detected violations of P-card policy and procedures.

Please refer to the accompanying survey slides for details of the survey responses.

Author's note: The survey had 23 statements (e.g., "Cardholders receive instructions on the proper use of P-cards" and "Employees demonstrate ethical behavior in their use of P-cards"). For each statement, respondents were asked, "How important is this?" and "How well is this being achieved?" They responded to each of these two questions on a four-tiered scale from "Very Important" to "Not Important" and from "Doing Little or Nothing Right" to "Doing Everything Right."

Responsible managers may wish to consider:

Monitoring Activities:

- Best practices in monitoring charge card programs include:
  o Performing periodic reviews of the number of charge card accounts in use for appropriateness of number.
  o Providing appropriate card limits that slightly exceed the highest actual purchase of the cardholder in the preceding year.
  o By a combination of the above, reducing the financial exposure to the county.

Information and Communication:

- The responsible general manager could direct managers to inform their cardholders to make sure their account numbers and expiration dates are marked out on all documents.

- Responsible managers could communicate with Procurement on any changes in P-card groups so that updates could be made timely in P-card management software to ensure reliable reporting.

- XXX could provide a process for cardholders to report suspected P-card misuse or abuse, such as through a mechanism for anonymous reporting of suspicious activity.

- The responsible general manager could communicate with Procurement regarding annual agreements in order to coordinate processes and procedures for cardholders when purchasing from annual agreements.

- XXX could communicate with Procurement on the need for bids in certain areas of purchasing related to P-cards. The need for annual agreements in certain areas will be monitored by Procurement, and OFP account managers may have recommendations based on their regular review of P-card purchase documentation.

- XXX could coordinate with Procurement to assist account managers and cardholders to make the monthly reconciliation process more efficient by evaluating their recommendations on an ongoing basis and implementing proposed solutions that may be effective.

- The responsible general manager could notify responsible managers to inform cardholders of the available budget toward the end of the fiscal year regarding P-card expenditures so that transactions are not flagged after the fact due to overspending in certain accounts.

REPORT COMMENTS K

1. Although the Business Ethics Committee (BEC) was formed, numerous employees at this location indicated they were not aware of the BEC and its purpose. In addition, most employees were not aware of the company's whistleblowing hot line.

   Without an awareness of a formal system to handle complaints and investigations, there is an increased risk of employees not communicating to management on matters of questionable or unethical conduct.

2. Operational employees indicated that management communicates the importance of ethics and integrity within the organization during new hire training via e-mail and verbal communication. However, employees indicated that in some cases, when some employees were close to attaining the sales target established by management, individuals would share employee numbers to help each other reach sales targets.

   Knowledge of improper practices of some employees in achieving performance goals could lead to other employees questioning what is acceptable and unacceptable behavior. Additionally, in instances where the sale of ancillary products is assigned to the incorrect employee, employees' personal sales statistics are misrepresented, which may impact the promotion selection process.

3. There is an opportunity for management to enhance its communication to employees regarding promotional criteria. Although the office had written promotional criteria, employees felt the criteria changed frequently and was not communicated to them, resulting in confusion.

   When promotional criteria is not communicated or lacks consistency, there is an increased risk of employee misunderstandings, which could result in morale issues and/or potential lawsuits.

4. There is an opportunity to strengthen the communication and support between locations. Employees indicated the lack of cooperation (i.e., transferring of inventory) between the locations is impacting employee morale and their ability to serve customers.

   When communication challenges exist between locations, there is an increased risk that organizational goals will not be achieved. Employees must not only understand their own role, but also how their role impacts others. Without open communication and cooperation between branches, employee morale, customer satisfaction, and profits could be negatively impacted.

5. There is an opportunity to enhance communication and the working relationships between department heads and administrative employees. A sample of employees noted that department heads rarely discuss expectations, goals, or career opportunities with employees. They did not discuss with employees the overall big picture of the office and how their positions fit into it. Additionally, employees did not feel that information was passed down to all levels of employees consistently and timely. Employees noted a lack of respect from department heads. They felt that they were treated as a lower class of people and did not receive daily support to perform their job duties.

When communication is not effective and there is not a good working relationship between management and employees, employee morale, motivation, and job effectiveness may be adversely impacted, leading to possible job dissatisfaction and turnover.

6. There is an opportunity to strengthen communication between the sales and administrative departments. Both departments indicated there was a lack of understanding regarding the various roles and responsibilities of employees in the other departments, leading to confusion and decreased cooperation between departments.

7. There is an opportunity to strengthen the level of professionalism in the work environment. Employees communicated instances where various levels of management made verbal comments that did not adhere to the principles of our conduct policies.

When employees exhibit behavior that does not comply with company standards, there is an increased risk of an uncomfortable work environment and possible employee litigation.

Guidelines for Formal Reporting of Soft Control Weaknesses

The audit report comments in this chapter are by no means perfect, but they fit the organizations for which they were written. As stated at the beginning of this chapter, most audit departments (in my experience) only report soft control weaknesses verbally. As long as positive change occurs, this may be sufficient.

Formal reporting is preferable, of course, but it becomes counterproductive if it creates an adversarial relationship with the managers being audited. Hopefully, the following guidelines help readers decide how best to report soft control weaknesses within their own organizations.

- **The organizational culture must support formal reporting.** If operating managers lose their jobs or suffer other harsh consequences unfairly, word will spread and other managers will be less cooperative with the auditors. Formal reporting can easily become a barrier to effective soft control auditing. A supportive culture is one in which the audit process is regarded as a learning experience — an opportunity for good managers to get better.

    There are times when serious problems *should* result in serious consequences, but full discussion of these issues is generally best done verbally. Any comments in audit reports should be kept general and completely objective.

- **Auditors must have persuasive evidence.** The subjectivity involved in soft controls makes this a challenge. The initial evidence of a soft control weakness usually comes from an auditor's perception of the environment or employee perceptions gathered through interviews or surveys. The audit departments in the case studies look for corroborating evidence before reporting a weakness. If none can be found, they usually report the perception of a weakness to the responsible manager as something the manager should be aware of and deal with, but do not report it to higher levels.

- **Report comments should be phrased carefully and provide full perspective.** It is very easy for higher-level managers who are not involved in the discussions that led to the comment to misunderstand it and blame the responsible manager unfairly.

Conclusion

There are limitations to how far auditors can go with formal reporting of soft control weaknesses. There are, in fact, limitations to how far auditors can go with soft control auditing. The challenge is one we will perhaps never be able to meet completely. The extent to which we are able to meet it, though, is the extent to which we fully meet our professional responsibility.

The audit departments represented in this study have found that upper management and audit committees value soft control auditing more highly than traditional audit work. They and the many other auditors I have worked with through the years who have embraced the challenge of evaluating soft controls believe that this is their most value-added audit work. The assurance it provides is what our stakeholders need most.

In almost every case, evaluating soft controls significantly raises the status and credibility of internal auditing. Hopefully, readers have found the tools, techniques, and guidelines they need to start down this challenging and rewarding path or take their efforts a few steps further.

Exhibit 1A

SA AT BELLSOUTH: THE AFTERLIFE

> The following article, "SA at BellSouth: The Afterlife," was written by Glenda Jordan, CIA, CCSA, CPA, CFE, Manager, Business Controls, BellSouth Corp. This article was reprinted with permission from the Fourth Quarter 2006 issue of the *CSA Sentinel,* published by The Institute of Internal Auditors, Inc., www.theiia.org.

Control self-assessment (CSA) was one of the hottest internal audit topics in the mid-1990s. Everyone wanted to understand what it was, what benefits it offered, and how to implement it, and there were heated debates about the definition and implementation style. While the debates continue, the focus is now on whether any version of CSA is a significant player in today's environment. Is CSA still alive? If so, what does it look like now? To answer this question from BellSouth's perspective, one has to understand the journey that CSA has taken within the organization.

CSA at BellSouth has undergone three major transformations since the company first embarked on the pilgrimage. The first version of BellSouth's CSA initiative was called Work Team Self-assessment, but the second and third versions didn't have official names. The core of the second version was the internal audit, so this version accurately can be described as the BellSouth CSA Audit Approach. CSA later became a working tool within pockets of the corporation, so the BellSouth Imbedded Approach is an appropriate name for the third version. The following commentary provides the key drivers, process design rationale, and outcomes of each of the three BellSouth CSA initiatives.

WORK TEAM SELF-ASSESSMENT INITIATIVE

Work Team Self-assessment (WTSA) Initial Drivers

In the early 1990s, BellSouth's chief corporate auditor (CCA) became aware of CSA. At that time, BellSouth knew the telecommunication industry would soon experience radical changes because of the convergence of technology that would allow cable companies to compete with traditional phone companies. The CCA believed that internal audit downsizing was inevitable and wanted to explore the possibility of implementing some form of CSA to ensure that there still would be reasonable oversight of the corporate control structure when internal auditing could no longer have the same scope coverage.

WTSA Process Design Rationale

After calling The Institute of Internal Auditors (IIA), BellSouth received two contact names — Tim Leech and Paul Makosz. Both gentlemen were pioneers of the CSA movement as a consequence of problem-solving techniques they developed at Gulf Canada, an independent oil and gas company. Representatives from the BellSouth Internal Audit Department attended training sessions held by both Leech and Makosz. BellSouth created a unique methodology based on input from several sources, including The IIA.

The implementation strategy was to partner with selected assistant vice presidents who had a need for CSA. Through this partnership, the WTSA team planned to demonstrate the value of CSA after obtaining reliable results. Reliable results included critical enhancements to reengineering projects prior to deployment and measurable key indicators like cost savings or customer satisfaction level increases as a result of improvements suggested within the WTSA process. For the next two years, BellSouth's Internal Audit Department allied with various departments and performed ad hoc WTSA workshops.

The largest effort was with the Network organization, a department within BellSouth. In telecommunications, a network organization generally includes the provisioning and maintenance of all assets required to route the call from origination to termination. Network had several ongoing control problems that management wanted resolved. So, Internal Audit teamed with Network to lead workshops throughout BellSouth. As a result, there were no audit findings associated with the WTSA topics during the next audit cycle. Other significant clients were BellSouth organizations that deployed major organizational changes (i.e., downsizing and outsourcing) where management wanted assurance that the business would still function in the new environment.

WTSA Outcomes — Lessons Learned

Everyone's individual concerns were addressed, and those who partnered closely with the WTSA team were positive about CSA. The WTSA process did not include any result summarization to the board or audit committee by Internal Audit, so customers (i.e., department management) appreciated getting control advice without experiencing any negative repercussions. However, despite positive experiences with the WTSA process, there was growing opposition. Because the CCA was open about potential downsizing to the Internal Audit Department as a driver for his involvement, other departments interpreted the message as Internal Audit wanting to transfer its job functions to the operating departments. In addition, some of the department heads that participated in CSA did not appreciate being audited shortly thereafter. Their belief was that because Internal Audit already had been in their department, they shouldn't have to be audited a second time. In reality, since WTSA did not include audit committee oversight, the audit still needed to be performed.

THE BELLSOUTH CSA AUDIT APPROACH

CSA Audit Initial Drivers

In early 1996, the CCA was transferred to assist in the formation of BellSouth's Long Distance entity, and a new CCA was appointed. The new CCA, however, was not a proponent of the WTSA process for the reasons previously mentioned. He believed that Internal Audit should prove it was adding value rather than preparing to downsize. Because the key WTSA players could substantiate the value WTSA had added, the new CCA asked a team of WTSA supporters to incorporate the strengths of WTSA into a new and improved internal audit approach, so the BellSouth version of the traditional CSA audit was born. Although the term *CSA audit* was used widely for similar methodologies, BellSouth never used that term internally. CSA supporters always believed the process should be owned by the business unit, but the new CCA believed the company did not have a ready appetite to volunteer for ownership at that time.

CSA Audit Process Design Rationale

Two critical CSA success factors were the forum for open communication across multiple organizational structures and key logic elements imbedded within the control model. Overwhelmingly, the element that everyone most valued in CSA was its ability to gather critical knowledge from many contributers at once. The CSA Audit Approach provided an opportunity to discuss the objectives, risks, and control design across organizational boundaries. A varying percentage of CSA clients appreciated learning the control design process and used the concepts in other aspects of their responsibilities after the CSA was complete. The CSA Audit Approach tailored the control model WTSA had used, but retained the aspects that BellSouth CSA clientele found most helpful.

For the next six years, BellSouth performed internal audits that opened and closed with facilitated sessions. The opening session gathered risks and key controls in a predetermined format. If time permitted, the auditors obtained input on the best way to test the key controls. The audit team also provided an overview of the process they were using upon request. Regardless of the scope of the opening facilitated session(s), the auditors always gave the client a copy of the audit test steps. The audit team was open to any suggestions on ways to make the audit more efficient and effective. The closing meeting also was a facilitated session where the auditors presented results formally and requested input for any corrective action needed.

CSA Audit Outcomes

Because some of the BellSouth international operations were not culturally prepared for open dialogue, audit teams adapted the original approach as needed. For example, Internal Audit led a facilitated session in Israel with minimal participant interaction. The audit team was prepared for this response by the local contact and compiled what it believed were the key risks and controls based on experiences in other international cellular companies. The audit team created paper forms and mailed soft copies of a multiple-choice questionnaire that asked the audit client to rank certain risks and controls. The audit team received a reasonable response using this more subtle approach.

Over time, some organizations across BellSouth continued to respond to the CSA Audit Approach well. Other business units didn't see as much value in spending resources in planning the audit participatively the second time. In addition, once Internal Audit opened the door to participation, it noted that some issues could be resolved more effectively with interdepartmental support or additional skill sets that were only needed temporarily.

THE IMBEDDED APPROACH

Imbedded Approach Drivers

BellSouth began implementing "early entry" audits in those areas where additional help was needed to resolve a control issue. Early entry audits were essentially control design reviews that, in some instances, included consulting to assist in the control design. Some of these early entry initiatives lasted months. It soon became apparent that sometimes the issue identified in the audit had a root cause far removed from the issue originally noted. As a result, the CCA created a Business Controls (BC) Group within the Internal Audit Department. This group was an internal consulting group and not a part of the internal audit staff. Some of the members had internal audit experience, but the key criterion for hire was specialized operations experience in one of BellSouth's key operating units. The CCA would then refer selected audit topics to the BC organization to assist in root cause analysis and/or risk mitigation implementation oversight. The CCA also would refer situations where a perceived control concern existed, but performing an audit did not seem to be the best use of resources.

Despite the fact that The IIA had broadened the professional standards and supported consulting activities within the internal audit profession, BellSouth executives were concerned about maintaining the perception of audit independence within BellSouth. In an effort to keep the consulting activities completely separate from the audit activity, which required independence, BC became a separate organization from Internal Audit in 2002, and began reporting to the Security Department. BC developed its own process, which included risk assessment, control design, and CSA techniques.

Imbedded Approach Process Design Rationale

The mission of this new work unit was to establish the use of business controls and risk management as a standard business practice within BellSouth. BC developed a simple, repeatable process that could be recorded in any spreadsheet or text document. This process included a series of up to 20 questions (depending upon the complexity of the function involved). These 20 questions did not require any accounting or specific control expertise. For example, questions regarding a particular control activity would include:

> Who performs this activity?
> How often is it performed?
> How does the person performing this activity know whether the outcomes are acceptable?
> What actions are taken if the results are not acceptable?

Imbedded Approach Outcomes

BC has varied in size since 2002, but averages 10 managers. Engagements still frequently originate from internal audit findings, but also come from several other main sources. BC often participates in new control design initiatives at the request of management. For example, BC ensured that CSA was performed during the design phase of implementing several custom billing solutions for some of BellSouth's larger customers.

BC also leads a Risk Analysis and Monitoring Team with representatives from all operating departments as well as all oversight organizations (Compliance, Ethics, Internal Audit, Legal, Risk Management, and Security). This team identifies issues across organizational boundaries and facilitates related root cause analyses. Team members use meeting discussions and a share point site to provide continued focus on key topics of concern across the corporation, thereby identifying areas where there is a need for BC to initiate the Imbedded Approach. BC continues to provide formal training on risk management and control design, with programs that vary in design from generic concepts for all directors and above to presentations tailored to performing CSAs to address specific predetermined business objectives.

BC has spent significant staff resources assisting BellSouth's Information Technology (IT) Department with various engagements, many of which were focused on ensuring that the general computer controls were compliant with the U.S. Sarbanes-Oxley Act of 2002. In an effort to maintain effective accountability and monitoring, the IT organization has developed a Web site where process, control, and execution owners sign off on key controls quarterly. This accountability process began with Sarbanes-Oxley controls, but also has expanded to other key controls. These quarterly "sign-offs" require answering key questions, including:

> How do you know the control is working?
> How would you know if the control was not working?

CSA has become a required quarterly activity in the IT Department, completely beyond the direct influence of BC. Although BC is not aware of any other departments using CSA as a repeatable ongoing monitoring mechanism at this time, some departments have expressed interest in the self-assessment process that IT has created.

ALIVE AND WELL

Is CSA still alive? At BellSouth it is. CSA has changed forms based on management and cultural needs, evolving to better meet business needs. BellSouth's BC Group serves as a centralized group that spans organizational boundaries, and the Internal Audit Department will perform a CSA-type audit for any audit clients who prefer a more participative form of auditing. The original WTSA team would be proud if they knew their efforts had, in part, set the stage for the Imbedded CSA Approach currently functioning in the IT Department.

Whether there is an interactive environment (like a WTSA workshop) or the ability for the IT Department to review its contractor responses within Web-based questionnaires, CSA provides a catalyst for effective communication that can sometimes be short-circuited in an organization as large as BellSouth. CSA, in its most basic form, provides reasonable assurance that business objectives will be met. Sound management practices provide the same outcome. Any technique that completely aligns with sound management practices will survive if it works effectively.

Glenda Jordan, CIA, CCSA, CPA, CFE, has supervised implementation of the Integrated Auditing Approach and CSA at BellSouth, as well as established internal audit offices throughout Latin America. She served on BellSouth's initial Sarbanes-Oxley Core Team, implementing the process for complying with Section 404 and continues to facilitate sustainability of Sarbanes-Oxley IT general controls. She is the author of *Control Self-Assessment: Making the Choice*, published by The IIA.

Exhibit 2A

UNIVERSITY OF MINNESOTA EMPLOYEE SURVEY

Instructions: For each statement, select the response that seems most appropriate. If you feel the statement doesn't apply to you or you have no opinion, please select N/A (Not Applicable).

"Management" refers to the department head/director and his/her leadership team if you work in an academic department or center, or to the dean and his/her leadership team if you personally work in or directly report to a Dean or Dean's Office.

		Strongly Agree	**Agree**	**Disagree**	**Strongly Disagree**	**N/A**
1	Management demonstrates the importance of integrity and ethical behavior to their employees.	SA	A	D	SD	N/A
2	Management is open to employee suggestions to improve productivity and quality.	SA	A	D	SD	N/A
3	Management sometimes overrides University policies, procedures or work place rules (e.g. takes shortcuts that are contrary to policy).	SA	A	D	SD	N/A
4	*Management* has the right knowledge, skills, and training to effectively perform their duties.	SA	A	D	SD	N/A
5	*Non-management* (support) staff has the right knowledge, skills, and training to effectively perform their duties.	SA	A	D	SD	N/A
6	Management effectively monitors and provides oversight and direction for the activities in my unit.	SA	A	D	SD	N/A
7	Management is concerned with and responsive to customer feedback or suggestions.	SA	A	D	SD	N/A

Exhibit 2A: University of Minnesota Employee Survey

	Strongly Agree	**Agree**	**Disagree**	**Strongly Disagree**	**N/A**
8. I understand workplace policies and rules, and have an effective resource for obtaining clarification of policies when needed.	SA	A	D	SD	N/A
9. Management has not effectively communicated my job duties and responsibilities to me.	SA	A	D	SD	N/A
10. Management would take appropriate corrective action if policy, procedure, or work place rule violations were detected.	SA	A	D	SD	N/A
11. I believe I would be protected from retaliation if I report a suspected violation.	SA	A	D	SD	N/A
12. I am familiar with how to report violations of law or policy, including the University's confidential reporting line.	SA	A	D	SD	N/A

Would you like to tell us anything else about the operations of your (college, department, center, or other term, as appropriate)?

NAME (optional) _____

Exhibit 2B

PRECISION DRILLING HR OR "HAPPINESS" SURVEY

HR Survey

Company:_____   Date:_____

Department:_____

		Survey Response (Rate 1-5)	Comments
1	Do you feel that you receive sufficient, timely, and relevant communications from your company and the corporate office?		
2	Do you feel that your company and the corporate office maintain good customer relationships?		
3	Do you feel you have sufficient resources to do your job?		
4	Do you feel that you receive fair treatment in your position within the company?		
5	Do you feel that the pay and benefits you receive is equitable and fair for the job you perform?		
6	What kinds of training have you received from the company? Do you feel this has been sufficient? Do you feel the company has a good philosophy on training initiatives?		
7	Are you aware of target zero? Do you feel the company is truly committed to this initiative?		
8	Do you feel there is a strong "tone at the top" (does mgmt walk the talk)?		

Exhibit 2B: Precision Drilling HR or "Happiness" Survey

		Survey Response (Rate 1-5)	**Comments**
9	Do you have any concerns around the ethics of your company, the corporate office, or any individuals?		
10	How would you rate your overall happiness level with your position and the company?		
11	Any other comments or concerns?		

Exhibit 2C

BOEING CUSTOMIZED SURVEY

Independent Review Example: Deployment of Key Objective			
0 = Don't know 1 = Disagree 2 = Somewhat Disagree 3 = Neutral 4 = Somewhat Agree 5 = Agree			
	Rating	Comment for each question (optional)
In my opinion, the objective is appropriate.		
A clear vision and strategy have been established for the objective.		
An effective plan has been established for the objective.		
Clear responsibility, accountability, and authority have been assigned for the objective.		
Clear and measurable performance measures for the objective have been identified and deployed.		
I have a clear understanding of my responsibilities for the objective.		
I understand the relationships between this objective and other related objectives.		
There are no significant conflicts between this objective and other objectives.		
All affected organizations are appropriately engaged in supporting the objective.		
I have sufficient time to execute my responsibilities for the objective.		
Plans are realistic in terms of cost, resources, and time estimates.		
So far, we have achieved the success that we should have achieved for this objective.		
If things are not going well with the objective, leadership/ management is open to hearing the truth.		

Exhibit 2C: Boeing Customized Survey

Independent Review Example: Deployment of Key Objective

0 = Don't know   1 = Disagree   2 = Somewhat Disagree   3 = Neutral   4 = Somewhat Agree   5 = Agree

	Rating	Comment for each question (optional)
I feel we have an effective management structure or approach for supporting the objective.		
I feel strong management support for the objective.		
In my opinion, the right things are being done to successfully implement the objective.		
We are working toward the objective at about the right pace.		

The next question uses a different response scale:
0 = Don't Know   1 = Deteriorating   3 = Staying Constant   5 = Improving

	Rating	Comment
In the past three months, support for the objective has been....		

Open-Ended Questions:

1. What do you see as the strengths of the objectives and how they have been deployed?

2. What do you see as the weaknesses of the objectives and how they have been deployed?

3. How do you feel the objectives and their deployment should be improved?

4. What would you do differently if you were in charge? (alternate to question #3)

Exhibit 2D

LOWES IT PROJECT MANAGEMENT SURVEY STATEMENTS

IT End User Survey Statements

Communication and Effectiveness
My input and feedback are actively solicited and considered throughout the project.
There is open communication across all levels of the project teams.
The IT project representatives assigned to my team understand my current business processes.
The IT project representatives assigned to my team leverage understanding of current processes in requirements development.
IT project objectives are clearly communicated within the project teams.
IT project status is accurately communicated to all stakeholders and management.
IT projects under development are reviewed on a regular basis to ensure my current needs will be met.
Scope change requests are resolved in a collaborative manner.
IT projects under development are managed to minimize operational disruption.
There are well-established, readily available and publicized channels through which my concerns may be expressed.
The IT Project Management process facilitates effective communication among all project participants.
IT Project Managers communicate openly and effectively with stakeholders.
There is an effective process in place to measure customer satisfaction on delivered projects.
IT projects are completed to the customer's satisfaction within the approved timeline.
IT projects are delivered with high quality.
PMO (Program Management Office) meetings facilitate the effective resolution of project issues.
Defined project management roles display increasing experience and skill level.

Exhibit 2D: Lowes IT Project Management Survey Statements

IT Personnel Survey Statements

Measuring Project Success
My department uses metrics to determine project and program effectiveness.
Projects have measurable objectives beyond project requirements, time and cost.
Project teams define and review goals and success criteria periodically as a project progresses.
Project Managers understand how their projects fit into the organization's overall goals and strategies.
My department continuously improves the quality on projects to achieve customer satisfaction.
My department incorporates lessons learned from past projects into its project management methodology.
Management Support
There is a knowledge transfer from internal and external resources leaving a project team.
Defined project management roles require increasing experience and skill level.
A professional development process facilitates career path progression.
Identifying and Mitigating Project Risks
My department uses risk management techniques to assess the impact of and mitigate risks during project execution (example include Risk Identification, Qualitative Risk Analysis, Quantitative Risk Analysis, Risk Response Planning).
Processes Surrounding the Activities of a Project
Policies that describe the standardization, measurement, control and continuous improvement of project management processes exist within the organization.
My department has the necessary processes and tools to assess the knowledge and experience levels of project resources and assign them to project roles appropriately.
My department uses common processes to effectively manage and integrate multiple projects.
Project Manager Success
My department uses a formal performance system that evaluates individuals and project teams on the project's overall results.
Project Managers have the flexibility to be creative in leading a project to provide a solution.

Communication and Effectiveness
There are well-established, readily available and publicized channels through which concerns of program stakeholders may be expressed.
Project status is communicated accurately and openly with stakeholders and management.
Program objectives are clearly communicated to all program stakeholders.
The needs of the business stakeholders and constituencies are clearly understood by project teams.
There is open communication across all levels of project teams.
Project teams identify unmet business needs and develop innovative solutions to address those needs.
Projects under development are reviewed on a regular basis to ensure the current needs of the business will be met by the final deliverable.
Projects I have been involved with were completed to the customer's satisfaction.
Projects I have been involved with were completed within the approved timeline.
There is an effective process in place to measure customer satisfaction.

Exhibit 2E

NEW YORK STATE COMPTROLLER'S OFFICE INTERNAL CONTROL SURVEY GUIDELINES

This section is available on the CD that accompanies this book.

Exhibit 2F

NEW YORK STATE COMPTROLLER'S OFFICE AUDIT REPORT

This section is available on the CD that accompanies this book.

Exhibit 3A

ALLINA ANNUAL RISK ASSSESSMENT INTERVIEW GUIDE

Allina Audit Services
Risk Assessment Questionnaire

As part of our planning process, Audit Services has prepared this questionnaire to solicit input from key management and operating personnel. Your candid responses will be appreciated and utilized in developing the Audit Plan for 2009.

Business Controls are those practices, procedures, and policies that enable or assist management to meet operating objectives.

- **Management** takes the lead role in clarifying business risk, develops business control processes, and implements monitoring mechanisms.

- **Audit Services** partners with management to evaluate the adequacy and effectiveness of business controls and risk management processes.

1. What do you consider the biggest business risks/issues to Allina Hospitals & Clinics for the next three years? To your division? To your department/function?

2. What organizational systems/processes will need redesign in the next three years?

3. What technology/tools will need replacement or upgrading in the next three years?

4. What impacts have you experienced, or do you have any specific concerns related to Excellian process changes and/or implementation (either past or future)?

5. What are the three to five most important things on which you are working this year?

6. Are there any plans in your business unit to develop a new program, expand an existing program or downsize an existing program during the next year? Or, has it occurred during the past year? Are any of concern?

7. Have there been any significant changes in management, or are any anticipated in the next year?

8. Are there any issues that you are uncomfortable raising with senior management? Why?

9. Are there any processes about which you have specific concerns related to:
    - Compliance
    - Appropriate Oversight
    - Efficiency & Effectiveness
    - Fraud
    - Misuse of assets
    - None
    - Other

10. What concerns do you have with anticipated regulatory changes?

Exhibit 3A: Allina Annual Risk Asssessment Interview Guide

11. Do you have any particular concerns related to a potential compliance issue (patient privacy, security of patient information, billing, charging, coding, or reimbursement)?

12. What do you believe is the biggest compliance risk to your business unit in the next three years?

13. What do you think should be the priorities for Audit Services during the next year? Are there any services Audit could/should be doing? Do you have any management requests? (Please specify)

Exhibit 3B

ALLINA AUDIT PLANNING DOCUMENT

Project Number and Name: *XXX xxx XXXXX Review*

Project Summary – *Complete this document before beginning the audit.*

Scope: *This is the business unit that is under review.*
-

Current Conditions/Situations: *Enter any facts about the business process/application/etc. that would help plan and execute the audit.*
-

Business/Operating Objectives: *Enter the objectives ("the thing aimed at, the purpose or end") that the business unit has, such as: compliance with regulations, accurate billing, secure applications, accurate general ledger account balances, patient safety. Objectives should not be confused with goals ("quantitative flavor, milestones along the path to achieving objective") or standards ("recognized example of correctness, perfection quantity or quality"). These objectives are set by management.*
-

Risks: *Enter the adverse effect that would occur if management doesn't have effective controls over its business processes. Ask — What would happen if something went wrong?*
-

Controls: *List out the potential controls that would generally be in place to mitigate the adverse effects of the risks identified.*
-

Audit Objectives: *Designed to determine whether the business/operating objectives are met, function as intended, and are accomplishing the intended objective. Audit objectives are set by the auditors.*

  Examples:
  - Assess the efficiency and effectiveness of controls for xxx;
  - Assess oversight and reconciliation of xxx;
  - Evaluate management oversight and due diligence of xxx;
  - Assess compliance with application regulations;
  - Identify opportunities for process improvement.

Exhibit 3B: Allina Audit Planning Document

Plans for Conducting the Review — Ideas

- Identify key contacts and departments.
- Develop an Internal Control Questionnaire (ICQ) or survey. Complete the ICQ through a personal interview with auditee (preferred) or have auditee respond by e-mail.
- Understand and document processes and controls (memorandum and/or flowchart) by performing walk-throughs and obtaining responses from ICQs.
- Identify what areas in the process should be tested and how tests are to be conducted in view of audit objectives and scope.
- Develop a preliminary audit program.

Audit Resource Planning

- Anticipated budgeted hours?
- Composition of audit team? IT, financial, and/or regulatory auditor?
- Dates of review?

Issue Track Recommendations pending?

Quotes in Business/Operating Objectives section from *Sawyer's Internal Auditing, The Practice of Modern Internal Auditing*, 4th edition, pp. 164-5

Exhibit 3C

ALLINA AUDIT PROGRAM EXCERPTS

From an Audit Program for IT Governance

Procedures
• *Objective: To assess the control environment for adequacy of design and effectiveness in:*
Aligning the corporate technology strategy with the business' strategic and operational objectives.
Defined roles and responsibilities in corporation's IT governance model.
IT decision-making processes, risk management, and resource management.
IT performance measurement, monitoring, and their reporting mechanisms.
To share the best practices of governance models.
General Interview Workpapers: .01 VP HI&S .02 Director IS Security .03 Manager IS Finance .04 CIO .05 Director IS, Financial Applications .06 VP Finance, Site or Area .07 VP Finance, Site or Area .08 VP Finance, Site or Area .09 CIO (Audit/Comp Committee member, Board of Directors) .10 VP Finance, Site or Area .11 Director System Architecture .12 VP Finance, Site or Area .13 Director IS .14 VP Site or Area .15 Director IS Service Management .16 Director IS Applications

Exhibit 3C: Allina Audit Program Excerpts

From an Audit Program for Readiness Review for Electronic Health Records

Procedures
Objective: • Evaluate implementation plan with regard to preparation for electronic health record at the centralized business office,   • Review integration of lessons learned from the hospitals' implementation, and   • Evaluate training for running dual billing systems.
Interview centralized billing office management.
Interview implementation consultants.
Interview internal implementation team management/staff.
Attend combined implementation team update meetings.
Attend health information management risk mitigation meetings.
Other meetings.
Review of business continuity plans.

From an Audit Program for Readiness Reviews of New Electronic Medical Records

Objective: The primary objectives include:
- Assess status of tasks from hospital implementation plan,
- Select sample of hospital departments and assess status from department readiness checklist, and
- Communicate possible improvements on hospital implementation plan and department readiness checklist.

Contact administrative assistant to determine which meetings to attend.

Meet with key person regarding tools for implementation.

Contact key person to discuss centralized scheduling registration.

Review hospital implementation plan.

Review a judgmental sample of high risk departments/areas to review (i.e., OR, CV, Lab, Radiology, Pharmacy, Nursing, ED).

Attend leadership team meeting.

Attend staffing meeting.

Attend a workgroup meeting.

Determine physician engagement:
    Plans for physician engagement.
    Review medication reconciliation process.
    Attend a communication meeting.

Examples of Potential Recommendations for the Readiness Reviews of New Electronic Medical Records

- Evaluate impact of insufficient staffing on go-live date.

- Ensure adequate training.

- Ensure accountability for leaders related to new system updates for a successful go-live.

- Update master templates/tools for completeness, accuracy, and limited access to formulas.

- Finalize and implement a system-wide education plan for post go-live needs.

- Test new processes and systems.

- Clarify manager role in reviewing reports.

Exhibit 3D
SECURIAN AUDITING DEPARTMENT CORE VALUES

Value	Our job is to provide assurance. We try to go beyond this by adding value in everything we do. We want big improvements, not *nitpicks*.
Productivity	We spend time on only things that matter. Our streamlined reports are easy to write but tell clients what they need to know.
Customer Service	When clients trust us, they tell us their concerns. We gain their trust through good service. If clients know we're on their side, they call for help. We want the phones to ring.
Knowledge	We strive to understand how things work — systems, processes, and people. We encourage professional development through certifications and continuing education. The more we know, the more value we add.
Teamwork	We learn from each other and respect each other's opinions. No one knows everything. A diverse knowledge and experience base gives us more ideas to tap. Teamwork makes the whole greater than the sum of the parts.
Rigor	Our audit process stresses rigorous process analysis. We would rather predict an error than search for a "needle in a haystack." We follow industry standards, but in a way that adds maximum value.
Objectivity	Objectivity is a state of mind. We stay objective by remembering our primary mission — providing assurance to the Board. We consult, but we don't make decisions for clients or own controls.
Life Balance	A flexible work environment gives us life balance. It also helps us attract and retain top talent, which makes us more effective.

Exhibit 3E

ING GROUP AUDIT STRATEGY MEMORANDUM

RAAP

Group Audit Strategy Memorandum

For 2009 Audit Plan

FOR CAS INTERNAL USE ONLY

This document is for CAS planning purposes only and does not constitute or represent the final agreed audit plan. The distribution of this document or parts of it to any parties outside of CAS is not permitted without the prior written consent from the Chief Auditor.

Version Control

Version	Last Update
1.0	

Exhibit 3E: ING Group Audit Strategy Memorandum

Table of Contents

1. Introduction ....
2. Business Line Summary Overview ....
3. Business Line Strategic Objectives and Value Drivers ....
4. Business Line Economic Capital Considerations ....
5. Conclusions ....
6. Business Line and Other Stakeholder Contacts ....

Best Practices: Evaluating the Corporate Culture

1. **Introduction**

    This objective of this document is to present information regarding global themes and areas of focus that will be the starting point for the 2008 Corporate Audit Services (CAS) audit strategy and related audit plans. These themes/focus areas were derived using various sources of information, including:

    - **MTP 2008-2010 – Executive Statement**
    - **Input from CAS Chief Auditors**
    - **Information obtained from various ING business unit and Group web sites**
    - **Monthly CAS meetings with ING Chairman**
    - **Quarterly Audit Committee Meetings**

    Any key changes in ING priorities arising from meetings with local management will be used to update the RAAP documentation on a quarterly basis. This will help to ensure that CAS overall is in alignment with changes in ING business priorities and risk profile.

    In advance of the official planning period, the CAS management team performed its own assessment of key global themes. This assessment was based on the previous year Audit Planning, updated to reflect current information regarding management attention areas, results of audit activities and last, but not least, prior year business MTPs.

2. **Excerpts from Executive Planning Letter**

    [CEO's statement regarding strategic objectives and value drivers]

3. **Key Focus Areas for Audit Activities**

    [CAS key focus areas based on information gathered]

    In addition, the CAS MT has identified the following global areas of focus for potential thematic audits.

Key Global Focus Areas	**Related Value Drivers**
Global Focus Area #1	
Global Focus Area #2	
Global Focus Area #3	
Global Focus Area #4	
Global Focus Area #5	

In consideration of the preceding focus areas, CAS will obtain input and steering from the "specialist" audit groups (i.e., Credit/Market/Insurance/Operational Risk and Compliance).

CAS has informed the ING chairman that a rolling plan will be used to ensure CAS covers all the above focus areas. The rolling plan of thematic audits will be reassessed during RAAP (i.e., 3 + 9 approach) on a quarterly basis so that we are in a position to adjust our audit plan for changes in ING priorities.

While it is recognized that the new CAS approach places strong emphasis on strategic objectives and value drivers, CAS teams should still take steps to ensure that important business line/business unit risk areas are not omitted from the audit plan (e.g., areas that have not been audited for a significant period of time, regulatory required audits, greenfields, remote entities). In addition, the CAS MT has identified global areas of focus for potential thematic audits.

4. CAS Global 2008 Internal Priorities

[List CAS internal priorities, including MTP highlights, KPIs, major projects, and initiatives.]

Exhibit 3F

ING BUSINESS LINE AUDIT STRATEGY MEMORANDUM

This section is available on the CD that accompanies this book.

Exhibit 3G

ING ORGANIZATIONAL UNIT AUDIT STRATEGY MEMORANDUM

This section is available on the CD that accompanies this book.

Exhibit 4A

PRECISION DRILLING ENTITY LEVEL INTERVIEW GUIDE

		Board	Sr Mgt	Ops Mgmt	Fin Mgmt	Employees	Other
Control Environment							
Integrity, ethical values, and behavior of key executives and Board of Directors							
CE-1	Does the Board of Directors show concern for integrity and ethical values?		X	X	X		
CE-2	Is there a code of Business Conduct and/or ethics Policy and has it been adequately communicated?					X	Audit
CE-3	Has all management personnel read and signed the Code of Business Conduct and/or Ethics Policy and reviewed it annually?		X	X	X	X	
CE-4	Has management through HR ensured that all new hires have been explained the Code of Business Conduct and/or Ethics Policy and each new hire has read and signed to acknowledge that they understand the policy?					X	HR
CE-5	Has management through HR ensured that all employees have annually reviewed and signed the Code of Business Conduct and/or Ethics to acknowledge that they understand the Policy?			X		X	HR
CE-6	Is there a separate Code of Business Conduct and/or Ethics Policy for the Board of Directors?	X					HR, Audit
CE-7	Have all members of the Board of Directors signed the Code of Business Conduct and/or Ethics Policy?	X					HR, Audit

Exhibit 4A: Precision Drilling Entity Level Interview Guide

		Board	Sr Mgt	Ops Mgmt	Fin Mgmt	Employees	Other
CE-8	Have all Directors filed their conflict of Interest declaration and have the conflict of Interest declarations been reviewed annually?		X		X		
CE-9	Is management's commitment to integrity and ethical behavior communicated effectively throughout the company, both in words and deeds?			X		X	
CE-10	Does management lead by example?					X	
CE-11	Are those in top management hired from outside made familiar with the importance of high ethics and controls?		X	X	X		
CE-12	Does management act to remove or reduce incentives or temptations that might prompt personnel to engage in dishonest, illegal, or unethical acts?			X	X	X	
CE-13	Do rewards, such as bonuses and stock options, foster an appropriate ethical tone (i.e., not given to those who meet objectives but, in the process, circumvent established policies, procedures, or controls)? Review on what basis bonuses and stock options are paid?			X	X	X	
CE-14	Does management take appropriate disciplinary action in response to departures from approved policies and procedures or violations of the code of conduct?		X	X	X	X	
Management's control consciousness and operating style							
CE-15	Is the management structure appropriate (i.e., not dominated by one or a few individuals) and is there effective oversight by the board of directors or audit committee?		X	X	X		

Best Practices: Evaluating the Corporate Culture

		Board	Sr Mgt	Ops Mgmt	Fin Mgmt	Employees	Other
CE-16	Does management's financial reporting philosophy, including its attitude toward the development of estimates, tend to be conservative?		X	X			Audit, Audit Committee
CE-17	Are biases that may affect significant accounting estimates and other judgments minimized?	X	X		X		Audit, Audit Committee
CE-18	Is there a mechanism in place to regularly educate and communicate to management and employees the importance of internal controls, and to raise their level of understanding of controls?		X	X	X	X	
CE-19	Does management give appropriate attention to internal control, including the effects of information systems processing?		X	X	X	X	
	Does management correct identified internal control deficiencies on a timely basis?		X	X	X		
CE-20	Are management incentives balanced (i.e., the portion of management compensation derived from bonuses, stock options, or other incentives does not promote an excessive level of interest in maintaining or increasing the entity's stock price or earnings trend)?						Audit
CE-21	Does management set realistic (i.e., not unduly aggressive) financial targets and expectations for operating personnel?		X	X	X		
Management's commitment to competence							
CE-22	Do personnel appear to have the competence and training necessary for their assigned level of responsibility or the nature and complexity of the entity's business?						

Exhibit 4A: Precision Drilling Entity Level Interview Guide

		Board	Sr Mgt	Ops Mgmt	Fin Mgmt	Employees	Other
CE-23	Does management possess broad functional experience (i.e., management comes from several functional areas rather than from just a few, such as production and drilling)?			X			HR
CE-24	Is departmental staffing appropriate (particularly with regard to knowledge and experience of management and supervisory levels within the accounting, information systems, and financial reporting areas)?			X	X	X	ACCT, IT
CE-25	Does management show a willingness to consult with the auditors on and address significant matters relating to internal control and accounting issues?	X					Audit
CE-26	Does management demonstrate a commitment to provide sufficient accounting and financial personnel to keep pace with the growth and/or complexity of the business?				X		ACCT
Board of directors' and/or audit committee participation in governance and oversight							
CE-27	Is the makeup of the board of directors, including the number of directors and their background and expertise, appropriate given the nature of the company?		X	X	X		
CE-28	Has the independence of outside board members been adequately reviewed, including affiliations and relationships and transactions with the company?						Audit, Audit Committee
CE-29	Is the board of directors and audit committee independent from management, such that necessary, and often probing, questions are raised?						

153

Best Practices: Evaluating the Corporate Culture

		Board	Sr Mgt	Ops Mgmt	Fin Mgmt	Employees	Other
CE-30	Does the board of directors and/or audit committee give adequate consideration to understanding management's processes for monitoring business risks affecting the organization?						Audit
CE-31	Does the audit committee represent an informed, vigilant, and effective overseer of the financial reporting process and the company's internal control, including information systems processing and related computer controls?					X	IT managers
CE-32	Does the audit committee include at least one "financial expert"?	X	X				Audit
CE-33	Does the audit committee adequately maintain a direct line of communication with the entity's external and internal auditors?	X	X				Audit
CE-34	Does the audit committee have a charter outlining its duties and responsibilities? Does the audit committee have adequate resources and authority to discharge its responsibilities?	X	X		X		Audit
Organizational structure and assignment of authority and responsibility							
CE-35	Is the organizational structure adequate for the size, operating activities, and locations of the company?		X	X			HR
CE-36	Is the overall organizational structure appropriate (i.e., not overly complex and not involving numerous or unusual legal entities, managerial lines of authority, or contractual agreements without apparent business purpose)?	X	X	X			
CE-37	Is there an appropriate structure for assigning ownership of data, including who is authorized to initiate and/or change transactions?						IT

Exhibit 4A: Precision Drilling Entity Level Interview Guide

		Board	Sr Mgt	Ops Mgmt	Fin Mgmt	Employees	Other
CE-38	Is ownership assigned for each application and database within the IT infrastructure?						IT
CE-39	Are there appropriate policies for such matters as accepting new business, conflicts of interest, and security practices?					X	Audit, IT, HR?
CE-40	Are they adequately communicated throughout the organization?					X	
CE-41	Are there adequate policies and procedures for authorization and approval of transactions at the appropriate level?				X		ACCT
CE-42	Is assignment of responsibilities clear, including responsibilities for information system processing and program development?					X	IT
CE-43	Does management review and make modifications to the organizational structure of the company in light of changed conditions?		X	X			HR
CE-44	Is there adequate supervision and monitoring of decentralized operations (including accounting personnel and information systems)?						
CE-45	Is there an appropriate segregation of incompatible activities (i.e. separation of accounting for and access to assets)?				X		Audit, Audit Committee
Human resources policies and practices
CE-46	Are there standards and procedures for hiring, training, motivating, evaluating, promoting, compensating, transferring, and terminating personnel that are applicable to all functional areas (e.g., accounting, marketing, information systems)?						HR

Best Practices: Evaluating the Corporate Culture

		Board	Sr Mgt	Ops Mgmt	Fin Mgmt	Employees	Other
CE-47	Are there screening procedures for job applicants, particularly for employees with access to assets susceptible to misappropriation?			X			HR
CE-48	Are policies and procedures clear and are they issued, updated, and revised on a timely basis? Are they effectively communicated to personnel at decentralized and/or foreign locations?			X		X	
CE-49	Are there written job descriptions, reference manuals or other forms of communication to inform personnel of their duties?					X	HR
CE-50	Is job performance periodically evaluated and reviewed with each employee?			X		X	HR

Exhibit 4B

PRECISION DRILLING ETHICS TRAINING

Precision Drilling

Ethical Awareness Session

Slide 1

Agenda

- Manager's Message
- Health, Safety and Environment
- Major Precision policies
    - Code of Business Conduct and Ethics Policy
    - IT Standard Practices
    - Disclosure Policy (Communications Policy)
    - Drug and Alcohol Policy
    - Discrimination, Harassment, & Workplace Violence Policy
- Guidelines for ethical decision making
- Scenario discussion and analysis
- Reporting procedures

Slide 2

Manager's Message

Precision is committed to maintaining a high standard of corporate governance that incorporates the principles of good conduct and high ethical behavior.

Employees are expected to act honestly and in good faith with a view to the interests of PD and its stakeholders.

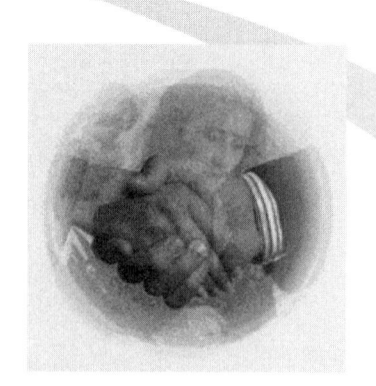

Identifying and reporting ethical issues and fraud is everyone's responsibility.

Slide 3

Exhibit 4B: Precision Drilling Ethics Training

Health, Safety and Environment Policy

Precision is dedicated to providing a safe and healthy workplace for all employees, complying with all applicable laws and protecting both the environment and the quality of life in the communities in which we work.

Slide 4

Did you know...

- An organization such as Precision typically loses up to 5% of annual revenues to operational fraud and abuse.

- Asset misappropriation accounts for 80% of fraud cases.

- Almost half of all corruption cases occur in the oil and gas sector.

- The typical perpetrator is a male between ages 41 and 50.

- Most fraud schemes are uncovered from employee tips.

Occupational fraud and abuse is a problem that affects all companies.

CFE Report to the Nation, 2006

Slide 5

Best Practices: Evaluating the Corporate Culture

Which person do you think would be more likely to commit fraud?

Slide 6

Code of Business Conduct and Ethics

- Compliance with laws, rules, and regulations
- Avoidance of conflicts of interest
- Maintain the confidentiality of information
- Protection and proper use of PD assets
- Decisions should benefit PD not personal interests
- Two ways to anonymously report concerns:
    - Internet
    - Phone

Slide 7

Exhibit 4B: Precision Drilling Ethics Training

Information Technology (IT) Standard Practices

Maintains the security and acceptable use of PD assets and helps to ensure the confidentiality, security and privacy of employee and customer information.

- Information Asset Security Policy
- Information Asset Acceptable Use Policy
- Information Asset Privacy and Confidentiality Policy

Slide 8

"I'm sure there are better ways to disguise sensitive information, but we don't have a big budget."

Slide 9

Best Practices: Evaluating the Corporate Culture

Disclosure Policy

Outlines PD's approach to communication of company information and provides guidelines for consistent disclosure practices.

- Authorized spokespersons – CEO, President & CFO
- Timing of disclosure
- Procedures for disclosure
- Communication with investors, media, financial analysts etc.

If you are asked questions refer to the President, CFO or Corporate Communications

Precision Drilling

Slide 10

Copyright 2002 by Randy Glasbergen.   www.glasbergen.com

"I know a lot of highly-confidential company secrets, so my boss made me get a firewall installed."

Slide 11

Drug and Alcohol Policy

Describes the responsibility of employees in maintaining a work environment free of alcohol and drugs.

- Work rules governing substance abuse
- Employee assistance available
- Alcohol and drug testing
- Testing guidelines

Slide 12

Drug and Alcohol Policy

Sorry

No jokes on this subject

Slide 13

Best Practices: Evaluating the Corporate Culture

Discrimination, Harassment and Workplace Violence Policy

Ensures employees are aware of their responsibility and right to a workplace free of discrimination, harassment and violence.

➢ Responsibilities
➢ Complaint and Investigation Procedures
➢ Communication/Appropriate Response

Precision Drilling

Slide 14

"I've been using the same computer since 1980. They can't replace it without violating the company's age discrimination policies."

Slide 15

Exhibit 4B: Precision Drilling Ethics Training

Fraud or Illegal Activities Policy

The goal is to enforce PD's commitment to conduct business with integrity, ethics and in compliance with all applicable laws.

- Definition of Fraud
- Roles and Responsibilities
    - Report suspicions of fraud
    - As an employee, manager, stakeholder, HR and audit services
- Reporting Process
- Consequences

Slide 16

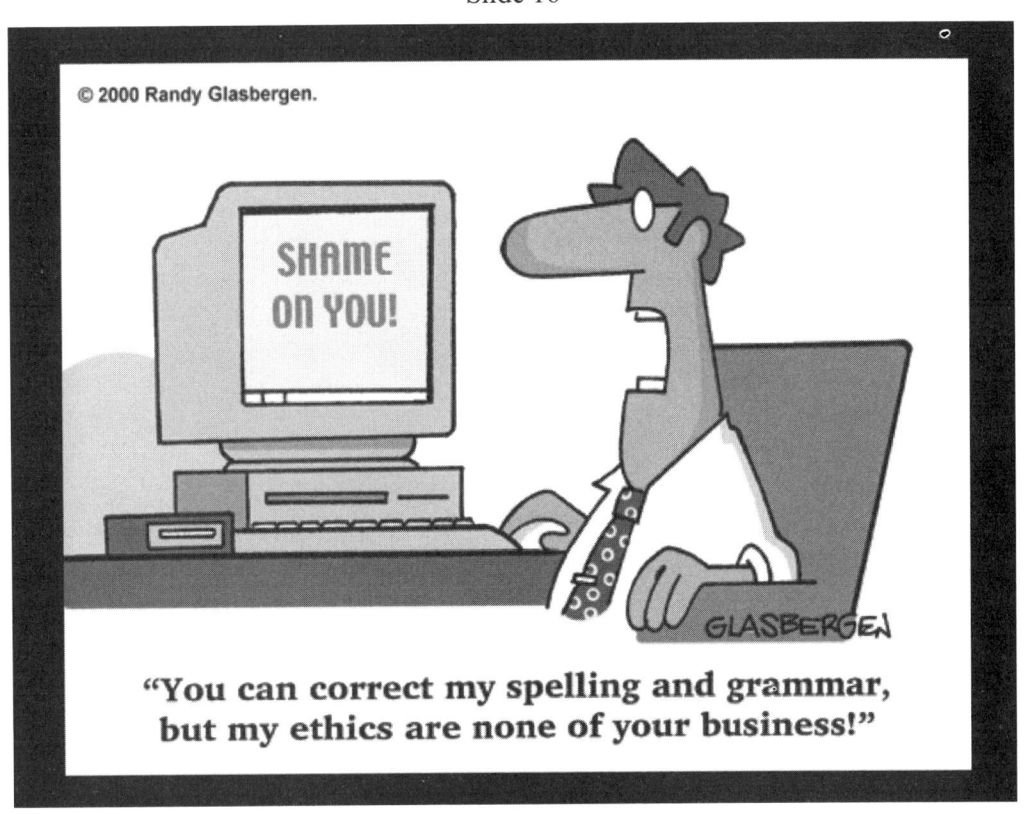

© 2000 Randy Glasbergen.

"You can correct my spelling and grammar, but my ethics are none of your business!"

Slide 17

165

Best Practices: Evaluating the Corporate Culture

Guidelines for Ethical Decision Making

When in doubt about a situation, take the "test"

- Would the action I'm considering violate any laws or company policies?

- Will this action result in a personal gain or benefit?

- Will I owe someone something as a result?

- Would an outside person, co-worker or the media perceive this action as unethical?

Precision Drilling

Slide 18

Ethical Scenarios for Discussion

Scenario # 1

- You are checking your PD email and a friend has sent you "Tuesday's Funnies." You find the email amusing but know some people could find it offensive, so you only forward the email to close co-workers.
    - Is this acceptable?

Scenario #2

- You are working in the finance department and an operations manager instructs you to overstate some revenue to help with the bonus pool this year.
    - Is this acceptable?

Precision Drilling

Slide 19

Ethical Scenarios for Discussion

Scenario #3
- A purchasing clerk in a PD warehouse is concerned about the number of orders to Company X recently. Her manager tells her "they are the best place to shop in town." The manager's brother-in-law is also a co-owner of Company X.
    - Is there a conflict of interest?

Scenario #4
- Jill overhears two managers talking at lunch about a "big" deal that will be approved next week. That evening she tells friends and family about the "big" deal and says now is a good time to buy PD stock.
    - Is this acceptable?

Slide 20

Ethical Scenarios for Discussion

Scenario #5
- You are talking to a co-worker about a fence you are building. He tells you scrap pipe works great as fence posts and there is some used pipe in the rig yard.
    - Are you allowed to take the used pipe?

Scenario #6
- You are working on Rig Y and noticed that a crew member appears to be intoxicated. You have noticed this behavior several times over the past month.
    - Is this acceptable?

Slide 21

Best Practices: Evaluating the Corporate Culture

Ethical Scenarios for Discussion

Scenario #7

- A major supplier is offering you a 3 day all expenses paid fishing trip to the coast.
  - Is it okay to go fishing?

Precision Drilling

Slide 22

If you have concerns

Where Do You Turn?

Precision Drilling

Slide 23

Exhibit 4B: Precision Drilling Ethics Training

Everyone has a responsibility to report

- **Talk with your <u>supervisor or manager</u> first. If you are reluctant to do so then:**

- Call (403) 716-4500 and ask for Audit Services
  (Unethical, fraud or illegal activities)

- Call (403) 716-4500 and ask for HR
  (Discrimination, harassment, workplace violence and drug and alcohol issues)

- Call our anonymous confidential phone line
  1-800-661-9675

Slide 24

ConfidenceLine

- Outside service provider
  - Anonymous
  - Confidential

- Submit concerns by phone or on our website

- All reports to *ConfidenceLine* go to Audit Services, legal counsel and the Audit Committee for assessment

Slide 25

Summary

Identifying and reporting ethical issues and fraud is everyone's responsibility.

"It is not what we do, but also what we do not do, for which we are accountable."
Moliére

Everyone benefits from an honest and ethical work place

Slide 26

Exhibit 4C

KAISER PERMANENTE AUDIT COMMITTEE PRESENTATION ON ENTITY-LEVEL CONTROLS

Annual Assessment on the Adequacy and Effectiveness of Processes for Controlling the Organization's Activities and Managing Its Risks

Slide 1

Best Practices: Evaluating the Corporate Culture

Annual Assessment

- The Internal Audit Department (IA) Charter states that one IA accountability is to:
  - Provide annually an assessment on the adequacy and effectiveness of the organization's processes for controlling its activities and managing its risks in the areas set forth under the mission and scope of work. *(For IA mission and scope of work, see Appendix III.)*
  - The Institute of Internal Auditors' professional standards also require this. There is no required format or content for the assessment.
- The IA evaluation is qualitative – not quantitative analysis.
  - It answers the question, "From the IA perspective, based on IA work, what is the status of the organization's internal controls and risk management for 2007 heading into 2008?"
- Caution: IA doesn't audit everything.
  - Due to **XXXX**, we can't just extrapolate from one audit to another.
  - For our 2007 audit reports, IA overall ratings were as follows:
    - Meets expectations   x% of reports
    - Needs attention   x% of reports
    - Does not meet expectations   x% of reports
- Based on IA work and interaction with our auditees and stakeholders, we can say that:
  - XXXX

Slide 2

Annual Assessment – Strengths and Opportunities are Outlined within the COSO Framework

COSO Cube – Internal Controls Framework

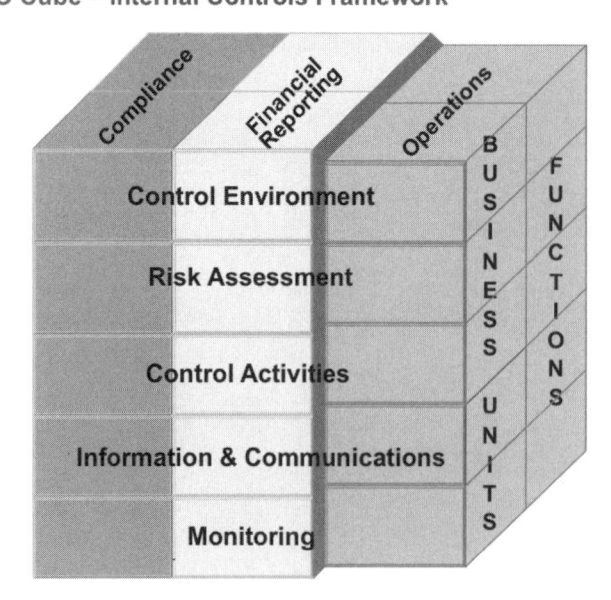

(COSO Cube diagram showing dimensions: Compliance, Financial Reporting, Operations; layers: Control Environment, Risk Assessment, Control Activities, Information & Communications, Monitoring; and Business Units, Functions)

Slide 3

Exhibit 4C: Kaiser Permanente Audit Committee Presentation on Entity-level Controls

Annual Assessment – Strengths

COSO Component	Signs of strength; positives that indicate good progress
Control Environment	• Leadership and Board "tone at the top" shows very strong support for internal controls, for corrective action, and for IA. • xxxx • Client interactions with IA are generally positive, engaged and focused on doing the right thing.
Risk Assessment	• Good work is done by a variety of management to assess and manage the key business risks, along with compliance and SOX assessments.
Information & Communication	xxxx
Control Activities	xxxx
Monitoring	xxxx

Slide 4

Annual Assessment – Opportunities

COSO Component	Signs of concern; inconsistencies that indicate we have some way left to go
Control Environment	xxxx
Risk Assessment	xxxx
Information & Communication	xxxx
Control Activities	xxxx
Monitoring	xxxx

Slide 5

Best Practices: Evaluating the Corporate Culture

Annual Assessment – Looking Ahead

- Looking ahead, IA anticipates XXXX.

Slide 6

Exhibit 4D

KAISER PERMANENTE CRITERIA FOR GOVERNANCE COMMITTEE REVIEW

AUDIT OF GOVERNANCE COMMITTEE OF BOARD OF DIRECTORS

Audit Objectives and Procedures

The audit evaluated the following governance objectives and the related processes and controls for the Committee:
- The Committee's Charter includes best practices.
- Corporate governance guidelines include best practices, in particular:
  - Director qualification standards
  - Code of ethics
  - Board convener
  - Annual performance and evaluation of the Board
- The Committee's activities enable it to fulfill its authority and duties, as described in the Charter, including key elements as follows:
  - Composition and qualifications of Committee members
  - Authority and duties:
    - Conflict of interests matters
    - Director and officers liability insurance arrangements
    - Corporate documents review
    - Strategic plan performance updates
- Activities and decisions of the Committee are documented.
- The Committee receives appropriate information from management to carry out its duties.

Audit procedures included the following:
- Observed Committee meetings (June and September 2008)
- Interviewed the Committee Chair, the Board Chair, and the Director of Board Services/Senior Counsel
- For the period January 1, 2007, through September 30, 2008, reviewed Committee activities, as documented in agendas, minutes, and Committee materials, in comparison with key elements of the Committee Charter
- Compared corporate governance guidelines and Committee Charter to governance best practices (see below for "best practice" information and resources)

Best Practice Information: The Conference Board's Commission on Public Trust & Private Enterprise and other resources
- Background:
  - The Conference Board is a business membership and research organization best known for the Consumer Confidence Index and the Leading Economic Indicators. The Conference Board provides business intelligence and best practice information.
  - The Conference Board convened the Commission on Public Trust and Private Enterprise to address the causes of declining public and investor trust.
  - Specifically, the Commission has addressed compensation, governance, and accounting issues. It has issued principles, recommendations, and specific best practice suggestions.

- We used the Commission's report, along with other resources, to assess the adequacy of the Committee's governance practices.
  - Other resources included Sarbanes-Oxley requirements and toolkits as relevant to the Committee, governance policies of Fortune 500 companies, and various guidelines and articles from governance, audit, and academic organizations.

- The following principles of corporate governance, taken from the Commission's report, support the adequacy of the Board and Committee governance process.
  - Relation of the Board and management
  - Fulfilling the Board's responsibilities
  - Director qualifications
  - Committee responsibilities
  - Board evaluations

Exhibit 4E

INTERVIEW GUIDE FOR COMPLIANCE AUDIT

Corporate Compliance Review Questionnaire

Employee: _____   Dept.:_____

Date of Interview: _____   Interviewer: _____

A. General Compliance Program Awareness

1. How would you describe the XXX Compliance Program?

2. What are the 5 components of the XXX Compliance Program?

3. What policies and procedures are there in the program?

4. Where can they be found?

B. Specific Compliance Program Knowledge

1. Who is the XXX Compliance Officer?

2. What are the general guidelines for accepting or giving gifts?

3. What is the inquiry/reporting process? How many ways can something be reported?

4. Can you report a potential violation without fear of retribution? Is there a fear from retribution policy included in the program?

5. Do you trust the policy? Do you believe that something can be reported truly anonymously? If not, why not?

6. Would you report a potentially unethical or illegal situation, and if so, to whom? If not, why not?

7. Do you feel that the same rules apply to all employees? Why or why not?

8. Have you ever referred to the Code of Business Conduct to answer a question? If not, when would you?

9. Have you ever reported a violation, and if so, were you satisfied with the action taken? Who did you make the report to? Was the Code of Conduct issue resolved?

10. What is the purpose of the annual Conflict of Interest form?

11. If your personal situation changes from the last Conflict of Interest form that you submitted, what should be done?

12. Government Contracts Compliance (as applicable):

    a. Do you work with government contracts?
    b. Are you aware of government purchasing regulations? Do you know what they are?
    c. Do you know where to find this information? Do you know how you can get additional assistance?
    d. What training has been provided to help ensure compliance with the government regulations?

13. How is the Code of Business Conduct to be addressed in nongovernment contracts?

14. What responsibilities do all employees have regarding protecting nonpublic information and dealing with publicly traded securities?

15. Are there Ethics policies for participating in external professional, service, charitable, or academic organizations?

16. What would an example of a third party endorsement be? Who can approve someone giving a third-party endorsement?

17. Under what circumstances can you accept an honorarium?

18. Does XXX allow the acceptance of funds from XXX companies?

19. Have you ever had knowledge of an improper activity but chose not to report it? Why didn't you?

20. Have you ever been asked to do anything that you believe violates the Code of Business Conduct or company policies?

21. If someone in your workgroup were suspected of unethical conduct, would you be comfortable assisting in investigating the matter? Why or why not?

22. Does XXX senior management encourage raising ethical concerns? Does your immediate management? If so, how?

23. Do you believe that XXX management respects and follows policies and ethical standards? What about XXX staff personnel? Why or why not?

24. Have you ever seen unethical behavior rewarded? Please describe in general terms.

Exhibit 4E: Interview Guide for Compliance Audit

25. How do you rate XXX's ethical standards compared to other companies?

   a. Higher than most
   b. Above average
   c. Average
   d. Below average
   e. Lower than most
   f. Don't know

C. Compliance Program Training and Communication

1. What do you think of the Compliance Program training program?

2. What was covered in the Program? When did you take it?

3. Do you feel the training was effective and relevant?

4. What do you think of the online annual refresher? What suggestions do you have for topics to be covered? At what intervals should the refresher be given?

5. Do you recall seeing any compliance articles in employee newsletters or in e-mails? Did you attend any of the Compliance Week events? If yes, did you read any or all of them? Were they useful and informative?

6. Has your department done anything to promote compliance awareness? If so, what have they done? Has anything been particularly helpful? If not, do you think they should? What kind of activities should be performed?

D. Compliance Program Improvement

1. What is your overall perception of the XXX Compliance Program?

   a. Comprehensive and effective
   b. Good for reference, but not enough detail
   c. Does not seem to address my issues (please explain)
   d. Good policies, but I have my doubts about enforcement
   e. It does not pertain to me

2. What suggestions do you have to improve the effectiveness of the compliance program?

Quick Compliance Quiz

1. It's OK to accept any gift from a vendor as long as it is only at Christmas or for your birthday. — T/F

2. If an employee believes he/she knows of an instance of someone violating the Code of Business Conduct, Human Resources must be notified immediately. — T/F

3. The Code of Business Conduct rules do not apply to senior management. — T/F

4. It's permissible to occasionally break a rule of the Code of Business Conduct if it benefits XXX and not me personally. — T/F

5. If I know of a reportable incident and do not report it, I can never be held accountable. — T/F

6. There are no restrictions regarding gifts or courtesies to or from vendor employees since we're all in the same "family." — T/F

7. If an employee has not taken the required compliance training yet, he/she cannot be held responsible for breaking any of XXX's Code of Business Conduct rules. — T/F

8. The only way a potential problem can be reported is to the Chief Compliance Officer. — T/F

9. Some departments are allowed to "bend the rules" because of the nature of the work they do. — T/F

10. The basic philosophy of the Code of Business Conduct is that it is better to do the right thing because it is the right thing to do. — T/F

Exhibit 4F

AQUILA COSO-BASED CAPABILITIES MATURITY ASSESSMENT

Aquila, Inc.

COSO-based Capabilities Maturity Assessment

Best Practices: Evaluating the Corporate Culture

Risk Assessment & Audit Services: **Risk Management Capability Characteristics COSO**

	Stage A	Stage B	Stage C	Stage D	Stage E
Control Environment					
Ethical Values — (policies)	A formal code of ethics policy does not exist.	An informal ethics policy exists but communication of policies is weak and inconsistent throughout the organization. Polices do not adequately cover dealings both internally and with external parties.	A formal ethics policy exists and is considered to adequately cover most aspects of ethical behavior involving internal employees and with external parties. Communication is adequate; however, not all aspects of the policy are well understood throughout the organization. The policy is only periodically updated.	A formal ethics policy exists and covers the majority of aspects related to ethical behavior involving internal employees and external parties. Policy communication is good and the majority of policy aspects are understood throughout the organization. The policy is regularly updated.	A formal ethics policy exists, is considered best practice, and continuously updated. Policy communication is excellent and fully understood throughout the organization. Policy is considered to cover all aspects of behavior internally as well as with external parties.
Ethical Values — Employees	Employees do not routinely display ethical behavior.	Employees are not consistently displaying ethical behavior when conducting Company activities with internal and/or external parties.	Most employees generally display ethical behavior in most aspects of day-to-day activities. Instances may occur where inconsistent communication of policy results in questionable behavior in regards to Corporate expectations.	The majority of employees regularly display ethical behavior in their day-to-day activities. Questions periodically surface regarding a specific aspect of expected behavior but these questions are appropriately and timely surfaced and addressed.	All employees regularly display ethical behavior in every aspect of day-to-day activities. Any question regarding appropriate activity is proactively addressed and resolved prior to any action.

182

Risk Assessment & Audit Services: **Risk Management Capability Characteristics COSO**

Exhibit 4F: Aquila COSO-based Capabilities Maturity Assessment

	Stage A	Stage B	Stage C	Stage D	Stage E
Control Environment (continued)					
Ethical Values — (reporting)	There are no means by which employees can report concerns regarding ethical behavior.	Informal methods exist to report questions on ethical behavior however, methods are not well established, communicated, or supported by the organization.	Formal methods exist and are considered adequate for employees to report questions on ethical values. Methods are communicated but not fully understood or utilized throughout the organization. Some questions may exist regarding confidentiality of reporting methods. Methods are only periodically updated.	Formal methods exist, are considered effective and well communicated throughout the organization. Methods are frequently reviewed and updated. Confidentiality of methods is considered good.	Formal methods exist and are considered best practice. Methods are continually reviewed and updated. Confidentiality rates are high.
Ethical Values — Discipline	There are no consequences within the organization for unethical behavior or noncompliance with policy.	Discipline for violation of the code of ethics is informal and not consistently executed throughout the organization.	Some formal disciplinary measures exist for violations to the code of ethics; however, methods may not be well communicated or understood throughout the organization. Also, methods may be inconsistently executed dependent on situation and parties involved.	Formal disciplinary measures exist for violations to the code of ethics. Communication and understanding of methods is considered good throughout the organization. Methods are consistently executed without bias to situation or individuals involved.	Formal and well-established measures exist for violations to the code of ethics. Communication and understanding of methods is excellent throughout the organization. Methods are not questioned and execution is fair and always consisted.

Best Practices: Evaluating the Corporate Culture

Risk Assessment & Audit Services: **Risk Management Capability Characteristics COSO**

	Stage A	Stage B	Stage C	Stage D	Stage E
Control Environment (continued)					
Mgmt internal control philosophy and actions	Management's understanding of internal control requirements is minimal and, as such, controls throughout the organization are inadequate.	Management has a basic understanding of internal controls requirements for various processes, however, operational needs and targets often overshadow those requirements. Internal controls throughout the organization are not considered effective. Deficiencies are not timely identified or corrected.	Management has a good understanding of internal control requirements for critical processes and is fairly committed to those controls. Internal controls for those processes are considered adequate. Internal control for less critical processes is not considered a priority and may be overlooked. Identification and correction of issues is considered adequate but may not always be executed timely. Identification of internal control deficiencies for less critical processes is not considered a priority and may be overlooked.	Management has an overall understanding and acceptance of internal control requirements for the organization. Internal controls are considered effective for the majority of processes. Correction of issues is considered effective but may vary dependent on the criticality of the process.	Management fully understands and is committed to establishing effective internal controls for all processes. Internal controls are considered highly effective for all processes. Timely identification and correction of any internal control deficiencies within the organization always occurs.
Overall Control Environment Evaluation	The overall control environment of the Company is considered ineffective and ad hoc.	The overall control environment of the Company is managed on a fairly informal basis and is not considered effective.	The overall control environment of the Company is considered adequate. Certain aspects of the environment may need attention and should be addressed to ensure they can be relied upon.	The overall control environment of the Company is considered effective. The majority of the environment is well controlled and can be relied upon.	The overall control environment of the Company is considered optimal. All aspects of the control environment are controlled at a very effective level and there is no question regarding reliability.

184

Exhibit 4F: Aquila COSO-based Capabilities Maturity Assessment

Risk Assessment & Audit Services: **Risk Management Capability Characteristics COSO**

	Stage A	Stage B	Stage C	Stage D	Stage E
Control Environment (continued)					
Method to identify business risks	Identification of business risks (e.g., entering new markets, offering new products/ services, privacy and data protection requirements, changes in the regulatory environment) is ad hoc and up to the individual efforts of employees/ management.	Methods to identify business risk are informal and not consistently executed or understood across the organization.	Methods to identify business risks are formal and considered adequate for the Company. Methods may not be consistently executed and reviewed to ensure they stay in line with the organization size and needs.	Methods to identify business risks are formal and considered effective for the Company. Methods are executed fairly consistently and periodically reviewed for effectiveness and their alignment with the organization's size and needs.	Methods to identify business risks are considered best of class and highly effective for the Company. Methods are executed consistently and continually reviewed for effectiveness to ensure their alignment with the organization's size and needs.
Overall Risk Assessment	The overall risk assessment process of the Company is considered ineffective and ad hoc.	The overall risk assessment process of the Company is conducted on a fairly informal basis and, overall, is not considered effective.	The overall risk assessment process of the Company is considered adequate. Certain aspects of the process may need attention and should be addressed to ensure it can be relied upon.	The overall risk assessment process of the Company is considered effective. The majority of aspects of the process is well defined and can be relied upon.	The overall risk assessment process of the Company is considered optimal. All aspects of the process are very effective and there is no question regarding reliability.

Best Practices: Evaluating the Corporate Culture

Risk Assessment & Audit Services: **Risk Management Capability Characteristics COSO**

	Stage A	Stage B	Stage C	Stage D	Stage E
Information and Communication					
Information and Communication—Systems Reliability	Systems do not provide for accurate and timely reporting of financial data.	Systems produce financial data; however, significant manual effort is incurred to ensure information is accurate. Timeliness of obtaining reporting information is an issue.	Systems are considered adequate for timely and accurate reporting of financial data. Some manual effort must occur to validate information and ensure its accuracy due to either interface issues or data reporting issues.	Systems are considered effective for timely and accurate reporting of financial data. Manual effort is minimal to validate information and ensure its accuracy.	Systems are considered optimal for timely and accurately reporting financial data.
Overall Management communication processes	Methods used by management to communicate important aspects of Company business to the employee population are ad hoc and not considered open, timely, and effective.	Methods used by management to communicate important aspects of Company business are varied and dependent on the nature of the issue. Communication is often unclear and inconsistent throughout the company. Management makes little effort to clarify the communication.	Methods used by management to communicate important aspects of Company business are considered adequate. Periodically, inconsistencies may occur in the communication and management does not always timely address these inconsistencies.	Methods used by management to communicate important aspects of the Company business are considered effective. Some instances occur of inconsistent communication; however, these are timely addressed and clarified by management.	Methods used by management to communicate important aspects of the Company business are considered optimal. Rare instances occur regarding inconsistent communication.

186

Exhibit 4F: Aquila COSO-based Capabilities Maturity Assessment

Risk Assessment & Audit Services: **Risk Management Capability Characteristics COSO**

	Stage A	Stage B	Stage C	Stage D	Stage E
Control Activities					
Overall Control Activities	The overall control activity process of the Company is considered ineffective and ad hoc.	The overall control activity process of the Company is conducted on a fairly informal basis and, overall, is not considered effective.	The overall control activity process of the Company is considered adequate. Certain aspects of the process may need attention and should be addressed to ensure it can be relied upon.	The overall control activity process of the Company is considered effective. The majority of aspects of the process is well defined and can be relied upon.	The overall control activity process of the Company is considered optimal. All aspects of the process are very effective and there is no question regarding reliability.
Correcting Deficiencies	Actions by management to correct deficiencies reported by internal audit or the external auditors are considered ad hoc and do not occur on a timely basis.	Actions by management to correct deficiencies reported by internal audit or the external auditors are sporadic and inconsistently executed. Actions do not regularly results in effective resolution of issues.	Actions by management to correct deficiencies reported by internal audit or the external auditors are considered adequate. Actions may not always be well coordinated or consistently executed on a timely basis.	Actions by management to correct deficiencies reported by internal audit or the external auditors are considered effective. Actions are fairly well coordinated and executed in an acceptable time period.	Actions by management to correct deficiencies reported by internal audit or the external auditors are considered optimal. Actions are extremely well coordinated and executed on a timely basis.
Overall Monitoring	The overall monitoring process of the Company is considered ineffective and ad hoc	The overall monitoring process of the Company is conducted on a fairly informal basis and, overall, is not considered effective.	The overall monitoring process of the Company is considered adequate. Certain aspects of the process may need attention and should be addressed to ensure it can be relied upon.	The monitoring process of the Company is considered effective. The majority of aspects of the process is well defined and can be relied upon.	The overall monitoring process of the Company is considered optimal. All aspects of the process are very effective and there is no question regarding reliability.

Exhibit 5A

AMERITECH ENTITY-WIDE SOFT CONTROL SURVEY

YOUR DEPARTMENT _____

In what state is your office located? IL   MI   OH   IN   WI   OTHER

AMERITECH RISK ASSESSMENT SURVEY

(PLEASE CIRCLE THE ONE RESPONSE THAT BEST DESCRIBES YOUR REACTION TO EACH STATEMENT)

KEY: SA = Strongly Agree **A** = Agree **D** = Disagree **SD** = Strongly Disagree **DK** = Don't Know

SECTION I: Company Culture

The company culture sets the tone of an organization, influencing the control consciousness of its people. It is the foundation for all other components of internal control. (PLEASE CIRCLE ONE FOR EACH.)

1.	Senior Management of my business unit demonstrates high ethical standards	SA	A	D	SD	DK
2.	Senior Management of my business unit strives to comply with laws/regulations affecting the company	SA	A	D	SD	DK
3.	My supervisor complies with laws/regulations affecting the company	SA	A	D	SD	DK
4.	The performance targets in my work unit are realistic and obtainable	SA	A	D	SD	DK
5.	Employees in my work unit have the knowledge, skill, and training to perform their job adequately..	SA	A	D	SD	DK
6.	My business unit learns from its mistakes	SA	A	D	SD	DK
7.	Personnel turnover has <u>not</u> impacted my work unit's ability to effectively perform its function................	SA	A	D	SD	DK

Exhibit 5A: Ameritech Entity-Wide Soft Control Survey

8.	Integrity of financial and operational results always takes priority over reporting acceptable performance targets...	SA	A	D	SD	DK
9.	Employees in my work unit are treated fairly and justly..	SA	A	D	SD	DK
10.	Employees in my work unit do not have to take unnecessary safety risks to perform their job..........	SA	A	D	SD	DK

11. If you disagree/strongly disagree with any of the above questions on the Company Culture, why do you feel this way?

_____

_____

SECTION II: Goals and Obstacles

Organizations identify and analyze potential obstacles to the achievement of their goals in order to determine how to manage these obstacles. (PLEASE CIRCLE ONE FOR EACH.)

12.	For the coming year I am accountable for defined, measurable objectives..	SA	A	D	SD	DK
13.	I have sufficient resources, tools, and time to accomplish my objectives..	SA	A	D	SD	DK
14.	In my department, we identify barriers and obstacles and resolve issues that could impact achievement of objectives	SA	A	D	SD	DK
15.	In my department, the processes supporting new products, services, technology, and other significant changes are adequately managed	SA	A	D	SD	DK
16.	My business unit adequately takes into account customer impacts in its decisions and actions........................	SA	A	D	SD	DK

17. If you disagree/strongly disagree with any of the above questions on Goals and Obstacles, why do you feel this way?

_____

_____

Best Practices: Evaluating the Corporate Culture

SECTION III: Policies and Procedures

Policies, procedures and other safeguards help ensure that objectives are accomplished. (PLEASE CIRCLE ONE FOR EACH.)

19.	The policies and procedures in my work unit allow me to do my job effectively	SA	A	D	SD	DK
20.	Employees who steal from the company (physical property, money, information, time) will be discovered	SA	A	D	SD	DK
21.	Employees who steal from the company and are discovered will be subject to appropriate consequences	SA	A	D	SD	DK
22.	Employees who break laws and regulations affecting the company will be discovered	SA	A	D	SD	DK
23.	Employees who break laws and regulations affecting the company and are discovered will be subject to appropriate consequences	SA	A	D	SD	DK

24. If you disagree/strongly disagree with any of the above questions on Policies and Procedures, why do you feel this way?

_____

_____

SECTION IV: Information and Communication

Pertinent information must be identified, captured and communicated in a form and time frame that enables people to carry out their responsibilities. (PLEASE CIRCLE ONE FOR EACH.)

25.	Our information systems provide management with timely reports on my unit's performance relative to established objectives	SA	A	D	SD	DK
26.	Mechanisms and incentives are in place for me to provide recommendations for process improvements.	SA	A	D	SD	DK
27.	The interaction between Senior Management and my work unit enables us to perform our jobs effectively	SA	A	D	SD	DK
28.	The communication across departmental boundaries within my business unit enables us to perform our jobs effectively	SA	A	D	SD	DK

Exhibit 5A: Ameritech Entity-Wide Soft Control Survey

29.	The communication across business unit boundaries enables people to perform their jobs effectively......	SA	A	D	SD	DK
30.	I have sufficient information to do my job..............	SA	A	D	SD	DK
31.	Senior management at Ameritech Corporate is informed and aware of my business unit's actual performance	SA	A	D	SD	DK
32.	A communication channel exists for reporting suspected improprieties...	SA	A	D	SD	DK
33.	Persons who report suspected improprieties are protected from reprisal	SA	A	D	SD	DK
34.	If I report wrongdoing to my supervisor, I am confident that the wrongdoing will stop.................................	SA	A	D	SD	DK

35. If you disagree/strongly disagree with any of the above questions on Information and Communications, why do you feel this way?

_____

_____

SECTION V: Evaluation and Feedback

Through evaluation and feedback processes, an organization assesses, tracks and monitors its performance over time. (PLEASE CIRCLE ONE FOR EACH.)

36.	Information reported to Senior Management reflects the actual results of operations in my work unit	SA	A	D	SD	DK
37.	I have enough information to monitor vendor performance...	SA	A	D	SD	DK
38.	I have enough information to monitor customers' satisfaction or dissatisfaction (either internal or external)..	SA	A	D	SD	DK
39.	External and/or internal customer feedback and complaints are followed up on in a timely and effective manner..	SA	A	D	SD	DK
40.	The quality of output in my work unit is measurable.	SA	A	D	SD	DK
41.	Employees in my work unit know what actions to take when they find mistakes or gaps in performance	SA	A	D	SD	DK

42. My supervisor reviews my performance with me at appropriate intervals .... SA A D SD DK

43. I know what action to take if I become aware of unethical or fraudulent activity .... SA A D SD DK

44. If you disagree/strongly disagree with any of the above questions on Evaluation and Feedback, why do you feel this way?

_____

_____

45. I suspect/know that fraudulent activity is occurring in my work place .... YES NO

If question 45 is answered YES, please complete the following.

45A. What is the activity referred to in question 45?

_____

_____

45B. Did you report it? Yes/No (Please circle)

45C. If no, why not?

_____

_____

(**NOTE:** If you wish to report any fraud, you may call the Ameritech Integrity Line at 1-800-628-8878)

Exhibit 5A: Ameritech Entity-Wide Soft Control Survey

MANAGEMENT 1996/1997 ANNUAL CONTROL SELF-ASSESSMENT

Mean Score
Ameritech Internal Control System
Self-Assessment Survey
Agreement with Adequacy of Control Components
(1993-1996)

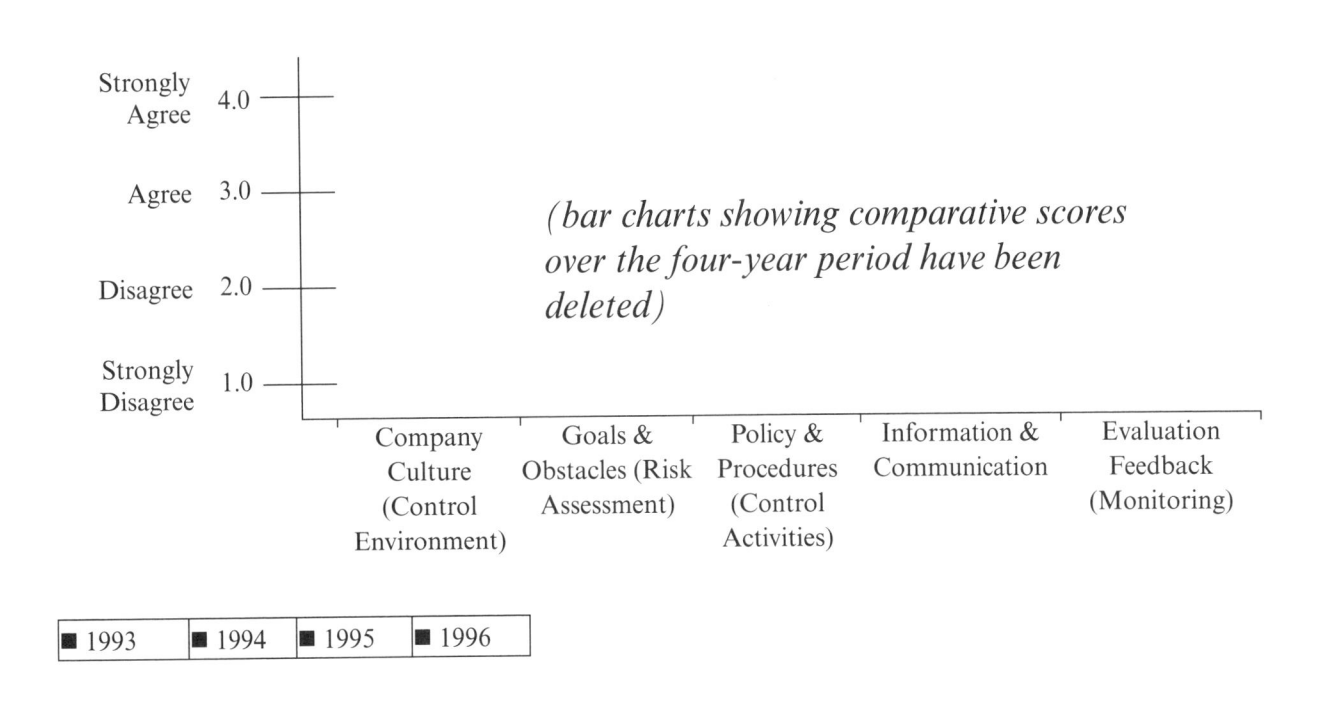

Strongly Agree — 4.0
Agree — 3.0
Disagree — 2.0
Strongly Disagree — 1.0

(bar charts showing comparative scores over the four-year period have been deleted)

Categories:
- Company Culture (Control Environment)
- Goals & Obstacles (Risk Assessment)
- Policy & Procedures (Control Activities)
- Information & Communication
- Evaluation Feedback (Monitoring)

■ 1993   ■ 1994   ■ 1995   ■ 1996

Exhibit 5B

UNITED STATIONERS SURVEY INVITATION LETTER

Annual Risk Assessment Survey

United Stationers Inc. and its subsidiaries perform an annual Risk Assessment Survey to assess the adequacy of its internal controls to support mandatory U.S. Securities and Exchange Commission requirements. The survey focuses on the Company's culture; goals and objectives; policies and procedures; information and communication; and evaluation and feedback.

As an associate working with other associates and customers on a daily basis, your perceptions and ideas are key to making improvements in the Company's internal control system. A strong internal control system consists both of policies and procedures and a culture that provides reasonable assurance that the Company and each of its functions will achieve financial and operational objectives with the highest ethical standards. In addition to ensuring financial results are accurate, a top-notch internal control system keeps the Company on course toward its vision and profitability goals and minimizes losses and surprises along the way. Everyone in the Company - not just the senior leadership team, accountants, and auditors - contributes to a strong internal control system.

For those of you in USSCO, please note that this survey is based on a compliance requirement. You will see just a few questions that overlap with those seen on the recent Associate Engagement Survey. In years to come, our goal will be to eliminate any redundancy between the two surveys. However, for 2008, since Lagasse and ORS Nasco did not participate in the Associate Engagement Survey this year, we must leave in these questions.

Please complete this survey by Friday, May 9, 2008. The survey should take about 15 – 30 minutes to complete and is accessed through the internet via a web page managed by Facilitate.com, a company who specializes in web based meeting and survey tools.

We promise you anonymity, therefore, we encourage you to be candid in your responses and comments. Your individual survey responses will remain confidential. Facilitate.com will only provide the summarized results to the Company. These results will be interpreted by the senior leaders of your organization and used to identify company-wide and functional area risks and improvement opportunities. Results and action plans are also shared with the Audit Committee of the Board of Directors. Last year's survey responses did not indicate that remediation was required for any particular control weakness, however, associates identified business risks and opportunities for improvement that were used as inputs to ongoing strategy and action plans.

Please click on the following link to begin the survey: https://secure.facilitate.com/USI.shtml. You will need your Cornerstone ID to complete the survey and you will be required to create a new password for this year's survey *(the survey does not use your Cornerstone password or last year's survey password)*.

Exhibit 5B: United Stationers Survey Invitation Letter

If you do not have access to the internet, please ask your supervisor to direct you to a personal computer with internet access. If you have logon issues or questions, please call Michele Laurence, Independent Facilitator, at (847) 627-7000 extension 73934 or send her an email at mlaurence@ussco.com.

If you'd like to openly discuss any part of this survey beyond your written comments, please call me at (847) 627-2150, or send me an email at skruse@ussco.com. As always, any issues or concerns can also be reported anonymously by calling our Company's Hotline at (877) 767-6021.

Thank you for taking the time to respond to this year's survey.

Sandy Kruse
Interim Vice President and General Auditor

United Stationers Inc.

Exhibit 5C

UNITED STATIONERS SURVEY STATEMENTS AND STRUCTURE FOR ONE GROUP

Risk Assessment Survey 2008 - All Other Exempt

SECTION 1: COMPANY CULTURE

The Company's culture reflects the tone set by top management and the overall attitude, awareness and actions of employees, the board of directors, owners and others concerning the importance of internal control and the emphasis placed on control in the company's policies, procedures, methods and organizational structure. It is the foundation for honest and ethical corporate behavior.

For each statement, indicate your level of agreement: SA = Strongly Agree, A = Agree, D = Disagree, SD = Strongly Disagree, DK = Don't Know.

101 Senior Management (2) demonstrates a commitment to integrity and ethical behavior by example in day-to-day activities. (See note (2) above for definition of Senior Management.)

102 Senior Management at the Company (1) complies with what I believe to be the laws/regulations affecting the Company. (See note (1) above for definition of Company.)

103 My supervisor and co-workers comply with what I believe to be the laws/regulations affecting the Company.

104 Senior Management is held accountable to company policies in the same way I am.

105 My organization (3) employs individuals with the necessary knowledge, skills, and training to perform their job adequately. (See note (3) above for definition of organization.)

106 The Company learns from its mistakes.

107 We put the right emphasis on satisfying the customer at this Company.

108 Reporting actual performance takes priority over reporting more favorable results.

109 Associates in my organization are treated fairly and justly.

110 I wouldn't hesitate to use the Company's Hotline to report wrongdoing because it's clear to me and everyone I work with that callers to the Company's Hotline are protected from reprisal.

111 At the Company, we do not "shoot the messenger" who delivers unfavorable information.

112 High Performance/Process Excellence Teams have had a positive impact on the Company and will lead to future improvement.

Exhibit 5C: United Stationers Survey Statements and Structure for One Group

113 The Company structure and policies provide associates with opportunities for growth.

114 Senior Management consistently demonstrates the importance of internal controls by developing, updating, and certifying Sarbanes-Oxley documentation.

SECTION 2: GOALS AND OBSTACLES

Goals and Obstacles reflect the setting of individual, functional, and corporate performance objectives as well as an analysis and understanding of relevant internal and external risks that could impact shareholder value. This in turn forms the basis for determining how risks should be managed.

For each statement, indicate your level of agreement: SA = Strongly Agree, A = Agree, D = Disagree, SD = Strongly Disagree, DK = Don't Know.

201 The Company has a clear vision for the future and a business plan to execute it.

202 Key Performance Indicators (KPI) and measurement criteria for achieving company-wide objectives have been communicated and are uniformly understood.

203 The performance targets in my organization are realistic and obtainable.

204 For the coming year, I am accountable for specific, measurable objectives.

205 My organization adequately takes into account customer impacts in its decisions and actions.

206 My organization adequately manages the process supporting new products, services, technology, and other significant changes.

207 Senior Management demonstrates the ability to modify its approach when unanticipated roadblocks surface.

208 My organization's goals and objectives are consistent with company-wide goals and objectives.

209 Associates in my organization know what actions to take when they find mistakes or gaps in performance.

210 In my organization, we are proactive in identifying obstacles that could impact the achievement of our objectives and we work successfully to resolve obstacles once they are identified.

211 In your opinion, what is the top business risk facing the Company?

212 In your opinion, what is the top financial risk in your organization? (Examples of financial risk include, but are not limited to: supervisory override of controls, assets/liabilities not recorded on Company's books, expenses not properly approved and promptly reported to Accounts Payable, sales/shipping cutoff not performed per policy, cycle count not performed per plan, dealer rebates and discounts not properly approved, supplier allowances and purchase discounts not reported to Finance, return credits not properly approved.)

Best Practices: Evaluating the Corporate Culture

SECTION 3: POLICIES AND PROCEDURES
Policies and Procedures are a combination of written documents and actions that codify management's directives and ensure these are carried out.

For each statement, indicate your level of agreement: SA = Strongly Agree, A = Agree, D = Disagree, SD = Strongly Disagree, DK = Don't Know.

301 The policies and procedures in my organization allow me to do my job effectively.

302 Unethical behavior in my organization is not tolerated.

303 Associates who steal from the Company (physical property, money, information, time) are likely to be discovered.

304 When discovered, associates who steal are appropriately disciplined.

305 Associates who break laws/regulations affecting the Company are likely to be discovered.

306 When discovered, associates who break laws/regulations affecting the Company are appropriately disciplined.

307 In my organization, policies and procedures are regularly reviewed and updated where appropriate.

308 I believe sales practices at the Company are ethical.

309 We take security and safety seriously at our facility.

310 I am aware, understand, and follow the policies and procedures that affect my job.

311 Management does not override internal controls in my organization.

312 I understand what I am personally allowed to authorize according to Company Policy 11: Corporate Approvals and Authorization Matrices.

313 In my organization, I believe that we comply with the authorizations allowed via the Corporate Approvals and Authorization Matrices.

314 Please identify the top opportunity to improve a process in your organization that you feel is inefficient or ineffective.

SECTION 4: INFORMATION AND COMMUNICATION
Information and communication systems support the identification, capture, and exchange of information in a form and timeframe that enable management and other appropriate personnel to carry out their responsibilities effectively.

For each statement, indicate your level of agreement: SA = Strongly Agree, A = Agree, D = Disagree, SD = Strongly Disagree, DK = Don't Know.

Exhibit 5C: United Stationers Survey Statements and Structure for One Group

401 Senior Management has accurate, relevant, and timely information to manage the Company's performance effectively.

402 Senior Management interacts with and supports my organization in achieving goals and objectives.

403 I have access to the right information to effectively attend to customers' (or internal clients') needs.

404 Senior Management encourages and rewards process improvement recommendations.

405 The communication and information shared across functions and departments in the Company enables people to do their jobs effectively.

406 Persons who report suspected wrongdoing are protected from reprisal.

407 If I report wrongdoing to my supervisor, I am confident that the wrongdoing will stop.

408 IT and other departments work together effectively to identify and resolve data/information needs.

SECTION 5: EVALUATION AND FEEDBACK

Evaluation and feedback is a process that assesses the quality of internal control performance over time.

For each statement, indicate your level of agreement: SA = Strongly Agree, A = Agree, D = Disagree, SD = Strongly Disagree, DK = Don't Know.

501 Senior Management at the Company monitors my organization using relevant Key Performance Indicators (KPI).

502 Customer feedback and complaints are followed up in a timely and effective manner.

503 The Company appropriately monitors customer satisfaction (using internal or external information).

504 My performance review is supported by quality measures that adequately indicate my performance level.

505 Monitoring procedures at the Company send up red flags to Senior Management when significant performance exceptions occur.

506 My supervisor provides me with developmental feedback at appropriate intervals.

507 (Question intentionally left blank.)

508 I suspect/know that fraudulent activity is occurring in my workplace (If "yes" please provide details). If you answered "no," proceed to question 601.

509 If you indicated "yes" on question 508 that you suspect/know that fraudulent activity is occurring, did you report it? If you answered "no," proceed to question 511.

510 If you indicated "yes" on question 509 that you reported fraudulent activity, to the best of your knowledge, what action was taken?

511 If you indicated "no" on question 509, why did you not report the fraudulent activity?

SECTION 6: ADDITIONAL COMMENTS

601 Please add any additional comments or observations that you would like to make regarding the Company's internal control system.

Exhibit 5D

UNITED STATIONERS SURVEY: DIFFERENCES AMONG THE GROUPS

This section is available on the CD that accompanies this book.

Exhibit 5E

"RISK WATCH" ARTICLE ON CITY OF AUSTIN ETHICS AUDIT

Measuring Ethical Climate Risk

By Colleen G. Waring

Why audit an organization's ethical culture? The key reasons center around requirements to evaluate the control environment. Specifically, audit shops that comply with Implementation Standard 2110. A1: Governance, of The IIA's *International Standards for the Professional Practice of Internal Auditing*, must "evaluate the design, implementation, and effectiveness of the organization's ethics-related objectives, programs, and activities." Moreover, throughout the world, publicly-traded companies are increasingly being required to conduct some form of evaluation of their controls, using an authoritative internal control model. These models — such as the Committee of Sponsoring Organizations of the Treadway Commission's (COSO's) *Internal Control–Integrated Framework* — include organizational culture as a key element.

In 2000, when the city auditor's office in Austin, Texas, audited the city departments' ethical climates, they were able to successfully document the fiscal benefits resulting from a strong organizational commitment to ethical conduct. Overall, the audit found evidence that fiscal and administrative benefits correlate to a stronger departmental ethical climate. Particularly, the audit demonstrated to city management that multiple measures of ethical climate are positively related to specific costs and other performance measures.

The City of Austin Audit

Although a variety of means have been used to audit organizations' ethical cultures, the basic methodologies are similar. All audits use survey data to establish the state of ethics, as indicated by employees, customers, or other stakeholders. Some audits have gone further and triangulated the survey information with hard data.

The Austin City Auditor's Office audit of organizational ethics involved use of existing survey data collected annually by the city's human resources department (stratified by city department), which was statistically correlated to selected fiscal and administrative outcome indicators, such as damage claims, complaints, lost-time injuries, and sick-leave usage.

DAMAGE CLAIMS Costs and number of successful damage claims against the city were highest among departments where employees reported greater awareness of unethical conduct. Damage claims — claims paid when the city is at fault in damaging a citizen's property — were used as an indicator of rule breaking by employees. Internal auditing's theory was that employees in departments who were following laws and standard operating procedures would be less likely to generate property damage. In the city organization, 57 percent of all damage costs are due to vehicle collisions.

We conducted several statistical correlations, one to correlate each department's claims cost and number to the department's individual average score on the statement, "I'm personally aware of an illegal act or ethical violation by a city employee in the past six months." For a second correlation, we put departments into two groups — those scoring below the mean on the statement where "disagree" or "strongly disagree" were the most frequent responses (labeled "low awareness") and those scoring above the mean where "agree" or "strongly agree" were the most frequently selected (labeled "high awareness"). Each group was correlated to its group's total costs of damage claims (see Figures 1 and 2, "Cost of Claims" and "Paid Claims").

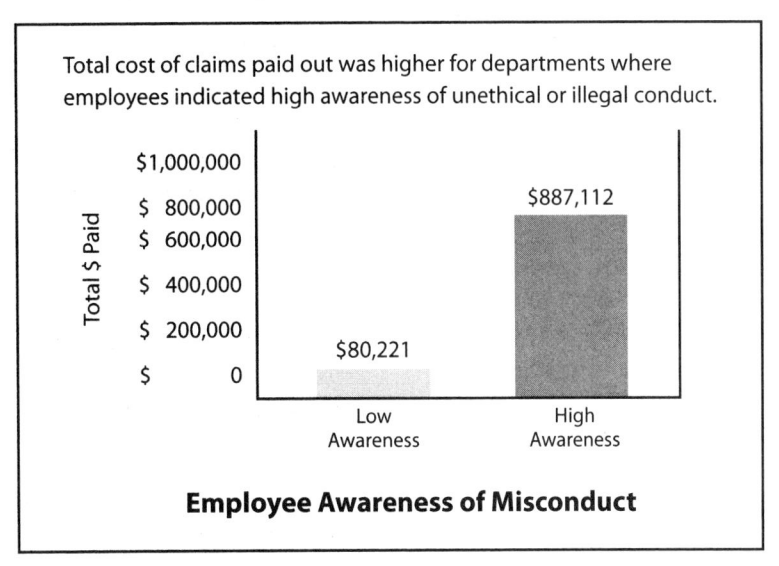

Figure 1: Cost of Claims

Total cost of claims paid out was higher for departments where employees indicated high awareness of unethical or illegal conduct.

- Low Awareness: $80,221
- High Awareness: $887,112

Employee Awareness of Misconduct

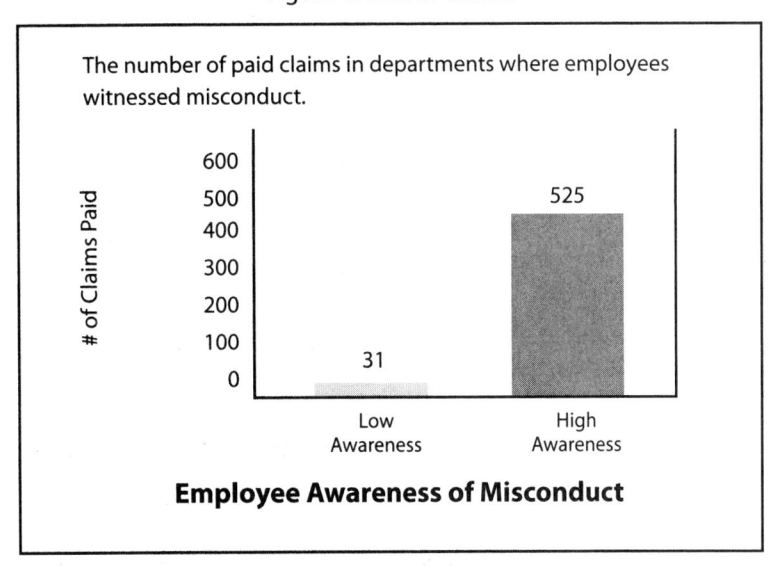

Figure 2: Paid Claims

The number of paid claims in departments where employees witnessed misconduct.

- Low Awareness: 31
- High Awareness: 525

Employee Awareness of Misconduct

When looking at cost and number of claims, both the individual and the grouped correlations to the awareness statement were statistically significant (i.e., not likely to be due to chance). We also conducted a third test to evaluate the extent to which the observed correlations might be due to other factors, such as the specific department's size or use of vehicles. For this test we used multivariate correlations to examine the strength of the different variables, including the ethical climate indicators. The correlation between the ethical climate indicator and the cost and number of claims continued to be statistically significant, even when controlling for size and vehicle use.

Best Practices: Evaluating the Corporate Culture

The number of successful damage claims also correlated with a second indicator — the employees' responses to a statement about the extent to which their managers "set a good example by following the laws and policies that apply to their jobs." This correlation was strong for individual departments and also when departments were grouped into two clusters, one that was above the mean ("strong ethical climate") and one that was below the mean ("weak ethical climate"). The correlation held even when controlled for department size and vehicle use.

COMPLAINTS Similarly, the number of complaints by the public was greater in departments where employees reported greater awareness of illegal or unethical behavior by city employees. We conducted correlations similar to those on paid claims, using data from the city's Public Information Office, which tracks complaints received from citizens. Individual departments' average responses to the awareness statement, "I'm personally aware of an illegal act or ethical violation by a city employee in the past six months," were significantly correlated to the number of citizen complaints. Moreover, when we grouped departments into two groups — above and below the mean — the correlation between number of claims and the climate indicator were significant (see Figure 3, "Complaints"). Again, we conducted a multivariate analysis to control for department size and the nature of the work — such as police or regulatory functions — and the relationship continued to be statistically significant.

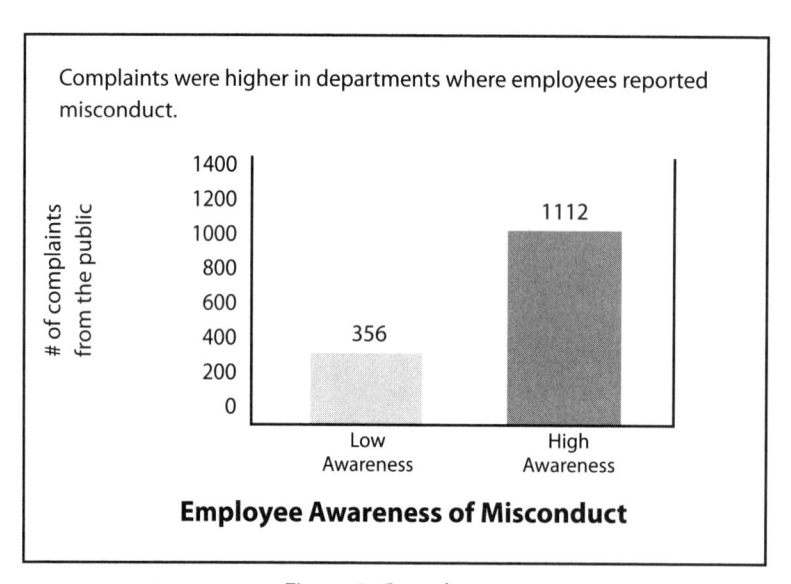

Complaints were higher in departments where employees reported misconduct.

Employee Awareness of Misconduct	# of complaints from the public
Low Awareness	356
High Awareness	1112

Figure 3: Complaints

The number of complaints by the public was lower in departments where employees agreed that "Managers in my work group set a good example by following laws and policies that apply to their jobs." Our analyses for this ethical climate indicator were identical to those on the awareness statement, and the results were also the same — statistically significant correlations, even after controlling for size and type of work of the departments.

LOST-TIME INJURIES The lost-time injuries also strongly correlated to two ethical climate indicators — awareness of unethical or illegal conduct, and examples set by managers. We theorized that injuries are more likely to increase when workers and managers take shortcuts and break safety rules. Moreover, because workers' compensation claims can be susceptible to fraudulent claims, a weak ethical climate would be likely to show higher injury rates. Again, the correlation was significant both for individual departments, and when the departments were grouped above and below the mean for the ethical climate indicators (see Figure 4, "Injuries"). Further, we conducted multivariate analyses to control for the size and inherent dangerousness of the work of some departments, and still the relationship between the ethical climate indicators ("awareness of illegal/unethical conduct" and "example set by managers") and the number of lost-time injuries was statistically significant.

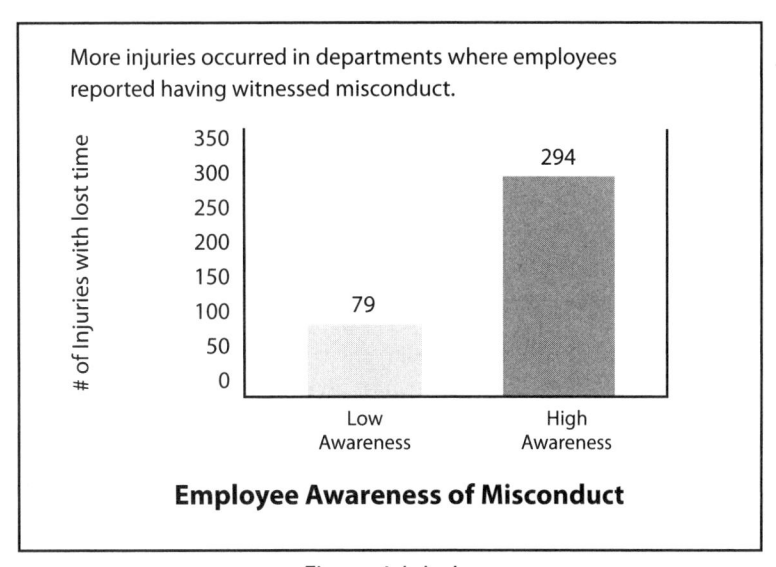

Figure 4: Injuries

SICK LEAVE High sick leave was concentrated in departments with weak ethics enforcement. In addition to the ethical climate indicators — awareness and example of managers — we correlated the outcome variables to a composite indicator representing departmental enforcement of ethical standards. The composite indicator was the averaged responses to four questions asking about the extent to which managers enforce and support ethical behavior and investigate and sanction ethical violations.

We theorized that stress-related illnesses and misuse of sick leave for nonmedical reasons were more likely to occur in departments with poor ethical climates. Specifically, 73 percent of the departments scoring below the average on their enforcement of ethical standards also had above-the-median sick leave usage. Conversely, only 25 percent of the departments showing above-average enforcement had high sick leave usage (see Figure 5, "Sick Leave").

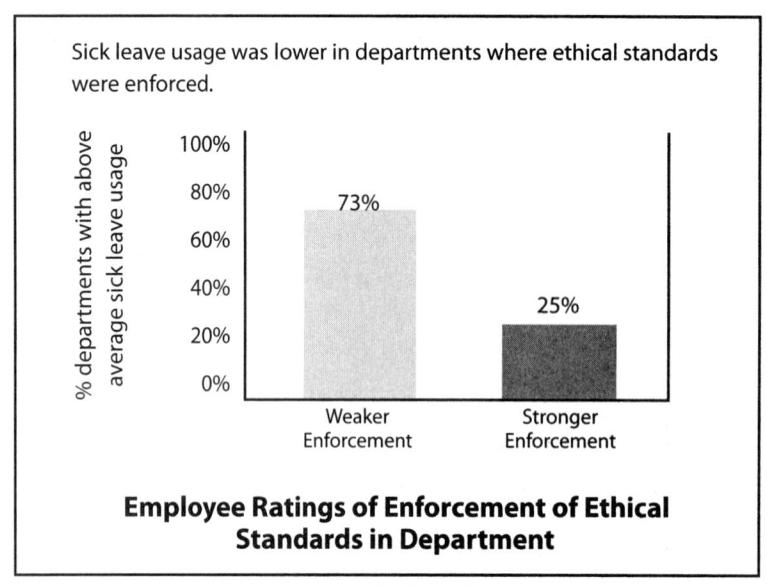

Best Practices: Evaluating the Corporate Culture

Figure 5: Sick Leave

Variances in Findings

Another important finding of the audit was the large variances among departments (see Figure 6, "Variances Among Departments"). The city needed to find ways to reduce the wide variation of ethical climate scores where fundamental corporate values should be roughly congruent across the organization.

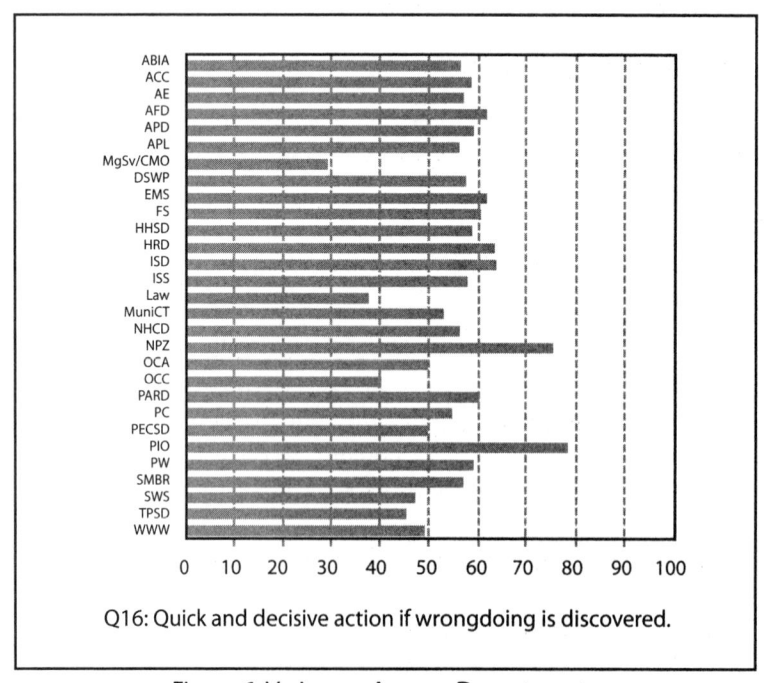

Figure 6: Variances Among Departments

Analytical techniques for this type of audit can be sophisticated or straightforward, depending on capacity of the audit organization. The Austin city auditor's original (2000) audit used statistical techniques that required a statistical software package and various data transformations to support the types of correlations being performed. However, we recently updated the results with 2003 data, using very straightforward data transformations only (i.e., averages and percentages) and employing the statistical correlation functionality available in Microsoft Excel. For our measures of significance, we supplemented Excel with Winstat, a downloadable add-in software for under $100. The updated results can be found on the city auditor's Web site at www.ci.austin.tx.us/auditor/downloads/indicators.pdf. In addition to the statistical analyses, the comparisons among departments that served as indicators that an overall corporate culture had not taken hold required no statistical correlations at all.

Committing to Ethical Behavior

An audit of an organization's ethical culture can provide information to management about the extent to which different units within the organization are conforming to the stated values. Plus, the audit project itself can help raise awareness and serve to reinforce the organization's commitment to its values and integrity.

Because the ethical climate indicators and the outcome measures vary, organizations can logically attempt to affect the latter by making changes in the former. Specifically, although the correlations demonstrated by the audit do not prove that the ethical climate is a "cause" of reduced claims, complaints, and so on, they do point to the ethical climate measures as a *leading* indicator that may be more amenable to change efforts than the *lagging* outcome indicators.

We found that the strong correlations between the ethical climate indicators and the measures of cost that are presented in the audit's results have served as a convincing argument for management to adopt efforts to improve its ethical climate.

Exhibit 5F

LENNOX INTERNATIONAL ENTITY-WIDE SURVEY

Lennox International, Inc.
Organizational Survey

Introduction

This survey has been designed to support Lennox International Inc.'s Code of Conduct redesign and update process. Fundamental to our work is encouraging and listening to input about how LII (as a whole) and its employees deliver on and live the Core Values of: Integrity and Trust; Accountability and Dependability; Valuing Individuals; Innovation; and Commitment to Quality. To that end, many of the questions included in this survey reflect the Core Value statements.

The purpose of the survey is to solicit input from employees regarding their awareness of, and views about, the ethical environment at LII.

Confidentiality

Please respond openly and honestly to this survey. Your individual responses are completely confidential and they will not be released to anyone at LII. No attempt will be made to identify individual respondents. An external firm will process all survey responses and only combined results will be provided to LII.

Results

Survey results will be summarized and communicated to the LII Business Conduct Office and Senior Management. Summary information will also be shared with LII employees through the Business Conduct newsletter and infosource. The results will then be integrated into the Code of Conduct review and update process.

Instructions

Please take a few minutes to complete the questionnaire. Should you have any questions regarding the questionnaire and/or the survey process, please feel free to contact the survey administrator at help@surveysupport.com.

Additional Comments

At the end of the survey, there is space for your additional comments and thoughts. Please take time to share these.

Exhibit 5F: Lennox International Entity-Wide Survey

Instructions: Please indicate the extent to which you agree with each statement below.

Please answer the following questions about the LII Executive Management Team <u>as a group</u> that includes the following individuals: XX, XX, XX, XX, XX, XX.

The LII Executive Management Team:

1. Talks about the importance of ethics and ethical behavior
2. Models ethical behavior
3. Sets a good example by doing the "right thing"
4. Provides employees with a clear picture of where the company is going
5. Is open and approachable
6. Is receptive to feedback
7. Will act upon the results of this survey

Please answer the following questions about your Business Unit Executive Leadership Team <u>as a group</u>.

My Business Unit Executive Team:

8. Talks about the importance of ethics and ethical behavior
9. Models ethical behavior
10. Sets a good example by doing the "right thing"
11. Provides employees with a clear picture of where the company is going
12. Is open and approachable
13. Is receptive to feedback
14. Will act upon the results of this survey

Please answer the following questions about your immediate Supervisor/Manager <u>as an individual</u>.

My immediate Supervisor/Manager:

15. Talks about the importance of ethics and ethical behavior
16. Models ethical behavior
17. Sets a good example by doing the "right thing"

18. Provides employees with a clear picture of where the company is going

19. Is open and approachable

20. Is receptive to feedback

21. Will act upon the results of this survey

In my experience:

22. Commitment to lawful and ethical behavior is a fundamental part of the way we do business

23. There is a published Company ethical code of conduct that guides employees' behavior at work

24. There is a clear and consistent set of values that guides the way we do business

25. Unethical behavior is tolerated

26. Employees are encourage to go their boss, HR representative, Legal Department, or Business Conduct Office with questions or concerns about ethical dilemmas

27. I can report concerns related to workplace ethical dilemmas without (fear of) retaliation

28. My coworkers talk about the importance of ethics and ethical behavior

29. I am able to provide input into decisions that affect my job

30. I feel valued for the work that I do

31. I understand how the work that I do is important to the overall success of the company

32. Employees trust each other

33. Employees are treated with respect

34. Employees are told the truth when something goes wrong

35. I trust my organization to do the right thing

36. I would recommend this organization to others as a great place to work

37. My values and the organization's values are very similar

38. I have personally felt pressure to compromise my organization's code of ethical conduct:
    Yes   No   Unsure

Exhibit 5F: Lennox International Entity-Wide Survey

39. I have personally observed someone stretching the rules at work:

   Yes   No   Unsure

40. During the past year, I have personally observed actions or behaviors that violated the law or my organization's code of ethical conduct:

   Yes   No   Unsure

   If Yes: Did you report the misconduct?

   Yes   No   Unsure

   **If Yes:* To whom did you report the misconduct? *Please select all that apply*

My manager	Human Resources	LII Ethicsline
Member of Senior Management	Legal Department/ Compliance Office	Other: Please specify: _____

   If you observed misconduct, but did not report the misconduct,
   Please contact the LII Ethicsline at 1-800-745-2382

Additional Comments:

DEMOGRAPHICS

The following questions are included for reporting purposes only. Once the survey results have been compiled, summaries will be given to each leader about their own Operating Unit and/or workgroup/department. This will provide each leader and manager with a clear picture of employees' awareness of and views about the ethical environment at LII (overall) and within their own department.

Please note: To maintain anonymity, survey results will be provided at the workgroup or department level *only* if at least 10 employees from that workgroup or department submit surveys.

1. How long have you worked for this organization?

   Less than one year
   1 to 3 years
   3 to 5 years
   5 to 10 years
   10 to 15 years
   Over 15 years

2. What is your job level/role in the organization?

   Hourly: Production
   Hourly: Clerical
   Salaried: Supervisor
   Salaried: Manager
   Salaried: Director
   Salaried: VP & Above

Best Practices: Evaluating the Corporate Culture

3. Which Operating Unit do you work for?

    Service Experts Inc. (SEI)

    Worldwide Refrigeration (WWR)

    Worldwide Heatcraft (WWHC)

    LII Parent Company (Headquarters)

Please provide the country, city and state/province of your work location:

Country: _____

City: _____

State or Providence: _____

Exhibit 5G

ROBECO ENTITY-WIDE SURVEY

Survey

Dear Robeco colleague,

PEOPLE MAKE THE DIFFERENCE!

Currently I am working on a (post academic) research paper regarding the Soft Controls within Robeco and the way they contribute to the Control Environment of Robeco. Soft Controls refer for example to the integrity of people and the culture of the organisation. I have made a list with statements that relate to Soft Controls of Robeco. This list is discussed with Corporate Compliance and will also be used in their upcoming integrity reviews.

I kindly ask you to take a mere **10 minutes** of your time to give your opinion on these statements. I sincerely hope that you will take part in this survey and submit the web based questionnaire before November 23, 2007.

To guarantee the absolute confidentiality of your answers, the questionnaire will be submitted to an independent institute that compiles the data for this research. Thus, no one (including myself) within Robeco will know the individual response.

The success of this survey relies on the honesty of the answers. Please take this in consideration.

Your co-operation will be highly appreciated!

Kind regards,

Rick Mulders

PLEASE CLICK ON THE HYPERLINK TO START THE QUESTIONNARE:

HTTP//WWW.ENQUETEVIAINTERNET/SOFTCONTROLS.NL

Please indicate your opinion according to the following scale:

Strongly Agree				Strongly Disagree	Don't Know
o---------o---------o---------o---------o					o
(1)	(2)	(3)	(4)	(5)	(6)

This scale system offers you six response possibilities, which enable you to give a nuanced opinion. You are kindly requested to choose only one opinion per statement.

The opinion (1) means: Strongly Agree
The opinion (2) means: Agree
The opinion (3) means: Undecided
The opinion (4) means: Disagree
The opinion (5) means: Strongly Disagree

I work for:
o   RAM
o   RAI
o   RD
o   Corporate Departments
o   Office of the Management Board (including IRIS)

Please indicate your managerial responsibilities (please follow the supervisor overview in the corporate directory):
o   no one (in)directly reports to me
o   less than 20 people (in)directly report to me
o   more than 20 people (in)directly report to me

		Agree	Disagree	Don't Know
1.	I am aware of the core values of Robeco.	o ------ o ------- o ------- o ------- o		o
2.	I acknowledge the core values of Robeco.	o ------ o ------- o ------- o ------- o		o
3.	The performance targets in my department are realistic and achievable.	o ------ o ------- o ------- o ------- o		o
4.	My manager knows the core values of Robeco.	o ------ o ------- o ------- o ------- o		o
5.	My manager acts upon the core values of Robeco.	o ------ o ------- o ------- o ------- o		o
6.	Employees in my department are treated fairly and justly.	o ------ o ------- o ------- o ------- o		o
7.	The Robeco policies regarding integrity are realistic.	o ------ o ------- o ------- o ------- o		o

Exhibit 5G: Robeco Entity-Wide Survey

		Agree	Disagree	Don't Know
8.	If I report wrong doing to my supervisor, I am confident that the wrong doing will stop.	o ------ o ------- o ------- o ------- o		o
9.	My manager informs me about the reasons of any special tasks I have to perform.	o ------ o ------- o ------- o ------- o		o

The following questions (from 10 to 20) refer to Robeco policies. Please take the Human Resources and Corporate Compliance policies into consideration in this respect.

10.	In my department we are aware of the Robeco policies.	o ------ o ------- o ------- o ------- o		o
11.	I know what the Robeco policies mean for my behaviour.	o ------ o ------- o ------- o ------- o		o
12.	In my department we act upon the Robeco policies.	o ------ o ------- o ------- o ------- o		o
13.	The Robeco policies allow me to do my job effectively.	o ------ o ------- o ------- o ------- o		o
14.	Robeco gives me enough help and information to understand the Robeco policies.	o ------ o ------- o ------- o ------- o		o
15.	I am aware of the risks if I do not comply with the Robeco policies.	o ------ o ------- o ------- o ------- o		o
16.	I know where to go if I have questions about the application of the Robeco policies.	o ------ o ------- o ------- o ------- o		o
17.	Breaches of compliance with external laws and policies in my department will be discovered.	o ------ o ------- o ------- o ------- o		o
18.	Robeco policies are set aside in my department if this is in favour of the client.	o ------ o ------- o ------- o ------- o		o
19.	There are not enough people in my department to work in accordance with the Robeco policies.	o ------ o ------- o ------- o ------- o		o
20.	If someone within my department is in breach with the Robeco policies he may get away with it.	o ------ o ------- o ------- o ------- o		o
21.	It does not matter how we achieve the objectives of my department, it is more important that we achieve them.	o ------ o ------- o ------- o ------- o		o
22.	My work pressure has increased considerably within the last two years.	o ------ o ------- o ------- o ------- o		o
23.	If my colleague behaves intolerable, I will address this to him/her.	o ------ o ------- o ------- o ------- o		o
24.	If my manager behaves intolerable, I will address this to him/her.	o ------ o ------- o ------- o ------- o		o

Best Practices: Evaluating the Corporate Culture

	Agree ──── Disagree	Don't Know
25. Reporting of intolerable behaviour within Robeco has negative consequences for the person who reports this.	o ── o ── o ── o ── o	o
26. Reporting of intolerable behaviour within Robeco has positive consequences for the person who reports this.	o ── o ── o ── o ── o	o
27. I have sufficient information about relevant developments within my department to perform my job adequately.	o ── o ── o ── o ── o	o
28. I am informed sufficiently about important developments within Robeco.	o ── o ── o ── o ── o	o
29. I know what is expected of me during the upcoming year.	o ── o ── o ── o ── o	o
30. Management of my department effectively communicates the objectives of the department to me.	o ── o ── o ── o ── o	o
31. If I do not function sufficiently, my manager will discuss this with me.	o ── o ── o ── o ── o	o
32. My department receives recognition within Robeco.	o ── o ── o ── o ── o	o
33. Managers in my department are sensitive to ethical considerations.	o ── o ── o ── o ── o	o
34. An atmosphere of mutual trust and open communication between management and employees has been established within my department.	o ── o ── o ── o ── o	o
35. An atmosphere of mutual trust and open communication between management and employees has been established within Robeco.	o ── o ── o ── o ── o	o
36. If I am not acting correctly, my colleague(s) will correct me.	o ── o ── o ── o ── o	o
37. The cooperation across Business Units and Corporate Departments enables people to perform their jobs effectively.	o ── o ── o ── o ── o	o

Exhibit 5G: Robeco Entity-Wide Survey

If you have any final remarks please state them here:

Thank you very much for participating in this survey. If you have any questions please do contact me.

Best Regards,

Rick Mulders
h.mulders@robeco.nl

Exhibit 6A

WORKSAFEBC PRE-INTERVIEW HANDOUT

Control Framework – Soft Controls

A. Introduction

This audit is one component of Internal Audit's assurance to the Audit Committee that the organization's controls are working effectively. The audit objective is to facilitate a self-assessment of the adequacy of soft controls at the divisional level. We will perform this audit for each division of the WCB.

We are conducting structured interviews with the Vice President and Directors in Worker & Employer Services (WES), and facilitating workshops for a sample of managers. We have designed a questionnaire to use in our interviews and workshops; it is based on a control framework generally accepted by international accounting and auditing associations.

Staff is excluded from the soft controls audit for this year.

The control framework we followed has 5 components and 17 factors within the components. We consolidated or omitted some of the factors to tailor our questionnaire to the audit objectives. An outline of the framework we used is presented below in Section B. Our questionnaire follows in Section C. The question numbers reference the framework, but do not follow it exactly:

- We excluded *3.0 Control Activities*, as this component addresses primarily hard controls. We will address this component through other internal audits
- We moved *2.0 Risk Assessment* to the end of the questionnaire for better flow with the final component of the interview (see below)

Participants should address the questions at the divisional and/or departmental level, as appropriate for their job function. After discussing each question, we will ask you to self assess the importance you place on the related factor/control and your confidence that it is operating effectively in your area. After the questionnaire, we will also ask you to rate the five WCB strategic objectives over two dimensions:

- How important is it for your division / department to support this initiative?
- How effectively is your division /department contributing to this initiative?

After each interview, we will send written minutes to the participant; we will not distribute the minutes to anyone else. When we have completed all of the interviews and workshops for your division, we will prepare a report summarizing the ratings and some of the comments. We will issue the report to the Vice-President, with a recommendation to share it with all participants. A copy of the final report will also be issued to the President/CEO, CFO and Corporate Controller.

B.   Control Framework

1.0   Control Environment *"Organization's Culture"*

    1.1   Integrity and ethical values

Integrity and ethical values should be established, communicated and practiced.

    1.2   Commitment to competence

People should have the necessary knowledge, skills and tools to support their department's goals.

    1.3   Assignment of authority and responsibility

Authority, responsibility and accountability should be clearly defined and consistent with goals, so that the right people make decisions and take actions.

    1.4   Organizational structure

The decisions and actions of different parts of the organization should be coordinated.

2.0   Risk Assessment *"Goals And Obstacles"*

    2.1   Objectives – entity wide

Corporate goals should be established, supported by written plans, and communicated to all employees.

    2.2   Objectives – activity level

Divisions /departments should establish goals consistent with the strategic plans of the organization. Goals and related plans should include measurable performance targets and indicators.

    2.3   Risk identification

Divisions / departments should identify the significant internal and external risks faced in reaching goals.

    2.4   Managing change

There should be processes to react to risks and changes that may threaten divisional goals.

3.0   Control Activities *"Policies and Procedures"*

Policies designed to support the achievement of an organization's objectives and the management of its risks should be established, communicated and practised so that people understand what is expected of them and the scope of their freedom to act.

Best Practices: Evaluating the Corporate Culture

4.0 Information and Communication

4.1 Information

Sufficient and relevant information should be identified and communicated in a timely manner to enable people to do their jobs.

4.2 Communication

There should be open communication, downstream, upstream and across activities, to support the organization's values and achievement of its goals.

5.0 Monitoring *"Evaluation & Feedback"*

5.1 Ongoing monitoring activities

Performance should be monitored against the targets and indicators identified in the plans and goals.

C. Self-Assessment Questionnaire

Issues/Instructions

- As much as possible, please base your assessment on current circumstances (WCB has had many recent changes)

- The context of responses should be at the divisional level, not organizationally, unless directed otherwise;

- If you cannot answer for the entire division, please address the question with respect to your own department

- Bulleted prompts below the questions provide issues you might consider in answering the question and rating the factor;

- In the box below the question and prompts, there is a statement that summarizes how the control should work for each factor

- During the interview/workshop, you will be asked to self assess, on a scale of 1 to 8 (8 is highest),
    - the importance of each factor in achieving your objectives and
    - your confidence that it is operating effectively in your area

Questions begin on Page 3, following.

Questions

1.1 How do management and employees demonstrate commitment to integrity and ethics?

- Understanding of values and consequences of non-compliance
    - Management
    - Employees
    - External parties
- Tone at the top
- Whistle-blowing
- Ethics and financial integrity v acceptable performance measures
- Examples: strengths and potential for improvement

Integrity and ethical values are established, communicated and practiced in my division / department.	Importance	Confidence
	1 2 3 4 5 6 7 8	1 2 3 4 5 6 7 8

1.2 How does your division / department ensure that its people have the necessary knowledge, skills and tools to do their jobs?

- Hiring practices
- Documented job descriptions / responsibilities
- Employee performance measurement – annual and ongoing
- Accountability
- Training and development (resources, effectiveness)
- Incentives
- Experience and opportunity
- Turnover

Employees in my division / department have the necessary knowledge, skills, and tools to do their jobs.	Importance	Confidence
	1 2 3 4 5 6 7 8	1 2 3 4 5 6 7 8

1.3 How does the assignment of authority, responsibility and accountability help ensure that the right people can make decisions and take actions?

- Key managers' authority, knowledge and skills
- Empowerment of line managers and staff

Authority, responsibility and accountability are clearly defined and consistent with the division's /department's objectives, so that the right people can make decisions and take actions.	Importance	Confidence
	1 2 3 4 5 6 7 8	1 2 3 4 5 6 7 8

Best Practices: Evaluating the Corporate Culture

1.4 How does the current organizational structure help or hinder your division / department in achieving its goals?

- Reporting relationships
- Enough people and resources
- Allocation of people and resources to key functions/activities
- Information flow
- Duplication

The decisions and actions of different parts of the organization are coordinated in a way that helps my division / department in meeting its goals	Importance	Confidence
	1 2 3 4 5 6 7 8	1 2 3 4 5 6 7 8

4.1 How do you ensure that sufficient information is provided to the right people at the right time to enable them to carry out their responsibilities?

- Process to request/develop reports
- Quality of existing reporting processes
- Quality of existing KPI's

Sufficient and relevant information is identified and communicated in a timely manner to enable people to carry out their responsibilities	Importance	Confidence
	1 2 3 4 5 6 7 8	1 2 3 4 5 6 7 8

4.2 How do your division / department's communication practices promote understanding and acceptance of values and ensure that everyone is working toward the same goals?

- Upstream – employee feedback and suggestions, whistle blowing
- Downstream – promote understanding of goals and values, rewards and consequences
- Cross-functional – promote teamwork, reduce duplication
- External – accept suggestions for improvement, communicate goals and values

The division / department has open lines of communication, upstream, downstream, cross functionally, and externally, that help our progress toward meeting goals.	Importance	Confidence
	1 2 3 4 5 6 7 8	1 2 3 4 5 6 7 8

5.1 How does your division / department monitor against targets and indicators to measure progress toward meeting goals?

- Control deficiencies and exceptions – detection and reporting
- Accuracy of financial information
- Customer satisfaction
- Employee training and feedback

Performance is monitored against the targets and indicators identified in the plans and goals.	Importance	Confidence
	1 2 3 4 5 6 7 8	1 2 3 4 5 6 7 8

Please address this question at the corporate level:

2.1 How well are WCB corporate goals supported by written plans and communicated to all employees?

- Existence and awareness of strategies, business plans and budgets
    - Management
    - Employees
    - Other stakeholders
- Input/feedback from key managers and employees

Corporate goals are established, supported by written plans, and communicated to all employees.	Importance	Confidence
	1 2 3 4 5 6 7 8	1 2 3 4 5 6 7 8

2.2 How do your division / department's goals align with the entity wide goals? What are the measurable targets and indicators?

- Which goals are supported
- Communication of missions and goals to
    - Line Managers
    - Staff
    - Consultants and other external parties
- Who is involved in objective setting
- Measurement criteria

My department establishes goals consistent with the strategic plans of the organization. Goals and related plans include measurable performance targets and indicators.	Importance	Confidence
	1 2 3 4 5 6 7 8	1 2 3 4 5 6 7 8

2.3 How do you identify and assess key risks to obtaining your division's /department's goals?

- What are key external risks (e.g. technology, competition, economic and political conditions)?
- What are key internal risks (e.g. employee retention, resources, tools and time, information systems)?
- How do you identify them and assess the likelihood and potential impact of their occurrence?

My department identifies and assesses the significant internal and external risks to achieving its goals	Importance	Confidence
	1 2 3 4 5 6 7 8	1 2 3 4 5 6 7 8

2.4 What processes are in place to react to risks and changes that may threaten your goals?

- What are key controls to mitigate risks?
- Corporate restructuring
- Other changes in operating environment
- New or redesigned information systems
- Rapid growth
- New technology

My division /department has processes to react to changes that may threaten its goals	Importance	Confidence
	1 2 3 4 5 6 7 8	1 2 3 4 5 6 7 8

Rating Guide – Control Framework Factors

Importance – How important is the effective operation of this control factor in achieving the division/department's goals?

8 This control is key to achieving the division /department's goals

7 .   .   .   .

6 .   .   .   .

5 This control is somewhat important in achieving the division's/department's goals

4 This control less important in achieving the division's/department's goals

3 .   .   .   .

2 .   .   .   .

1 This control is not important in achieving the division's/department's goals

Confidence – How confident are you that this control factor is operating effectively at the divisional/ departmental level?

8   Very confident: Successful actions are predominant and obstacles, if any, do not hinder the effectiveness of this control

7

6

5   Somewhat confident: The number of successful actions is greater than the obstacles. The control is in place, but the obstacles hinder its effectiveness to some extent

4   Less confident: The number of obstacles is slightly greater than the successful actions, and improvements are required to ensure that the control is effective

3

2

1   Not confident: Successful actions are few or non-existent, and obstacles are so prevalent that the effectiveness of the control is significantly impaired

Rating Guide – WCB Initiatives

Importance – How important is it for your division / department to support this initiative?

8   It is very important for our division/department to support this initiative

7

6

5   It is somewhat important for our division/department to support this initiative

4   It is less important for our division/department to support this initiative.

3

2

1   It is not important for our division/department to support this initiative

Confidence - How effectively is your division / department contributing to this initiative?

8   Successfully: Successful actions are predominant and obstacles, if any, do not hinder the division / department's ability to contribute to the initiative.

7

6

5   To some extent: The number of successful actions is greater than the obstacles, but the obstacles impair the division / department's ability to support this initiative somewhat

4   To a lesser extent: The number of obstacles is slightly greater than the successful actions, and improvements are required to ensure that the division / department is contributing effectively

3

2

1   Not contributing: Limited or no successful actions exist and/or obstacles are so prevalent that the contribution is significantly impaired.

Exhibit 6B

WORKSAFEBC PRE-INTERVIEW PRESENTATION

Soft Controls 2006
Internal Audit Assurance Project

Objectives and Approach

WorkSafeBC
WORKING TO MAKE A DIFFERENCE
worksafebc.com

Slide 1

Audit Objective

- To assess the adequacy of soft controls within your division
- This audit is part of our annual assurance to the Audit Committee that the organization's internal controls are working effectively

Slide 2

Internal Control

- WHEN
- WHO
- WHY
- WHAT

- A process
- effected by an entity's board of directors, management and other personnel
- designed to provide reasonable assurance regarding the achievement of objectives in the following categories:
  - effectiveness and efficiency of operations
  - reliability of financial reporting
  - compliance with applicable laws and regulations

Slide 3

Exhibit 6B: WorkSafeBC Pre-Interview Presentation

Audit Approach for Hard Controls

- How
  - Substantive audit procedures
  - Structured walkthroughs
  - Business Unit Financial Controls Checklist
- What
  - Paper-work
  - Policies and procedures
  - Segregation and delegation of duties

This is the traditional approach you may be familiar with

Slide 4

Self Assessment For Soft Controls

- How
  - Structured interviews
  - Facilitated workshops
  - Surveys
- What (examples)
  - Attitudes
  - Skill level and training
  - Communication
  - Goal setting

Soft controls help ensure the effectiveness of hard controls

Slide 5

Why Interviews vs. Surveys

- Discuss questions and issues for consistency of understanding before rating
- Ability to probe for more depth
- Identify potential solutions

Slide 6

After the Interview

- Copy of minutes to participant to verify accuracy and add any other comments / concerns
- Final Report to the Vice-President/Chief Financial Officer and Controller with recommendation to share with other participants
- Report summarizes ratings and comments, compares assessments of different groups / levels
- Executive Summary to the Audit Committee

Slide 7

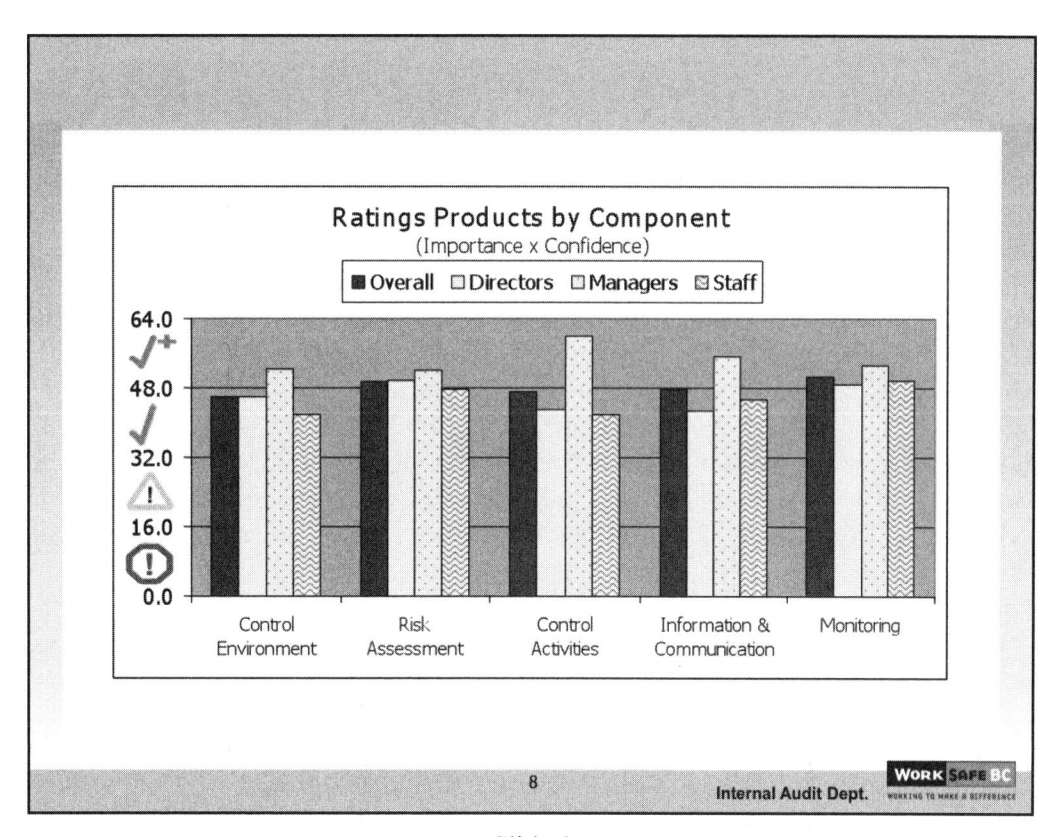

Exhibit 6B: WorkSafeBC Pre-Interview Presentation

Slide 8

231

Exhibit 6C

WORKSAFEBC SOFT CONTROLS QUESTIONNAIRE

Introduction

The objective of this audit is to facilitate a self-assessment of soft controls within WorkSafeBC, following a generally accepted control framework. This audit is one component of Internal Audit's assurance to the Audit Committee that the organization's controls are working effectively.

Soft controls include values, attitudes and other measures that cannot be audited in the traditional sense. A breakdown in soft controls is often a factor in hard control failures (e.g., fraud, financial loss, reputation loss). To assess soft controls, we followed a control framework that is recognized internationally by accounting and auditing associations[1].

To assess soft controls, we have designed a questionnaire based on a control framework that is recognized internationally by accounting and auditing associations. The framework has five components:

Control Environment: The Control Environment sets the tone of an organization. It includes integrity and ethical values, commitment to employee competence, assignment of authority and responsibility, and the organizational structure.

Risk Assessment: Risk Assessment is the identification and analysis of risks relevant to achievement of stated objectives. This component includes establishment and communication of goals, risk identification and assessment, and change management.

Control Activities: Control Activities help ensure that people take necessary actions to progress toward objectives and mitigate risks to their achievement. They include documented policies and procedures and the day-to-day practices that ensure they are carried out (this audit does not include substantive tests to gather hard evidence of control activities).

Information and Communication: The information required to take action must be identified, captured and provided to the right people in a timely manner. Communication must flow in all directions to promote understanding of values, achievement of objectives, and mitigation of risks.

Monitoring: Monitoring activities measure progress toward achieving objectives, and identify any internal controls deficiencies or exceptions.

---

[1] We followed the COSO Internal Control Framework. COSO, which stands for the Committee of Sponsoring Organizations, was sponsored by The Institute of Internal Auditors, the American Institute of Certified Public Accountants, the American Accounting Association, the Institute of Management Accountants and the Financial Executives Institute.

Instructions

Participants should address the questions at the divisional and/or departmental level, as appropriate for their job function.

After discussing each question, we will ask you to self assess the importance you place on the related factor/control and your confidence that it is operating effectively in your area. The ratings should reflect current circumstances.

After each interview, we will send written minutes to the participant; we will not distribute the minutes to anyone else. At the workshops, the minutes will be recorded and available for review on the projector screen. When we have completed all of the interviews and workshops for the Executive Group, we will prepare a report summarizing the ratings and comments. We will issue the report to the President, with a recommendation to share it with all participants. A copy of the final report will also be issued to the Chief Financial Officer and the Corporate Controller, with a summary paragraph provided to SEC and the Audit Committee.

Questions

1.0 Control Environment *"Organization's Culture"*

1A How do management and employees demonstrate commitment to integrity and ethics?

- Understanding of values and consequences of noncompliance
    - Management
    - Employees
    - External parties
- Tone at the top
- Management intervention/override
- Whistle-blowing
- Specific examples of strengths and potential for improvement

Integrity and ethical values are established, communicated and practiced in my division/department.	Importance	Confidence
	1 2 3 4 5 6 7 8	1 2 3 4 5 6 7 8

Best Practices: Evaluating the Corporate Culture

1B   How does your division/department ensure that its people have the necessary knowledge, skills and tools to do their jobs?

- Hiring practices
- Documented job descriptions/responsibilities
- Employee performance measurement – annual and ongoing
- Training and development (resources, effectiveness)
- Experience and opportunity
- Turnover

Employees in my division/department have the necessary knowledge, skills, and tools to do their jobs.	Importance	Confidence
	1 2 3 4 5 6 7 8	1 2 3 4 5 6 7 8

1C   How does the assignment of authority, responsibility, and accountability help ensure that the right people can make decisions and take actions?

- Appropriate balance between authority to "get the job done" and involvement of superiors where needed
- Key managers' authority, knowledge, and skills
- Empowerment of line managers and staff
- Clear boundaries of authority

Authority, responsibility, and accountability are clearly defined and consistent with the division/department's objectives, so the right people can make decisions and take actions.	Importance	Confidence
	1 2 3 4 5 6 7 8	1 2 3 4 5 6 7 8

1D   How does the current organizational structure help or hinder your division / department in achieving its objectives?

- Reporting relationships
- Appropriate allocation of people and resources to functions/activities
- Information flow
- Duplication

The decisions and actions of different parts of the organization are coordinated in a way that helps my division/department to meet its objectives.	Importance	Confidence
	1 2 3 4 5 6 7 8	1 2 3 4 5 6 7 8

Exhibit 6C: WorkSafeBC Soft Controls Questionnaire

2.0 Risk Assessment *"Goals And Obstacles"*

Please address this question at the corporate level:

2A How well are WorkSafeBC corporate (entity-level) goals supported by written plans, communicated to and understood by all employees?

- Existence and awareness of goals and strategies
  - Management
  - Employees
  - Other stakeholders
- Clarity on what the entity wants to achieve
- Specific enough to relate to your division/department
- Input/feedback from key managers and employees is considered

The organization establishes and documents entity-wide goals, which are understood by all employees.	Importance	Confidence
	1 2 3 4 5 6 7 8	1 2 3 4 5 6 7 8

2B How do your division/department's (activity-level) goals and objectives align with the entity-level goals?

- The entity-level goals that are supported
- Communication of activity-level objectives and strategies downstream
  - Line Managers
  - Staff
  - Consultants and other external parties
- Downstream communication of linkage to entity-level goals
- Relevance of divisional/department objectives to all significant business processes
- Adequacy of resources relevant to activity level objectives
- Who sets the goals and objectives, and who provides input

For discussion to clarify question:

2B.1 What are your division/department's **key** activities, and how do they tie into the departmental/divisional objectives and the corporate goals?

My division/department establishes goals and objectives consistent with the goals and strategies of the organization.	Importance	Confidence
	1 2 3 4 5 6 7 8	1 2 3 4 5 6 7 8

2C How do you identify and assess the key risks to obtaining your division's/department's objectives?

- Processes to identify risks and assess the likelihood and potential impact of their occurrence
    - Risks from external sources (see 2C.1 for examples)
    - Risks from internal sources (see 2C.1 for examples)
    - Linkage to activity-level objectives

For discussion to clarify question:

2C.1 What are the key risks that threaten achievement of your division/department's objectives?

- Key external risks (e.g., politics and legislation, stakeholder expectations, industry and economic changes)
- Key internal risks (e.g., employee retention, resources, tools and time, information systems)

	Importance	Confidence
My division/department has processes to identify and assess the significant internal and external risks to achieving its objectives.	1 2 3 4 5 6 7 8	1 2 3 4 5 6 7 8

2D What processes are in place to react to risks and changes that may threaten your objectives?

- Processes to anticipate, identify and react to routine events/activities, e.g.
    - Resource limitations
    - Access to data and people
- Processes to react to non-routine changes
    - Corporate restructuring
    - Turnover/reassignment of personnel
    - Regulation changes
    - Technological changes
    - Economic and political changes
- Key controls to mitigate risks identified in 2C.1

	Importance	Confidence
My division /department has processes to react to risks and changes that may threaten its objectives.	1 2 3 4 5 6 7 8	1 2 3 4 5 6 7 8

Exhibit 6C: WorkSafeBC Soft Controls Questionnaire

3.0 Control Activities *"Policies and Procedures"*

3-A How do management and staff know the appropriate actions and their own responsibilities in carrying out the division/department's key activities?

- Nature of policies/manuals/other documentation
- Completeness of the information
    - Laws/policies documented
    - Procedures to carry out policies documented
    - Key controls included in policies / manuals / other documentation
    - Question 1.3 – clear assignment of responsibility
- Method of employees access
- Process to keep policies/manuals current
- Processes and controls are understood and practiced day-to-day

	Importance	Confidence
There is clear guidance to support the achievement of the division/department's objectives and the management of its risks. People understand the actions they need to take.	1 2 3 4 5 6 7 8	1 2 3 4 5 6 7 8

4.0 Information and Communication

4-B How do you ensure that sufficient information is provided to the right people at the right time to enable them to take action to meet objectives and mitigate risks?

- Information required to perform activities (inflow)
    - Quality of information systems
    - Appropriate access to information systems
    - Input to developing information systems to meet needs
    - Quantity/quality of organization-wide information
- Information required to evaluate activities
    - Information to calculate KPI's
    - Timely reports for budget activity and evaluation
- Information outflows – internal
    - Info required by other depts to perform their activities
    - Reporting to Financial Services Managers (budget variances / BUFCC)
    - Reporting to SEC
- Information outflows – external
    - Employers
    - Claimants
    - Publications (e.g., Annual Report) & Media

	Importance	Confidence
Sufficient and relevant information is identified, captured and provided to the right people in a timely manner, enabling them to take action to meet objectives and mitigate risks.	1 2 3 4 5 6 7 8	1 2 3 4 5 6 7 8

Best Practices: Evaluating the Corporate Culture

4-C How do your division/department's communication practices promote understanding and acceptance of values and ensure that everyone is working toward the same goals?

- Upstream – employee feedback and suggestions, whistle blowing
- Downstream – promote understanding of goals and values, rewards and consequences
- Cross-functional – promote teamwork, reduce duplication
- External – accept suggestions for improvement, communicate goals and values

	Importance	Confidence
Open lines of communication, upstream, downstream, cross functionally, and externally, promote understanding and acceptance of values and assist the division/ department in meeting their objectives.	1 2 3 4 5 6 7 8	1 2 3 4 5 6 7 8

5.0 Monitoring *"Evaluation & Feedback"*

5-D How does your division/department monitor against targets and indicators to measure progress toward meeting objectives?

- Measurement criteria for stated objectives, e.g.,
    o Nature of performance indictors
    o Quality of performance indicators
    o Processes to evaluate customer satisfaction
- Reasonableness of targets
    o Short term and long term achievability
    o Consideration for short term impacts (e.g., turnover)
- Supervisory review of controls
- Detection and reporting of control deficiencies and exceptions
- Processes to ensure accuracy of financial information
- Processes to review budgets and variances
- Any external evaluations of controls, performance, or quality

	Importance	Confidence
Performance is monitored against the targets and indicators identified in the business plans. Controls are assessed and any deficiencies reported to the appropriate management level.	1 2 3 4 5 6 7 8	1 2 3 4 5 6 7 8

Rating Guide – Control Framework Factors

Importance – How important is the effective operation of this control factor in achieving the division/department's objectives?

8   This control is key to achieving the division/department's objectives.

7   .   .   .   .

6   .   .   .   .

5   This control is somewhat important in achieving the division's/department's objectives.

4   This control less important in achieving the division's/department's objectives.

3   .   .   .   .

2   .   .   .   .

1   This control is not important in achieving the division's/department's objectives.

Confidence – How confident are you that this control factor is operating effectively at the divisional / departmental level?

8   Very confident: Successful actions are predominant and obstacles, if any, do not hinder the effectiveness of this control.

7   .   .   .   .

6   .   .   .   .

5   Somewhat confident: The number of successful actions is greater than the obstacles. The control is in place, but the obstacles hinder its effectiveness to some extent.

4   Less confident: The number of obstacles is slightly greater than the successful actions, and improvements are required to ensure that the control is effective.

3   .   .   .   .

2   .   .   .   .

1   Not confident: Successful actions are few or nonexistent, and obstacles are so prevalent that the effectiveness of the control is significantly impaired.

Exhibit 6D

WORKSAFEBC DIVISIONAL AUDIT REPORT

This section is available on the CD that accompanies this book.

Exhibit 6E

WORKSAFEBC EXECUTIVE INTERVIEW MATERIAL

short form questionnaire

Purpose/Objective:

This memo will accompany the calendar invitation when setting up meetings with Executive and Directors who where interviewed in prior soft control audits and are incumbent in that position.

Criteria:

Capture the following points

- Reliance on:
    o Continuity of key personnel
    o Applicable portions of HR survey
    o Prior interviews
- Update for current year
- Focus on those control questions not addressed in HR survey
- Additional focus on risk identification to help with our audit planning
- Full questionnaire for new employees, or employees in new positions
- Reporting to Dave Anderson, but SEC presentation upon conclusion of project

Work Done:

On an annual basis, Internal Audit is required to report to the Audit Committee on the state of the organization's internal controls. Our soft control audit is crucial because it is the primary audit that allows us to obtain representation from all areas of the organization.

Our approach this year is to use a short form questionnaire and primarily rely on the information obtained from prior year's soft control audits as well as the results from last year's HR survey. There is a lot of overlap in the engagement model used by HR and the COSO internal control framework we use for our internal controls analysis.

The short form questionnaire has been developed with only those parts of COSO not addressed by the HR survey. This short form questionnaire is being used here because you have participated in prior audits where the full questionnaire was used. The full questionnaire will still be used for new directors, or for employees in new positions. The entire copy of the questionnaire is available upon request.

ATTACH PARTIAL QUESTIONNAIRE

The rating system has been changed from an 8 point scale to a 4 point scale. The new scale is attached:

ATTACH SCALE

With the assistance of an Audit Manager, I will be conducting each interview with all executive staff, and a random sample of the directors. In addition to the interviews, a short 14 questions survey will be sent to a random sample of managers and staff across the organization. The workshop approach will not be used this year.

Unlike prior years, a separate report for each division will not be prepared this year. The focus will be on a corporate level evaluation of internal controls. The final report will be sent to Dave Anderson, President CEO, with a copy to Steve Barnett, the Chief Financial Officer, and Brian Erickson, Corporate Controller. However, the results of this audit will be presented at a SEC meeting shortly after the report is issued.

After the interview, we will send back the minutes and ratings, so you can review them for accuracy.

We appreciate you taking the time to meet with us. Please call or email me if you have any questions.

Don Pawluk
Director, Internal Audit

Exhibit 6E: WorkSafeBC Executive Interview Material

Soft Controls Questionnaire

Introduction

The objective of this audit is to facilitate a self-assessment of corporate level soft controls, following a generally accepted control framework. This audit is one component of Internal Audit's assurance to the Audit Committee that the organization's controls are working effectively.

Soft controls include values, attitudes and other measures that cannot be audited in the traditional sense. A breakdown in soft controls is often a factor in hard control failures (e.g. fraud, financial loss, reputation loss). To assess soft controls, we followed a control framework that is recognized internationally by accounting and auditing associations. The framework has five components:

Control Environment: The Control Environment sets the tone of an organization. It includes integrity and ethical values, commitment to employee competence, assignment of authority and responsibility, and the organizational structure.

Risk Assessment: Risk Assessment is the identification and analysis of risks relevant to achievement of stated objectives. This component includes establishment and communication of goals, risk identification and assessment, and change management.

Control Activities: Control Activities help ensure that people take necessary actions to progress toward objectives and mitigate risks to their achievement. They include documented policies and procedures and the day-to-day practices that ensure they are carried out (this audit does not include substantive tests to gather hard evidence of control activities).

Information and Communication: The information required to take action must be identified, captured and provided to the right people in a timely manner. Communication must flow in all directions to promote understanding of values, achievement of objectives, and mitigation of risks.

Monitoring: Monitoring activities measure progress toward achieving objectives, and identify any internal controls deficiencies or exceptions.

Instructions

Participants should address the statements at the corporate level, or as appropriate for their job function. A number of bulleted items follow each statement as possible discussion points for the topic.

After discussing each statement, we will ask you to self assess the importance you place on the related factor/control and your confidence that it is operating effectively in your area. The ratings should reflect current circumstances.

After each interview, we will send written minutes to the participant; we will not distribute the minutes to anyone else. Results will be consolidated for one corporate level report. There will not be any divisional level reports prepared. The final report will go to the President, Chief Financial Officer, Corporate Controller and the division's Financial Services Manager, with a summary paragraph provided to SEC and the Audit Committee.

Questions

1.0 Control Environment *"Organization's Culture"*

1.1 Integrity and ethical values are established, communicated, and practiced.	Importance	Confidence
	1 2 3 4 5 6 7 8	1 2 3 4 5 6 7 8

- Annual ethics meeting with Staff
- Managers Annual Declaration of Compliance
- Understanding of values and consequences of non-compliance
    - Management
    - Employees
    - External parties
- Tone at the top
- Management intervention/override
- Whistle-blowing
- Specific examples of strengths and potential for improvement

2.0 Risk Assessment "Goals And Obstacles"

2.3 My division/department has processes to identify and assess the significant internal and external risks to achieving its objectives.	Importance	Confidence
	1 2 3 4 5 6 7 8	1 2 3 4 5 6 7 8

- Annual Business Plan
- Enterprise Risk Management program
- Processes to identify risks and assess the likelihood and potential impact of their occurrence
    - Risks from external sources
    - Risks from internal sources
    - Linkage to activity-level objectives

For discussion:

2.3.1 What are the key risks that threaten achievement of your division/department's objectives?

- Key external risks (e.g., politics and legislative expectations, stakeholder expectations, industry and economic changes)
- Key internal risks (e.g., employee retention, resources, tools and time, information systems)

2.4 My division /department has processes to react to risks and changes that may threaten its objectives.	Importance	Confidence
	1 2 3 4 5 6 7 8	1 2 3 4 5 6 7 8

- Processes to anticipate, identify and react to routine events/activities, e.g.
    o Resource limitations
    o Access to data and people
- Processes to react to non-routine changes
    o Corporate restructuring
    o Turnover/reassignment of personnel
    o Regulation changes
    o Technological changes
    o Economic and political changes
- Key controls to mitigate risks identified in 2C.1

3.0 Control Activities *"Policies and Procedures"*

3.1 There is clear guidance to ensure people understand the actions they need to take to support the achievement of the division/department's objectives and the management of its risks.	Importance	Confidence
	1 2 3 4 5 6 7 8	1 2 3 4 5 6 7 8

- Policies/manuals/other documentation
- Completeness of the information
    o Laws/policies documented
    o Procedures to carry out policies documented
    o Key controls included in policies/manuals/other documentation
- Method of employees access
- Process to keep policies/manuals current
- Processes and controls are understood and practiced day-to-day

4.0 Monitoring *"Evaluation & Feedback"*

5.1 Performance is monitored against the targets and indicators identified in the business plans. Controls are assessed and any deficiencies reported to the appropriate management level.	Importance	Confidence
	1 2 3 4 5 6 7 8	1 2 3 4 5 6 7 8

- Corporate KPI's
- Measurement criteria for stated objectives, e.g.
    - Nature of performance indictors
    - Quality of performance indicators
    - Processes to evaluate customer satisfaction
- Reasonableness of targets
    - Short term and long term achievability
    - Consideration for short term impacts (e.g., turnover)
- Supervisory review of controls
- Detection and reporting of control deficiencies and exceptions
- Processes to ensure accuracy of financial information
- Processes to review budgets and variances
- Any external evaluations of controls, performance or quality

Rating Guide – Control Framework Factors

Importance – How important is the effective operation of this control factor in achieving the division/department's objectives?

4   This control is key to achieving the division/department's objectives.

3   This control is somewhat important in achieving the division's/department's objectives.

2   This control less important in achieving the division's/department's objectives.

1   This control is not important in achieving the division's/department's objectives.

Confidence – How confident are you that this control factor is operating effectively at the divisional/departmental level?

4   Very confident: Successful actions are predominant and obstacles, if any, do not hinder the effectiveness of this control.

3   Somewhat confident: The number of successful actions is greater than the obstacles. The control is in place, but the obstacles hinder its effectiveness to some extent.

2   Less confident: The number of obstacles is slightly greater than the successful actions, and improvements are required to ensure that the control is effective.

1   Not confident: Successful actions are few or nonexistent, and obstacles are so prevalent that the effectiveness of the control is significantly impaired.

Exhibit 6F

WORKSAFEBC MANAGER/EMPLOYEE SURVEY

1. **The Standards of Conduct program is an effective deterrent to unethical behaviour.**

	Low	Med Low	Med High	High	N/A
How IMPORTANT is the statement to achieving corporate objectives?	○	○	○	○	○
How CONFIDENT are you that the statement is working effectively?	○	○	○	○	○

2. **Processes are in place to IDENTIFY risks/threats to achieving objectives. ***

	Low	Med Low	Med High	High	N/A
How IMPORTANT is the statement to achieving corporate objectives?	○	○	○	○	○
How CONFIDENT are you that the statement is working effectively?	○	○	○	○	○

3. **Processes are in place to ASSESS the risks/threats. ***

	Low	Med Low	Med High	High	N/A
How IMPORTANT is the statement to achieving corporate objectives?	○	○	○	○	○
How CONFIDENT are you that the statement is working effectively?	○	○	○	○	○

Best Practices: Evaluating the Corporate Culture

4. **Processes are in place to respond to events or activities that could have an impact upon achieving objectives.** *

	Low	Med Low	Med High	High	N/A
How IMPORTANT is the statement to achieving corporate objectives?	○	○	○	○	○
How CONFIDENT are you that the statement is working effectively?	○	○	○	○	○

5. **Appropriate policies and procedures are in place for each of your major functions.** *

	Low	Med Low	Med High	High	N/A
How IMPORTANT is the statement to achieving corporate objectives?	○	○	○	○	○
How CONFIDENT are you that the statement is working effectively?	○	○	○	○	○

6. **Employees who steal from the company (i.e. physical property, money, information, time) will be discovered.** *

	Low	Med Low	Med High	High	N/A
How IMPORTANT is the statement to achieving corporate objectives?	○	○	○	○	○
How CONFIDENT are you that the statement is working effectively?	○	○	○	○	○

7. **Controls described in policy and procedures manuals are actually applied the way they are intended.** *

	Low	Med Low	Med High	High	N/A
How IMPORTANT is the statement to achieving corporate objectives?	○	○	○	○	○
How CONFIDENT are you that the statement is working effectively?	○	○	○	○	○

Exhibit 6F: WorkSafeBC Manager/Employee Survey

8. **Supervisory staff periodically checks to ensure policies and procedures are working.** *

	Low	Med Low	Med High	High	N/A
How IMPORTANT is the statement to achieving corporate objectives?	○	○	○	○	○
How CONFIDENT are you that the statement is working effectively?	○	○	○	○	○

9. **Management has enough information to monitor external customer satisfaction.** *

	Low	Med Low	Med High	High	N/A
How IMPORTANT is the statement to achieving corporate objectives?	○	○	○	○	○
How CONFIDENT are you that the statement is working effectively?	○	○	○	○	○

10. **Management has enough information to monitor internal customer satisfaction.** *

	Low	Med Low	Med High	High	N/A
How IMPORTANT is the statement to achieving corporate objectives?	○	○	○	○	○
How CONFIDENT are you that the statement is working effectively?	○	○	○	○	○

11. **In the event that there is a breakdown of controls, policies and procedures are reassessed and modified as needed.** *

	Low	Med Low	Med High	High	N/A
How IMPORTANT is the statement to achieving corporate objectives?	○	○	○	○	○
How CONFIDENT are you that the statement is working effectively?	○	○	○	○	○

Best Practices: Evaluating the Corporate Culture

12. **Information reported to senior management reflects the actual performance of operations in my department.** *

	Low	Med Low	Med High	High	N/A
How IMPORTANT is the statement to achieving corporate objectives?	○	○	○	○	○
How CONFIDENT are you that the statement is working effectively?	○	○	○	○	○

13. **Procedures are in place for reporting internal control deficiencies to those who can take necessary action.** *

	Low	Med Low	Med High	High	N/A
How IMPORTANT is the statement to achieving corporate objectives?	○	○	○	○	○
How CONFIDENT are you that the statement is working effectively?	○	○	○	○	○

14. **To assess soft controls, we follow a framework that is recognized internationally by accounting and auditing associations. Please read the following 5 components and provide any comments, either favourable or unfavourable, as it relates to WorkSafeBC.**

    CONTROL ENVIRONMENT: Sets the tone of an organization. It includes integrity and ethical values, training of staff, management's philosophy and operating style, organizational structure, assignment of authority and responsibility and human resources policies and procedures.

    RISK ASSESSMENT: The process of identifying and analyzing the risks with achieving objectives. This includes establishing and communicating goals, identifying and assessing risks, and change management.

    CONTROL ACTIVITIES: Help ensure that people take necessary actions to achieve their objectives (i.e., mitigate risks). They include documented policies and procedures and the day-to-day practices that ensure they are carried out.

    INFORMATION AND COMMUNICATION: Information involves the timeliness of identifying, capturing and providing the information to the right people. Communication is the flow of information in all directions in order to promote understanding of values, achievement of objectives, and mitigation of risks.

    MONITORING: The measurement of progress toward achieving objectives, and identifying the status of internal controls or exceptions.

# Exhibit 6G

SARASOTA COUNTY COSO-STRATEGIC RISK-HPO FRAMEWORK CROSS-REFERENCE

Sarasota County Clerk of the Circuit Court and County Comptroller
INTERNAL AUDIT DEPARTMENT
Cross-Walk: COSO Focus Points / Strategic Risks / Elements of High Performance

Strategic Business Risks

A. Negative Publicity	F. Non-compliance with Laws and Regulations
B. Legal Liability Exposure	G. Unreliable Financial or Operational Reporting
C. Fraudulent Activities	H. Business Interruption
D. Inaccurate Budgets/Plans	I. Compromise of Sensitive Data
E. Insufficient Funding/Loss of Revenue	J. Waste or Loss of Assets/Resources

Impacts on HPO Elements Associated with:

a. Vision	e. Leadership
b. Values	f. Environment
c. Mission/Niche	g. Operational Plan
d. Theory of Business	h. Results

Q#	Business-Risk Mitigation - Strategic Focus Point	Relevent Risks	Mngt Control Component	Elements as Defined by the HPO Model
1	Managers reinforce the need for ethical decision-making	(A,B,C,E,F,G,I,J)	Control Environment	b, c
2	Executives reinforce the need for ethical decision-making	(A,B,C,D,F,G,I,J)	Control Environment	b, c
3	In doing their work, people follow pertinent laws, regulations, and policies	(A,B,C,E,F,I)	Control Environment	b, c
4	People use appropriately the County resources entrusted to them	(A,B,C,I,J)	Control Environment	b, c, d, e
5	People in our departments do not accept personal gifts or other things of value from anyone with whom they do business	(A,B,C,F,I,J)	Control Environment	b, c, d, e
6	People are free of outside interests that conflict with the duties and responsibilities of their jobs	(A,B,C,J)	Control Environment	b, c, d, e
7	The job training employees receive improves customer service/outcomes	(B,C,F,G,I,J)	Control Environment	b, c, d, e
8	We orient new employees to their jobs	(B,C,F,G,I,J)	Control Environment	b, c, d, e
9	People understand the desired outcomes most important to fulfilling their mission and objectives	(E,G,J)	Business Risk Assessment	a, c, d, g, h
10	People routinely accomplish those outcomes most important to their mission and objectives	(A,B,C,D,E,F,G,H,I,J)	Business Risk Assessment	a, c, d, g, h
11	People have a healthy work environment	(A,B,F,H,J)	Business Risk Assessment	a, c, d, g, h
12	People have a safe work environment	(A,B,F,H,J)	Business Risk Assessment	a, c, d, g, h
13	People are safe from potential physical harm	(A,B,F,H,J)	Business Risk Assessment	a, c, d, g, h
14	People are safe from potential emotional harm	(A,B,F,H,J)	Business Risk Assessment	a, c, d, g, h
15	If there is a major computer systems failure, we could resume effective operations with minimum disruption	(A,B,F,G,H,J)	Business Risk Assessment	a, c, d, g, h
16	We could continue effective operations if we need to evacuate our facilities for 2-3 days	(A,B,F,G,H,I,J)	Business Risk Assessment	a, c, d, g, h
17	Our practices minimize the chance an employee could be accused of improper behavior	(A,B,D,F,G,I,J)	Control Activities	b, d
18	Cash and other valuables entrusted to us are physically protected from theft or harm	(A,C,J)	Control Activities	b, d
19	Our irreplaceable records are physically protected from theft or harm	(A,B,F,H,I,J)	Control Activities	d
20	Access to confidential information is restricted	(A,B,C,F,I,J)	Control Activities	d
21	People communicate across organizational boundaries	(B,C,D,E,F,G,I,J)	Information & Communication	a, c, f, g, h
22	Access to key business records and confidential information is monitored routinely	(A,B,C,F,I,J)	Monitoring Activities	a, c, f, g, h
23	Supervisors are notified routinely when significant issues or concerns arise	(A,B,C,D,E,F,G,H,I,J)	Monitoring Activities	a, c, d, h
24	Our managers are responsive to issues brought to their attention	(A,B,C,D,E,F,G,H,I,J)	Monitoring Activities	a, c, d, h
25	Our executives are responsive to issues brought to their attention	(A,B,C,D,E,F,G,H,I,J)	Monitoring Activities	a, c, d, h

Exhibit GH

SARASOTA COUNTY EXECUTIVE DIRECTOR MEETING AGENDA

Prepared by:_____
Date:_____

Project Number: _____

Dept/Process:

Audit Planning Program
Step # 5 – Contact Cognizant Executive Director

AGENDA

Audit Focus:

- Reasonable assurance business risks have been identified and addressed
- Compliance with legal and regulatory requirements
- Compliance with county standards, polices, and procedures.

Discussion:

The Greatest Operational Risks	Range of Risk Tolerance

The top three conditions, which, should they occur, would warrant immediate attention:

- ○ _____
- ○ _____
- ○ _____

The top three conditions, which, should they occur, would warrant attention within one year:

- ○ _____
- ○ _____
- ○ _____

What are your top three operational governance processes that mitigate mission critical business risk.

- ○ _____
- ○ _____
- ○ _____

Specific risk mitigation practices you feel are carried out well by the responsible manager.

Any specific operational concerns.

Exhibit 6I

SARASOTA COUNTY PROCUREMENT CARD AUDIT MATERIAL

This section is available on the CD that accompanies this book.

Exhibit 6J

SARASOTA COUNTY OVERALL ASSESSMENT OF MANAGEMENT CONTROL FORM

Prepared by: _____
Date: _____
Reviewed by: _____

Project Number: _____

Department/Function/Process: _____

Survey Program Step # 9 Overall Assessment of Management Control

Management Control Components and Focus Points
Evaluation Scale
(Place a check mark in the appropriate column)

	1 None	2 Marginal	3 Satisfactory	4 Good	5 Excellent
1. Control Environment					
a) Strengths					
☐ Culture, Integrity, and Ethical Values			☐	☐	☐
☐ Commitment to employee competence			☐	☐	☐
☐ Senior Management oversight			☐	☐	☐
☐ Management's vision and leadership			☐	☐	☐
☐ Organizational structure			☐	☐	☐
☐ Assignment of authority and responsibility			☐	☐	☐
☐ Human resources policies and practices			☐	☐	☐
b) Concerns					
☐ Culture, Integrity, and Ethical Values	☐	☐			
☐ Commitment to employee competence	☐	☐			
☐ Senior Management oversight	☐	☐			
☐ Management's vision and leadership	☐	☐			
☐ Organizational structure	☐	☐			
☐ Assignment of authority and responsibility	☐	☐			
☐ Human resources policies and practices	☐	☐			
2. Risk Assessment					
a) Strengths					
☐ Objective setting processes			☐	☐	☐
☐ Risk identification and risk analysis processes			☐	☐	☐
☐ Managing change			☐	☐	☐
b) Concerns					
☐ Objective setting processes	☐	☐			
☐ Risk identification and risk analysis processes	☐	☐			
☐ Managing change	☐	☐			

Exhibit 6J: Sarasota County Overall Assessment of Management Control Form

Project Number: _____

Prepared by: _____
Date: _____
Reviewed by: _____
Page 2 of 2

Department/Function/Process: _____

Survey Program Step # 9 Overall Assessment of Management Control

	1 None	2 Marginal	3 Satisfactory	4 Good	5 Excellent
Management Control Components and Focus Points *Evaluation Scale* (Place a check mark in the appropriate column)					
3. Control Activities					
a) Strengths					
☐ Policies and Procedures			☐	☐	☐
b) Concerns					
☐ Policies and Procedures	☐	☐			
4. Information and Communications					
a) Strengths					
☐ Information systems			☐	☐	☐
☐ Communication processes			☐	☐	☐
b) Concerns					
☐ Information systems	☐	☐			
☐ Communication processes	☐	☐			
5. Monitoring Activities					
a) Strengths					
☐ Ongoing monitoring activities			☐	☐	☐
☐ Internal control self-assessment activities			☐	☐	☐
☐ Internal and external audit activity			☐	☐	☐
☐ Upward reporting of deficiencies			☐	☐	☐
b) Concerns					
☐ Ongoing monitoring activities	☐	☐			
☐ Internal control self-assessment activities	☐	☐			
☐ Internal and external audit activity	☐	☐			
☐ Upward reporting of deficiencies	☐	☐			

Exhibit 6K

SARASOTA COUNTY AUDIT REPORT — EXPLANATION OF COSO CRITERIA

Project 2008-49
Management Controls Over Business Center P-Card Administration
PUBLIC WORKS
March 2008

Criteria for Evaluation of Management's Control of Business Risk

The Nature of Internal Auditing

Internal auditing is an integral part of the constitutional duties assigned to the Clerk of the Circuit Court and County Comptroller as Auditor of the Board of County Commissioners. The Clerk's Internal Audit Department provides independent, objective assurance, attestation, and other services designed to add value and help improve County operations. This is accomplished by bringing a systematic, disciplined approach to evaluate the effectiveness of County business risk management, control, and business-governance processes. Our audit work is performed under guidance provided by the professional auditing standards of the Institute of Internal Auditors and the U.S. General Accountability Office.

The Nature of Business Risk Management, Control, and Governance Processes

Business risk management, control, and governance processes are all those activities designed and engaged in by the Board of County Commissioners, County Administration, executives, directors, and staff to provide reasonable assurance of (1) reliable financial and operating data and reports, (2) compliance with laws and regulations, (3) effective and efficient business practices, and (4) safeguarding the public resources and assets entrusted to them. Reasonable assurance that these core business objectives can be achieved is dependent upon the presence of the five components of management control listed below:

- The Control Environment
- Risk Assessment Practices
- Control Activities
- Information and Communications, and
- Monitoring Activities.

To control business risk, all five components must operate effectively and in unison, and all County employees share in that responsibility. Please read Appendix F on pages 15 and 16 for additional information.

The Nature of Reportable Issues

The Institute of Internal Auditors defines these as situations that are of such significance that they require the attention of the senior leadership.

Critical Conditions
Any condition that has caused, or is likely to cause, errors, omissions, fraud or other adversities of such magnitude as to force immediate corrective actions to mitigate the associated business risk and possible consequent damage to the organization.

Important Conditions
Any condition that has caused, or is likely to cause, errors, omissions or other adversities that increase business risk and possible consequent damage to the organization, but does not require immediate corrective actions to mitigate the associated impact on operations or outcomes. Important conditions require attention within the short term (typically less than one year from disclosure).

The Nature of Opportunities for Enhancement

These represent improvements to the system of management control that the responsible manager may wish to consider as time and resources permit.

Exhibit 6K: Sarasota County Audit Report — Explanation of COSO Criteria

Project 2008-49
Management Controls Over Business Center P-Card Administration
PUBLIC WORKS
March 2008

APPENDIX F

DEFINITION OF MANAGEMENT CONTROL

Management control is broadly defined as a process, affected by managers and other people, that provides reasonable assurance of achieving the three primary objectives for which all businesses strive:
- Effective and efficient operations, including achievement of performance goals and safeguarding of assets against loss
- Compliance with laws and regulations
- Reliable operational and financial data and reports

COMPONENTS NECESSARY FOR EFFECTIVE MANAGEMENT CONTROL

THE CONTROL ENVIRONMENT
The foundation for effective control. It sets the tone for the organization, and influences the control consciousness of its people. It addresses:
- Integrity, ethical and cultural values
- Competence of the organization's people
- The manager's philosophy and operating style
- Assignment of authority and responsibility
- Organization and development of human resources
- The attention and direction given by senior management

RISK ASSESSMENT
The process of recognizing and prioritizing operational risks and obstacles.
- Statement of clear objectives
- Recognition of critical risks and obstacles
- Identification of factors critical for success
- Identification of significant changing conditions

CONTROL ACTIVITIES
Flow from Risk Assessment. Control Activities are the policies and procedures that managers establish to minimize risks and obstacles to desired outcomes. Examples include:
- Guidance, processes and practices
- Safeguarding resources
- Information systems and processing controls
- Approvals, authorizations, verifications, and reconciliations
- Division of work and separation of responsibilities

INFORMATION and COMMUNICATION
Provide the knowledge people need to meet responsibilities.
- The systems of information gathering
- The systems of internal/external communications flowing down, across and up the organization
- Internal and external data for decision-making
- Employees' understanding of their control responsibilities
- Employees' understanding how their work fits into the "big picture"

MONITORING ACTIVITIES
Involve assessment of control effectiveness by appropriate people on a timely basis.
- Measurement of outcomes
- Comparison of expected and actual results
- Performance comparisons and variance analyses
- Review of work assignments
- Upward reporting to senior management of significant concerns and issues

APPENDIX F

Project 2008-49
Management Controls Over Business Center P-Card Administration
PUBLIC WORKS
March 2008

APPENDIX F

CRITERIA FOR ASSESSMENT OF EFFECTIVE MANAGEMENT CONTROL

Management control can be judged effective if the responsible managers and senior leadership have reasonable assurance that they understand the extent to which desired outcomes are being achieved; the extent to which operational and financial data is being prepared reliably; and the extent to which legal and regulatory requirements are being met.

This reasonable assurance exists when the five components of control are present and operating effectively. When this happens, the system of control should bring to light and routinely correct any critical or important conditions. These would be events that are likely to cause errors, omissions or other adversities of such magnitude that prompt the corrective actions required, thereby mitigating the associated business risk and possible consequent damage. The expectation is that, in the normal course of operations, critical or important conditions can be identified, addressed and corrected, and not allowed to become persistent or pervasive. When significant issues are not detected and corrected, or when they become persistent or pervasive, then it can be inferred that operations are out of control.

Should any one of the five components of the control framework be absent or seriously flawed, then it would be highly unlikely that effective control could exist. In practice, the need for efficient operations implies that the benefits derived from controls should exceed the cost to implement and maintain control processes. This acknowledges that there is a certain amount of residual risk associated with an effective system of management control.

INHERENT LIMITATIONS

The effectiveness of controls changes over time. Moreover, controls designed to prevent all problems would not be cost effective. Limitations which may hinder the effectiveness of a system of controls include resource constraints, faulty judgments, unintentional errors, circumvention by collusion, and management overrides. The presence of these limitations may not always be detected by the audit process.

The vision of The IIA Research Foundation is to understand, shape, and advance the global profession of internal auditing by initiating and sponsoring intelligence gathering, innovative research, and knowledge sharing in a timely manner. As a separate, tax-exempt organization, we do not receive funding from IIA membership dues but depend on contributions from individuals and organizations, and from IIA chapters and institutes, to move our programs forward. We also would not be able to function without our valuable volunteers. To that end, we thank the following:

RESEARCH SPONSOR RECOGNITION

Visionary Circle
Paul J. Sobel, CIA

Chairman's Circle

Stephen D. Goepfert, CIA	Itau Unibanco Holding SA
3M Company	Lockheed Martin Corporation
Cargill Inc.	Microsoft Corporation
Chevron Corporation	PricewaterhouseCoopers LLP
ExxonMobil Corporation	Southern California Edison Company

Diamond Donor
IIA Chicago

THE IIA RESEARCH FOUNDATION
BOARD OF TRUSTEES

President: Paul J. Sobel, CIA, *Mirant Corporation*
Vice President – Strategy: Mark J. Pearson, CIA, *Boise Inc.*
Vice President – Research: Philip E. Flora, CIA, CCSA, *Texas Guaranteed TG*
Vice President – Development: Wayne G. Moore, CIA, *Wayne Moore Consulting*
Treasurer: Stephen W. Minder, CIA, *YCN Group LLC*
Secretary: Douglas Ziegenfuss, PhD, CIA, CCSA, *Old Dominion University*

Members

Neil Aaron, *The McGraw-Hill Companies*
Eric N. Allegakoen, CIA, CCSA, *Adobe Systems*
Richard J. Anderson, CFSA, *DePaul University*
Javier O. Arrieta, CIA, *Laboratorios Farma*
Sten Bjelke, CIA, *IIA Sweden*
Robert B. Foster, *Fidelity Investments*
James A. LaTorre, *PricewaterhouseCoopers LLP*
Marjorie Maguire-Krupp, CIA, CFSA, *Coastal Empire Consulting*
William Middleton, CIA, *New South Wales Department of Education*
Leen Paape, CIA, *Nyenrode Business University*

Jeffrey Perkins, CIA, *TransUnion LLC*
Edward C. Pitts
Michael F. Pryal, CIA, *Michael Pryal and Associates*
Carolyn Saint, CIA, *Lowe's Companies, Inc.*
Mark L. Salamasick, CIA, *University of Texas at Dallas*
Elizabeth Samuel, CIA, *IIA South Africa*
Susan D. Ulrey, CIA, *KPMG LLP*
Carmen Prevost Vierula, CIA, *Bank of Canada*
Shi Xian, *Nanjing Audit University*

THE IIA RESEARCH FOUNDATION
BOARD OF RESEARCH AND EDUCATION ADVISORS

Chairman
Philip E. Flora, CIA, CCSA, CFE, CISA, *Texas Guaranteed TG*

Members

George R. Aldhizer III, PhD, CIA, *Wake Forest University*
Lalbahadur Balkaran, CIA, *Ernst & Young LLP*
Kevin W. Barthold, CPA, CISA, *City of San Antonio*
Thomas J. Beirne, CFSA, CPA, CBA, *The AES Corporation*
Audley L. Bell, CIA, CPA, CFE, CISA, *Habitat for Humanity International*
John K. Brackett, CFSA, *RSM McGladrey, Inc.*
Thomas J. Clooney, CIA, CCSA, CPA, CBA, CSP, *KPMG LLP*
Kathryn Constantopoulos, CIA, *Deloitte & Touche LLP*
Jean Coroller, *Ernst & Young LLP*
Mary Christine Dobrovich, *Jefferson Wells International*
Susan Page Driver, CIA, CPA, CISA, *Texas General Land Office*
Ana Maria Escalante Penaloza, CIA, *IIA Bolivia*
Donald A. Espersen, CIA, CBA, *despersen & associates*
Randall R. Fernandez, CIA, *Adams Harris*
John C. Gazlay, CPA, CCSA
Dan B. Gould, CIA
Ulrich Hahn, CIA, CCSA, CGAP
John C. Harris, CIA, *Aspen Holdings/FirstComp Insurance Company*
Sabrina B. Hearn, CIA, CPA, CMA, CHFP, *University of Alabama System*
Peter M. Hughes, PhD, CIA, CPA, CFE, *Orange County*
David J. MacCabe, CIA, CGAP, MPA
Gary R. McGuire, CIA, CPA, *Lennox International Inc.*
John D. McLaughlin, *Smart Business Advisory and Consulting LLC*
Steven S. Mezzio, CIA, CCSA, CFSA, CPA, CISSP, CBA, *Resources Global Professionals*
Deborah L. Muñoz, CIA, *CalPortland Company*
Claire Beth Nilsen, CFSA, CRCM, CFE, CRP
Frank M. O'Brien, CIA, *Olin Corporation*
Amy Jane Prokopetz, CCSA, *Farm Credit Canada*
Mark R. Radde, CIA, CPA
Vito Raimondi, CIA, *Zurich Financial Services NA*
Jesus Antonio Serrano Nava, CIA, *Banco Azteca*
Kyoko Shimizu, CIA, *The Board of Audit of Japan*
Katherine E. Sidway, CIA, *Ernst & Young LLP*
Iva Sucha, CIA, *IIA Czech Republic*
Linda Yanta, CIA, *Eskom*

The IIA Research Foundation Headquarters Support

Richard F. Chambers, CIA, CCSA, CGAP, *Executive Director*
David Polansky, *Director of Finance*
Bonnie L. Ulmer, *Vice President, Research*
Joe Sorrentino, *Director, Retail Operations*
Nicki Creatore, *Operations Manager*
Erin Weber, *Business Development Manager*